How Weak Regionalism in East Asia Works Well

This book investigates the reasons why regionalism in East Asia has been much weaker than in Western Europe and North America. It focuses particularly on economic factors, examining the regional and global linkages of production networks.

Through a focused exploration of regional and global production networks, it argues that East Asia was not as regionally concentrated as was Western Europe or North America, lacking a regionally oriented productional basis to support the institutional arrangement of East Asia as a stand-alone economic community. Moreover, the regional production networks of each national economy in the region are influenced by a different set of value-added components from different global and regional origins. This divergence in their positions accounts for the mushrooming of divergent initiatives and projects for regional institutional arrangement. Finally, the institutional choices of the states to join Comprehensive and Progressive Agreement for Trans-Pacific Partnership (CP/TPP) and/or Regional Comprehensive Economic Partnership (RCEP) are found to be strongly influenced by the sectoral focuses and priorities of their economies.

Demonstrating how the unique economic factors of each nation override other considerations for greater regional integration, this book will be a valuable resource to students and scholars of international trade, Asian politics and economics.

Luna Ge Lai is an Assistant Research Fellow at the Institute for International Affairs, the Chinese University of Hong Kong, Shenzhen, China.

China Policy Series

Series Editor: Zheng Yongnian

Professor and Director of the Institute for International Affairs, the Chinese University of Hong Kong, Shenzhen, China.

13. China's Trade Unions
How Autonomous Are They?
Masaharu Hishida, Kazuko Kojima, Tomoaki Ishii and Jian Qiao

14. Legitimating the Chinese Communist Party since Tiananmen
A critical analysis of the stability discourse
Peter Sandby-Thomas

15. China and International Relations
The Chinese view and the contribution of Wang Gungwu
Zheng Yongnian

16. The Challenge of Labour in China
Strikes and the changing labour regime in global factories
Chris King-chi Chan

17. The Impact of China's 1989 Tiananmen Massacre
Edited by Jean-Philippe Béja

18. The Institutional Dynamics of China's Great Transformation
Edited by Xiaoming Huang

19. Higher Education in Contemporary China
Beyond expansion
Edited by W. John Morgan and Bin Wu

20. China's Crisis Management
Edited by Jae Ho Chung

21. How Weak Regionalism in East Asia Works Well
Beyond the Flying Geese Model
Luna Ge Lai

For more information about this series, please visit: https://www.routledge.com/China-Policy-Series/book-series/SECPS

How Weak Regionalism in East Asia Works Well

Beyond the Flying Geese Model

Luna Ge Lai

Routledge
Taylor & Francis Group
LONDON AND NEW YORK

First published 2025
by Routledge
4 Park Square, Milton Park, Abingdon, Oxon OX14 4RN

and by Routledge
605 Third Avenue, New York, NY 10158

Routledge is an imprint of the Taylor & Francis Group, an informa business

British Library Cataloguing-in-Publication Data
A catalogue record for this book is available from the British Library

ISBN: 978-1-032-61328-4 (hbk)
ISBN: 978-1-032-61329-1 (pbk)
ISBN: 978-1-032-61332-1 (ebk)

DOI: 10.4324/9781032613321

Typeset in Times New Roman
by SPi Technologies India Pvt Ltd (Straive)

Contents

Figures

Tables

Preface

This book investigates the structural causes to the problem in East Asian regionalism. From the 1980s to the 2010s, multiple states were involved in various intergovernmental initiatives and projects to develop a set of institutional arrangements for organizing transborder production and distribution in East Asia. There was a great sense of a problem in East Asian regionalism due to a lack of a single, region-wide institutional arrangement for East Asia to operate as a stand-alone economic community. This led to the rise of multiple contending initiatives and projects for such an institutional arrangement. Finally, this resulted in the emergence of two separate and competing sets of arrangements.

Liberal institutional theory and market force theory have been put forward to explain this problem in East Asian regionalism. Liberal institutional theory suggests that East Asian states had little experience in international institutional building and lacked a shared regional identity. Market force theory, on the other hand, argues that the failure of liberal institutionalist lens may not be a failure at all, but rather the powerful working of market forces in transregional trade, investment, manufacturing, and marketing in East Asia. These explanations, while noting the role of international institutions and market forces, miss out a set of very important forces influencing East Asian regionalism.

This book seeks to identify the structural dynamics behind the complexity and high tension in the institutional preferences of individual East Asian nations for regional economic organization. It constructs international economic structures—global, regional, and sectoral—for visual analysis and indicator comparison, and identifies the structural forces and their logical relation with states' behavior in East Asian regionalism. The book investigates the relationship in three cases: the global economic structure and the material basis for East Asia as a stand-alone economic community; regional economic structures and states' desires and interests in multiple initiatives and projects for institutional arrangement in the region; and the sectoral economic structures of CP/TPP, RCEP, and institutional choices of the states.

The structures and institutions of East Asian regionalism to me are not only intriguing models about modern economic development but also the embodiment of hard work, determination, and wise decisions of East Asian people. In 2010, I did a summer job at an assembly line of a baby stroller factory in

Shenzhen, China, owned by a Taiwanese American. I learnt many amazing stories from my workmates who migrated to this coastal city to sell their cheap labor in this sweatshop of excessive-work culture to enable their children to go to university. During my Master's study at the University of International Business and Economics, Beijing, I also learnt from my teachers that FTA negotiation is often a process of power-based dialogue. As part of this, my teachers spent days and nights on writing a paper on the trade and income effects of a China-Japan-South Korea Free Trade Agreement (FTA). This kind of interaction with my teachers and my work experience in the factory aroused my interest in the evolving roles of China and its East Asian neighbors in the international division of labor.

I have benefited from the advice of many academics and friends when I first pursued my interest in international economics and FTA negotiations during my Master's study. Professor Rui Zhuang, Professor Xiaohong Hua, and Professor Liqiang Yang were my former teachers whose ideas inspired me to study regional economic integration. At the same time, I worked part-time as a Junior Associate at the Beijing Office of International Centre for Trade and Sustainable Development (ICTSD). Andrew Crosby and Dr Shuaihua Cheng were my work supervisors whose professionalism and commitment to trade policy-making further motivated me to pursue an academic career overseas. I owe them a debt of gratitude for their support over the past few years.

While writing this book, I am most indebted to my primary PhD supervisor Professor Xiaoming Huang, whom I met in 2016 as an M.A. student in economics. At that time, I was working on my M.A. thesis on the China-New Zealand Free Trade Agreement. His interpretation of the unbalanced trade and investment flows between China and New Zealand from the International Political Economy perspective was so enlightening and made me realize the limitations of my pure economic empirical calculations. Thanks to his encouragement, I applied for a PhD in International Relations at Victoria University of Wellington and started this challenging and rewarding journey. During my whole journey, Professor Huang has always been ready to help me with his rich knowledge of East Asian International Relations. I appreciate very much the time and energy he has devoted to my thesis. Most importantly, Professor Huang's enthusiasm about the structures of production networks in East Asia refreshes me when I get tired of this "bloody big book".

My secondary PhD supervisor, Dr Ben Thirkell-White, also contributed significantly to this study. He has wizardry and can explain complex theories and research frameworks by drawing pictures. Moreover, his brilliant ideas and insightful comments on my thesis have inspired me.

In addition to the comments of my supervisors, I am grateful to a number of teachers at Victoria University who welcomed me to their lectures: Dr Jason Young (Approaches to International Relations), Professor Xiaoming Huang (International Relations of East Asia), Dr Ben Thirkell-White (International Political Economy), Professor Susy Frankel (International Trade Law), Professor Siah Hwee Ang (International Business), Professor Arthur Grimes

(Economics and Policy), Dr Nokuthaba Sibanda (Applied Statistics), and Dr Xavier Marquez (R Studio Training).

I gratefully acknowledge the financial support for my doctoral study provided by Victoria University of Wellington and the China Scholarship Council. Also, Without the generosity of some research institutes and academics, I would not have had access to some data that has played a crucial role in building the very foundation of this thesis, the methodology in particular. I owe great thanks to the Research Institute for Global Value Chains (RIGVC) of University of International Business and Economics (UIBE) for organizing the 2018 Global Value Chains (GVCs) training workshops and offering a scholarship to me. Special thanks go to Professor Fei Wang, Professor Kunfu Zhu, and Professor Jiansuo Pei for their guidance on methodology during and after the workshop. I am also grateful to the members of the OECD-ICIO team and ADB-ICIO team for their data support. Special thanks go to Mahinthan J. Mariasingham and his team for the swift response and kind support on the processing of input-output tables. I would like to thank Professor Takashi Yagi at Meiji University for inviting me to be a visiting scholar in 2019. Professor Yagi kindly introduced me to his research networks, lectures and seminars. I met Dr Satoshi Inomata from IDE-JETRO, Rintaro Matsuda from Meiji University, Dr Hui Li from Qingdao University, and Luciano Cintio Carment from Sydney University who offered selfless support on the methodology. I also appreciate the great opportunity to work as a Hinrich research fellow at the policy support unit, APEC Secretariat (Singapore) in 2022. What resonates with me most about this fellowship is the beautiful research work of the Hinrich Foundation and APEC Secretariat, particularly relating to sustainable trade and supply chain connectivity.

In addition, special thanks are due to three examiners of my PhD thesis: Professor Fei-Ling Wang, Professor Gerald Chan, and Dr. Matthew Castle. They have made insightful comments that help improve the thesis. I also benefited from the feedback of Duncan Campbell, Dr Lifang Peng, Dr Deborah Laurs, Kirsten Reid, Dr Caroline McDonald, Andrew Wilford, and Professor Yongnian Zheng. Duncan read my whole thesis carefully and offered witty comments. Dr Peng read the abstract, Chapters One and Two critically. Dr Laurs and Kirsten Reid are my student learning advisors during my PhD, whom I met almost every week to improve my writings. Dr McDonald read Chapters Four, Five, and Eight cheerfully. Andrew Wilford is always happy to help proofreading upon my urgent requests. Their annotations helped me polish the writing. Professor Zheng provided constructive comments and encouraged me to publish this thesis. I would like to express my appreciation.

Moreover, I would like to express my gratitude to my parents, friends, and partner. My parents always support whatever decision I make to pursue academic excellence. During my study and life in New Zealand, I express my gratitude to two homestay happy couples. Meihua Han and Yiji Gao have fed me homemade dumplings for four years, which considerably satisfy my "Chinese stomach". Michele Allison (an amateur triathlete and a world champion in her age group) and Richard Allison shared their Kiwi way of life: work hard and play harder. The following friends have helped me in various ways: Shaun Hopkins, Wendy Gao, Andrew Donoghue, Mengzhu Yan, Lifang Peng, Junjun Cheng, Jonette Crysell, Yan Ma, Roseanne Harland, Isabel Li, Thomas Song, Pavithra Jayawardena, Mengdi Zhang, Jie Huang, Yue Sun, Dylan Stent, Nguyen Khac Giang, Ganlong Wang, and Melody Yu. This thesis would not have existed in its present form without the unwavering support of my "long-suffering" partner, Yongyi Liu.

Abbreviations

ABMI	Asian Bond Market Initiative
ADB	Asian Development Bank
AEC	ASEAN Economic Community
AFC	Asian financial crisis
AIO	Asia Input-Output Database
AMSR	Agriculture-manufacturing-services ratio
APEC	Asia-Pacific Economic Cooperation
ASEAN	Association of Southeast Asian Nations
BRI	Belt and Road Initiative
CEPA	Closer Economic Partnership Arrangement (mainland China and Hong Kong)
CJK	China-Japan-South Korea
CMIM	Chiang Mai Initiative Multilateralization
CPTPP	Comprehensive and Progressive Trans-Pacific Partnership
DVA	Domestic value-added
EAFTA	East Asia Free Trade Area
EAS	East Asia Summit
ECFA	Economic Cooperation Framework Agreement (mainland China and Taiwan)
EEC	European Economic Community
EOI	Export-oriented industrialization
EU	European Union
FDI	Foreign Direct Investment
FG	Flying geese
FTA	Free trade agreement
FVA	Foreign value-added
GATT	General Agreement on Tariffs and Trade
GDP	Gross domestic product
GPNs	Global production networks
GRC	Global and regional connectivity
GVA	Global value-added
GVC(s)	Global value chain(s)
IAEA	International Atomic Energy Agency

ICAO	International Civil Aviation Organization
ICIO	Inter-Country Input-Output
IES	International economic structure
IMF	International Monetary Fund
IPR	Intellectual property rights
ISDS	Investor-State Dispute Settlement
ISI	Import substitution industrialization
MFA	Multi-Fiber Arrangement
MFN	Most favored nation
MNCs	Multinational corporations
MRIO	Multi-regional input-output
NAFTA	North American Free Trade Agreement
NGO(s)	Non-governmental organization(s)
NIE	New Institutional Economics
NIEs	Newly industrialized economies
ODM	Original design manufacturers
OECD	Organization for Economic Cooperation and Development
OEM	Original equipment manufacturers
OFDI	Outward foreign direct investment
PRC	People's Republic of China
RCEP	Regional and Comprehensive Economic Partnership
RCI	Regional Concentration Index
R&D	Research and development
ROOs	Rules of origins
ROW	Rest of the world
RTA	Regional trade agreement
RVA	Regional value-added
RVC(s)	Regional value chain(s)
SOE(s)	State-owned enterprise(s)
SSR	Self-sufficiency rate
TiVA	Trade in value added
TPNs	Transborder production networks
TPP	Trans-Pacific Partnership
UN	United Nations
UPU	Universal Postal Union
USMCA	US-Mexico-Canada Agreement
WHO	World Health Organization
WIOD	World Input-Output Database
WTO	World Trade Organization
WWI	World War I
WWII	World War II

1 Introduction

1.1 The Problem in East Asian Regionalism: Weakness

It is argued that we live in "a world of regions" (Peter J. Katzenstein, 2015, p. 1). Regionalism is a global phenomenon in the world economic system. This is true of the European Union (EU), where regionalism has been a consistent feature of its economic structure since World War II. It is true of North America, where the North American Free Trade Agreement (NAFTA) functions as a trilateral trade bloc.[1] Regionalism also applies to East Asia where regional economic institutions are emerging. The world is indeed demarcated by regionalist proposals for the EU, NAFTA, and many more regions.

However, East Asian regionalism distinguishes itself from the EU and NAFTA model because there is no single unitary regional framework. East Asia is defined here as consisting of 15 economies: Southeast Asia or ASEAN (Association of Southeast Asian Nations)—Brunei, Cambodia, Indonesia, Laos, Malaysia, Myanmar, the Philippines, Singapore, Thailand, and Vietnam; and Northeast Asia—China, Hong Kong, Taiwan,[2] Japan, and South Korea. Southeast Asia is building various projects, which, instead of uniting the region, have somewhat divided it (Pitakdumrongkit, 2016, p. 250), and Northeast Asia appears even less integrated and seems like a "non-region" (Wissenbach, 2013, p. 219).

Instead of a single inward-looking regional bloc, some sub-regional and trans-regional frameworks such as ASEAN, APEC (Asia-Pacific Economic Cooperation), CP/TPP (Comprehensive and Progressive/Trans-Pacific Partnership), and RCEP (Regional Comprehensive Economic Partnership) have been created. None of these frameworks are modeled on the EU and NAFTA-style institutionalization. Their membership mechanisms were deliberately designed as being inclusive. Their functions were strictly limited to intergovernmental coordination rather than supranational governance. The end goals of these East Asian regional frameworks were not political and economic integration but rather mechanisms that allow international cooperation. Figure 1.1 demonstrates the different scopes of membership for ASEAN, APEC, CP/TPP, and RCEP.

DOI: 10.4324/9781032613321-1

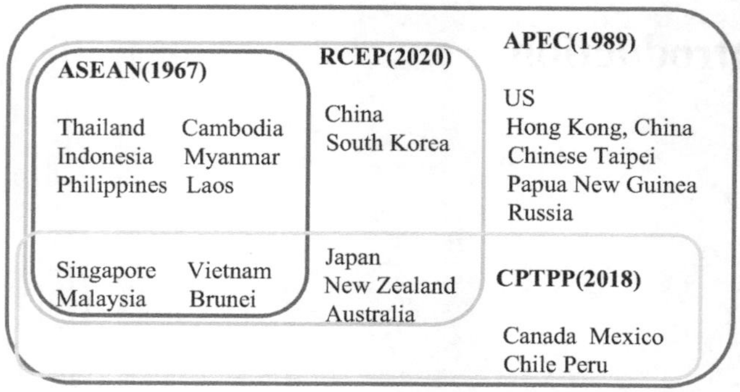

Figure 1.1 Members of ASEAN, APEC, CP/TPP, and RCEP.

ASEAN member economies[3] signed a free trade agreement (FTA) in 1992 and the ASEAN Economic Community (AEC) was established in 2015, which were two major milestones in the organization's regional economic integration agenda (Wood, 2017, p. 1). However, ASEAN countries lack the factual solidarity to act as a whole; instead, national interests and capabilities still dominate. For example, the ASEAN FTA does not have a common external tariff. When an external partner establishes an FTA with ASEAN, it has to sign ten bilateral agreements with individual ASEAN member economies rather than a single multilateral pact with ASEAN as a collective body (Ravenhill, 2016).

APEC, established in 1989, comprises 21 member economies[4] from the Asia-Pacific region. APEC has the widest membership across the Asia-Pacific and includes global economic powers such as the United States, China, Japan, and even Russia. It adopts the weakest institutional form of open regionalism and voluntary commitments. Open regionalism refers to "the practice of making trade concessions available to member and non-member economies alike" (Ravenhill, 2001, p. 6). Voluntary commitments suggest no legally binding commitments and no mechanisms for resolving disputes.

More recently, two conflicting and legally binding preferential trade agreements across the Asia-Pacific—CP/TPP[5] and RCEP—were signed in 2018 and 2020, respectively. With respect to membership, CP/TPP does not include China, while RCEP does not include the United States. CP/TPP is led by developed economies such as Japan, Singapore, Australia, and New Zealand. RCEP, advocated for by ASEAN developing economies and China, is a "backbone" for the economic integration of ASEAN and its six FTA partners (Mukherjee, 2019, p. 1). In terms of functions, each of the two frameworks has a distinct set of rules for transborder trade, investment, and manufacturing organization. CP/TPP goes beyond traditional tariffs and extends into the behind-the-border issues and domestic regulations such as trade in services, investment, intellectual property rights (IPR), and even state-owned enterprises (SOEs). RCEP, in contrast, is built on ASEAN and its six bilateral FTAs and mainly focuses on traditional tariff barriers.

After decades of institutional development, instead of a single economic community, East Asian economies are divided among different and sometimes contending regional institutional arrangements. Thus, compared to the EU and NAFTA, regionalism in East Asia is weak. Weak regionalism is defined as a problem of East Asian regionalism in terms of three patterns: (1) a lack of a single unitary regional framework; (2) multiple and competing initiatives between the ideas of East Asia and the Asia-Pacific; (3) now two divergent frameworks—CP/TPP and RCEP. All of these regional economic frameworks seek "the right institution" but none appear to be working well.

This book proposes a structural theory to demonstrate the relationship between structural forces and institutional outcomes as an overlooked factor that can contribute to explaining East Asian regionalism. Two conventional approaches, liberal institutionalism and market force theory, have attempted to explain this weakness. Liberal institutional theory argues that well-designed and implemented institutions have the potential to facilitate regional economic integration. Accordingly, the problem of weak regionalism in East Asia lies in the institutional ineptness of East Asian states in that they are not willing to sacrifice national interests for a supranational-regional authority. Market force theory, on the other hand, maintains that the externally oriented nature of market forces in East Asia is precisely antithetical to strong regionalism. My structural theory transcends institutional ineptness and market force entrepreneurism and identifies the underlying international economic structures that, in my view, lead to weak regionalism.

This chapter begins with an examination of the experience of East Asian regionalism from the late 1980s to the 2010s. Then, three patterns of weak regionalism in East Asia will be analyzed. After establishing the weak regionalism of East Asia, I will outline my research problem and the structure of this book.

1.1.1 The Experience of East Asian Regionalism

To better understand the origin and development of weak regionalism, I suggest that we first revisit the experience of East Asian regionalism from the period of "institutional deficit" (John Ravenhill, 2001, p. 2) to that of "institutional overreach" (Li, 2011, p. 5). The period of institutional deficit saw a lack of regional economic institutions until the establishment of APEC in 1989. The period of institutional overreach from 1989, by contrast, witnessed too many institutions competing with one another, yet no one force emerged to promote regional governance. As the Cold War ended, East Asian countries started to view regional trade agreements positively. In the subsequent decades, there has been a mushrooming of regional institutional frameworks: APEC, ASEAN FTA, ASEAN+1, ASEAN+3, China-Japan-South Korea trilateral cooperation, CP/TPP, and RCEP.

The change of East Asian regionalism from institutional deficit to institutional overreach has resulted in three stages of development of regionalism in the 1990s–2010s. In the first stage of 1989–1997, East Asia adopted a reactive approach toward the worldwide trend of regionalism and developed APEC and ASEAN FTA, which were known for their principle of open regionalism. The second stage of the late 1990s and 2000s saw the rise and fall of an exclusionist East Asian regionalism in the aftermath of the 1997 Asian financial crisis (AFC). The third stage in the 2010s highlighted the emergence of two mega-regional FTAs—CP/TPP and RCEP, disguised as regionalism for global economic governance. These three waves of regionalism, however, have not unified East Asian economies into a single regional economic community.

1.1.1.1 Phase I (1989–1997): Reactive and Open Regionalism

East Asia, which traditionally embraced global multilateralism, was hesitant to develop regionalism. For many years, East Asian countries had been firmly grounded in the key principles of the GATT (General Agreement on Tariffs and Trade)/WTO (World Trade Organization) system[6]: non-discrimination, reciprocity, and multilateralism. Leaders in the region were committed multilateralists, seeking access to global markets to fuel the export-oriented growth models. They were long immune to the intensifying regionalist tendency. The post-1945 liberal international order gave rise to processes of globalization, and these processes enabled East Asian countries to rapidly develop their economies through trade liberalization. First, securing and expanding access to the global market was of critical importance to East Asian countries. A well-functioning GATT/WTO system thus was most in line with the economic interests of East Asian countries. Therefore, traditionally, East Asian economies were beneficiaries and firm supporters of multilateral trading systems centered on GATT/WTO. They tended to believe that regionalism might threaten the multilateral trading system.

However, in the late 1980s, influenced by two factors, regionalism became the second-best choice for East Asian countries to strengthen global economic relationships. First, there were rising concerns about potential breakdowns, or at least stagnation, in the multilateral trading system. In the early 1990s, multilateral talks under GATT proceeded "at a glacial pace" (Baldwin, 1993, p. 409). Proposals to liberalize agricultural trade, to grant equal treatment for foreign firms, and to cut tariffs along the lines of the US's "zero-for-zero initiative" failed. In order to expand the scope of trade rules, countries were negotiating to establish a wholly new body, WTO, which was established in 1995. Second, regional liberalization was sweeping the world trading system like wildfire. In Europe, regional integration strengthened with the shift from European Economic Community to the EU, while the Canada-US FTA took effect in 1989. Compared to Western Europe and North America, the FTA negotiation process of East Asian countries proved significantly slower.

Due to the fears of the stagnation of the GATT/WTO system and being left out from other regional blocs, especially NAFTA and the EU, East Asia developed its first two regional economic institutions: APEC (1989) and ASEAN FTA (1992). APEC and ASEAN share two defining features in institutional design—both are reactive and open. First, these institutions are reactive for being a means of countering the proceeding regional institution-building in Europe and North America. East Asian countries accepted regionalism such as APEC and ASEAN due to their fear that they would be left outside of emerging trade blocs in the world. Both APEC and ASEAN were driven in large part by the domino effect of regionalism, a circumstance in which nations excluded from a trade agreement launch their own negotiations to redress trade diversion.

Second, APEC and ASEAN have "open regionalism" as their core objectives. Open regionalism seeks to "promote economic integration amongst participants without discrimination against other economies" (Drysdale & Vines, 1998, p. 103; Pitakdumrongkit, 2016, p. 249). In other words, open regionalism means openness and inclusiveness to countries outside of formal membership. Table 1.1 sets out the regional efforts of APEC and ASEAN that were ordered around the key idea of open regionalism.

Table 1.1 Principle of Open Regionalism in APEC and ASEAN

APEC	*APEC Bogor Goals*	*ASEAN FTA*	*ASEAN Charter*
Inclusiveness and support for the global economic system			
"None believes that APEC should be directed to the formation of a trading bloc" (1989 APEC Ministerial Meeting, agenda 2—Global Trade Liberalization—The Role of the Asia-Pacific Region).	"To support an expanding world economy and an open Multilateral trading system" (Leaders' Declaration point 2(2)) and to enhance regional and global growth).	The primary motive of ASEAN FTA is to "intensify cooperation among the members of ASEAN to increase their international competitiveness and integration with the world" (ASEAN Secretariat, 2015).	To promote "the centrality of ASEAN in external political, economic, social and cultural relations while remaining actively engaged, outward-looking, inclusive and non-discriminatory" (Article 2(m)).
Support for multilateralism and non-discrimination			
"Every economy represented in Canberra relies heavily on a strong and open multilateral trading system" (1989 APEC Ministerial Meeting, agenda 2—Global Trade Liberalization—The Role of the Asia-Pacific Region).	"[Opposed] to the creation of an inward-looking trading bloc that would divert from the pursuit of global free trade" (Leaders' Declaration point 6).	"With its commitment to open regionalism, ASEAN pursues active external economic relations with countries and regional groupings around the world in parallel to its internal integration efforts" (ASEAN Secretariat, 2015).	"Adherence to multilateral trade rules and ASEAN's rules-based regimes to move towards elimination of all barriers to regional economic integration, in a market-driven economy" (Article 2(2) (n)).

As Table 1.1 shows, APEC was designed as an "Asia-Pacific" way to achieve a free, open, and globally oriented trade and investment regime. It adopted an "open regionalism" approach to promote regional economic cooperation in a voluntary, unilateral, and flexible way. One of APEC's flagship initiatives, the Bogor Goals, was put forward in 1994, calling for two timelines—the realization of free and open trade and investment by 2010 for industrialized economies and by 2020 for developing economies. However, the first goal did not come about in 2010, and the second goal can hardly be achieved within the time framework. APEC's failure to meet the Bogor Goals reinforced governments' skepticism over whether open regionalism can deliver the anticipated outcome of regional cooperation. Similarly, ASEAN develops an "ASEAN way", which is associated with "a high degree of discreteness, informality, pragmatism, expediency, consensus building, and non-confrontational bargaining styles" (Amitav Acharya, 1998, p. 58). The ASEAN way brings major powers together in a wider regional and international setting, attracts foreign direct investment as a single investment destination, and improves the region's competency as a unitary production base.

1.1.1.2 Phase II (the Late 1990s and 2000s): An Exclusionist Regional Economic Community

The 1997 AFC marked a clear shift of East Asian regionalism from open regionalism to an exclusionist regional economic community. The AFC exposed the weaknesses of open regionalism, as both APEC and ASEAN illustrated an inability to avoid or mitigate financial crises. As an alternative, the pace of East Asian regionalism and community building picked up (Webber, 2001). The AFC also exposed the existing links among economies in the region and each country's vulnerability to economic problems that beset their neighbors (Haggard, 2000). This sense of vulnerability gave a strong impetus to the search for regional collective action that could help safeguard the region against future crises.

Professor Zhang Yunling, one of the leading Chinese researchers on East Asian regionalism, argues that East Asian community building is driven by four wheels (2002). The first wheel is the ASEAN+3 process, which covers the entire area of East Asia. The second wheel is the ASEAN+1 process, that is, ASEAN's bilateral cooperation with China, Japan, and South Korea. The third wheel is the CJK, i.e., cooperation between China, Japan, and South Korea. Finally, the fourth wheel is the cooperation within ASEAN itself. Driven by the four wheels, East Asian governments engaged in unprecedented collaboration on financial and trade matters.

First, sparked by the AFC, ASEAN+3 was initiated as an alternative platform for ASEAN and APEC. ASEAN+3 includes the ten members of ASEAN plus China, Japan, and South Korea, and thus is named the "newlyweds" of Southeast Asia and Northeast Asia. Webber considers the developments in East Asian regionalism in the mid-2000s as "Two funerals and a wedding"—the decline of ASEAN and APEC in contrast to the rise of ASEAN+3 (2001, p. 339). The remarkable achievement under the ASEAN+3 framework is the enhancement of regional self-help and support mechanisms in monetary and financial cooperation. The Chiang Mai Initiative in 2000, its multilateralization in 2010 as Chiang Mai Initiative Multilateralization (CMIM),[7] and the Asian Bond Market Initiative (ABMI)[8] in 2002 have been key steps to realize a long-term vision for "monetary regionalism" (Dieter & Higgott, 2003).

Both CMIM and ABMI are part of the regional liquidity fund mechanisms which aim to improve immunity to another financial crisis. However, both cases are often cited as examples of limited monetary regionalism (Dieter & Higgott, 2003; Kawai, 2015). On one hand, an important feature of the CMI is the IMF link, which dictates that only 10% of funds can be released without the approval of IMF. For the remaining 90%, the approval of the IMF will be required. This IMF-delinked portion was raised to 20% in 2005 and 30% in 2012. The debate over whether to increase the IMF unlinked portion from 30% to 40% has dragged on for years and is not resolved yet. The legacy of IMF stigma is too much of a hurdle to overcome. On the other hand, the ABMI has not made impressive gains either. The ABMI also appears to complement the IMF-led global financial architecture. Asian bond markets still lagged in both breadth and depth. Therefore, the framework of ASEAN+3 is not a regionalist approach but designed to "complement existing features of the global financial architecture" (Grimes, 2006). Therefore, despite growing interactions, the ASEAN+3 framework is not solid enough to pull individual nations together.

Second, the ASEAN+1 FTAs provide an insufficient level of regional cooperation. The majority of regional institutional frameworks in East Asia follow the so-called ASEAN+ logic, with ASEAN at the center creating concentric circles of regionalism in East Asia. For instance, in the field of trade, ASEAN has concluded a variety of ASEAN+1 FTAs. ASEAN signed its first three FTAs with China (2005), South Korea (2007), and Japan (2008). The ASEAN+1 FTAs are viewed by many as the basis for ASEAN+3, which can evolve from the amalgamation of the "ASEAN+1" FTAs. They were regarded as a foundation for the more ambitious vision of "an East Asia Free Trade Area" (ASEAN-China Expert Group on Economic Cooperation, 2001, p. 30). However, the ASEAN+1 approach is problematic. First, the coexistence of ASEAN-centered FTAs with different rules creates the "noodle bowl syndrome" of too many institutional frameworks (Baldwin, 2008, p. 2). These frameworks vary greatly in the level of tariff liberalization, services liberalization, and rules of origin (Fukunaga & Isono, 2013). It should be noted that ASEAN+1 FTAs are not uniform in structure. On trade in goods, for example, ASEAN and its FTA partners not only use different tariff classifications for their tariff concessions but also use different schedules for their FTAs with different countries. In addition, tariff concessions from the same country differ depending on the FTA involved, and tariff elimination rates are different across ASEAN+1 FTAs. Trade in services and investment are not concluded for all ASEAN+1 FTAs, either. Also, there is doubt or uncertainty about the idea of ASEAN centrality in regional cooperation. The leadership of ASEAN in East Asian regional cooperation has been called into question and is likened to "ponies pulling the cart" (Zhai, 2009). Moreover, ASEAN also signed FTAs with extra-regional members such as Australia-New Zealand and India in 2004. The inclusion of these new members leads to a bigger regional framework, ASEAN+6, which further undermines the original core of an exclusionist East Asian regionalism.

Third, the ongoing trilateral economic cooperation among China, Japan, and South Korea (CJK) has advanced in a stop-and-go fashion for almost two decades. In contrast to Southeast Asia, the Northeast Asia sub-region has been late to develop regionalism. The trilateral FTA was proposed in 2002. The CJK Trilateral Summit was established in 2007. The negotiation of the CJK trilateral FTA was initiated in 2013, and the most recent update is the 16th round of talks in 2019. The three governments have employed a "low-profile" approach, allowing them to sustain the momentum to promote regional cooperation (Takashi, 2012). Efforts to institutionalize trilateral cooperation have experienced back and forth, even on and off, over time, due to politics on different fronts. Unlike the ASEAN-centered approach, Northeast Asian trilateralism remains at the periphery of East Asian regionalism.

Fourth, ASEAN has been by far the most advanced effort to build a regional economic community, but it has fallen short of the high standard and time frame it has set for itself. ASEAN has come a long way since ASEAN FTA was established in 1992. ASEAN has been working on its roadmap with a vision to create an AEC by 2015. The level of economic integration in Southeast Asia, however, has not been satisfactory. Although the FTA is already in place, there are still a substantial amount of items that are not included in the agreement, and the usage level of preferential tariff is still low.[9] Even the creation of a manufacturing base is mostly led by multinational corporations. While there are efforts for balanced economic development among member states, ASEAN has yet to narrow the development gaps among them.

Despite the four wheels-driven endeavors, an exclusionist East Asian regionalism has not taken shape so far. An East Asian economic community has increasingly been called into question and labeled as an unfeasible dream. The regional trade system in East Asia was at a crossroads in the late 2000s. Many governments in the region have begun to look toward new "mega-regional" trade deals.

1.1.1.3 Phase III (the 2010s): Disguised Regionalism to Make Trade Rules for the Asia-Pacific Region and Beyond

In the 2010s, the limits of global multilateralism (such as WTO) and bilateralism created strong incentives for states to devise a region-wide trade architecture for East Asia: mega-regional frameworks. Globally, the WTO's Doha Round[10] had become extremely fraught as tension and disagreements between major trading countries in the developed and developing world impeded progress. The Nairobi Ministerial Conference in 2015 finally put an end to the Doha Round, which became the first-ever fruitless round since GATT was invented in 1947 (Martin & Mercurio, 2017). The failure of the Doha Round can be seen as a sign of a larger problem: there were growing tensions between developed and developing economies on whether and how far negotiations should go beyond traditional tariffs.

Meanwhile, the trade architecture built on bilateral FTAs is also problematic. Bilateral FTA networks are metaphorically compared to a tangled bowl of noodles, featuring the entanglement of hundreds of FTAs with various rules, tariffs, and institutional arrangements (Baldwin, 2008, p. 2). As of December 2020, East Asian economies have signed a large number of FTAs: Singapore (25), South Korea (18), Japan (17), China (15), Malaysia (14), Thailand (13), Vietnam (13), Indonesia (10), Philippines (10), Brunei (8), Laos (8), Hong Kong (7), Taiwan (6), Myanmar (7), and Cambodia (6). In industries organized in transborder production networks, East Asian firms must manage the transaction costs of compliance with the complex set of rules. Economists argue that the "noodle bowl" problem can act as a new trade barrier in and of itself.

In this context, two competing mega-regional agreements—CP/TPP and RCEP—emerged to multilateralize the "noodle bowl". Table 1.2 illustrates key

Table 1.2 Key Features of the CP/TPP and RCEP Agreements

Mega-FTAs	*CP/TPP*	*RCEP*
Launch negotiations	Mar. 2010	Nov. 2012
Conclude negotiations	TPP: Feb. 2016CP/TPP: Mar. 2018	Nov. 2020
Take into effect	CP/TPP: Dec. 2018	Expected date: 2021
Primary goal	A new "twenty-first-century" FTA to remove behind-the-border non-tariff barriers	Manage the noodle bowl effect of the ASEAN+X model
Relation to regional architecture	Trans-regional (Asia-Pacific)	Affirms the principle of ASEAN centrality
Scope and coverage	"WTO-X" aspirations—non-tariff issues targeted	"WTO-consistent" and WTO+"—mostly focused on tariffs
Major sponsor	TPP: US-led; CP/TPP: Japan-led	ASEAN-led
Membership	Australia, Brunei, Canada, Chile, Japan, Malaysia, Mexico, New Zealand, Peru, Singapore, United States, and Vietnam Withdrawal of the United States: Jan. 2017	ASEAN, China, Japan, South Korea, India, Australia, and New Zealand; Withdrawal of India: Nov. 2019
Significant absent members	China, Indonesia, and South Korea	United States

Notes: For a more detailed comparison between RCEP and CP/TPP, see the website of the Asian Trade Center: http://asiantradecentre.org/talkingtrade//myvwg5yr21a93pkjc45bwzx3wtbc3z

features of the CP/TPP and RCEP agreements. CP/TPP is, on the whole, considerably more ambitious than RCEP. A distinguishing feature of CP/TPP is its primary goal of crafting a new "twenty-first-century" FTA. It attempts to remove the behind-the-border non-tariff barriers that affect the ability of firms to enter, operate in, and exit foreign markets. It addresses potential non-tariff barriers to trade, covering public health and product safety standards, labor and the environment, international investment, digital trade and e-commerce, and SOEs. RCEP is the "ASEAN-centered answer" to the "noodle bowl" effect, aiming primarily at harmonizing existing rules and their application within various ASEAN+1 FTAs (Mukherjee, 2019, p. 1). In its scope and coverage, RCEP lacks regulations on behind-the-border non-tariff barriers and is mostly focused on traditional tariffs. While RCEP does not go as far as CP/TPP in ensuring comprehensive coverage of trade in goods and services, it substantially opens up access in countries that maintain relatively high trade barriers. RCEP represents the first time for many members to engage in trade arrangements with each other, especially between China, Japan, and South Korea.

Trade economists argue that RCEP and CP/TPP are "disguised multilateralism" (Camroux, 2012). Rather than building regional economic communities, they are trans-regional and trying to develop an extensive set of rules and regulations in the Asia-Pacific and beyond (Deborah K. Elms, 2021; Shen, 2018). Both CP/TPP and RCEP serve as a kind of preparation for setting future multilateral rules.[11] Both assume consistency in regional platforms and use it as a basis for negotiating tomorrow's WTO rules (Horn et al., 2010). The ambitions in the CP/TPP agreement largely reveal the aspirations of developed countries in trade negotiations. The modest and tariff-focused commitments in the RCEP agreement are a response on the part of developing economies to CP/TPP.

In summary, there were contending initiatives for an economic community in the region, from APEC and ASEAN to ASEAN+3, to CP/TPP and RCEP, and many less prominent ones in between. However, all of these proposals and projects have not led to the formation of a single, region-wide architecture for economic integration and cooperation.

1.1.2 The Patterns of Weak Regionalism

Having reviewed the experience of East Asian regionalism, I discuss weakness in East Asian regionalism in three broad patterns. There has been no single and region-wide architecture for economic integration and cooperation. There have been too many contending initiatives for an economic community in the region. Two trans-regional, overlapping, and contending economic frameworks, CP/TPP and RCEP, have emerged to dominate the region.

1.1.2.1 Not an East Asian Economic Community

Perhaps the most important pattern associated with weak regionalism in East Asia is a lack of a single, region-wide architecture for economic integration and cooperation. The only true East Asian regional framework, ASEAN+3, is already "running out of steam" due to an apparent lack of common resolve in regional monetary and trade integration (Hund, 2003, p. 407).

ASEAN+3 had commitments in regional monetary integration but failed to realize the promises. At the beginning of the century, regional leaders called for creating a common East Asian currency.[12] For example, the CMIM and the ABMI marked important milestones that highlighted the members' strong commitment. However, later the idea of a common trading currency for East Asia has been shifted from the regional to the global level. Rather than developing a Yen or RMB regional bloc, the big economic powers of the region—Japan and China—put more emphasis on the internationalization of its currency globally. As a result, the discussion on the East Asian currency idea has been closed off, and the ASEAN+3 framework has not made substantial progress in monetary cooperation.

The idea of establishing an East Asia Free Trade Area (EAFTA) ended up as a "visionary fancy" (Hund, 2003, p. 410). The China-Japan-South Korea trilateral FTA is the most difficult and complex threshold in the entire East Asian regional economic integration process. Within the trilateral framework, there is coexisting bilateral cooperation. The China-South Korea FTA came into force in 2015. The Japan-South Korea FTA negotiations were launched as early as 2003 but have been stalled for years. Worst of all, there is no bilateral FTA negotiation between China and Japan. The EAFTA would be not realized without constituting an FTA between these two regional economic powers. Thus, it is becoming increasingly clear that ASEAN+3, in its present shape, does not have the potential to evolve as a region-wide trade bloc in its own right.

1.1.2.2 Too Many Contending Initiatives

Instead of one unitary and exclusive East Asian economic community, East Asian countries propose contending institutional frameworks: ASEAN, APEC, East Asia Summit (EAS),[13] CP/TPP, RCEP (also known as ASEAN+6), and many less prominent ones in between.

Rather than a supranational institution, ASEAN is an intergovernmental project. When ASEAN reaches functional cooperation on economic projects, the strong commitment to non-interference and its resulting institutional inefficiency makes it difficult to deal smoothly with controversial issues (Jetschke, 2009; Yukawa, 2017). ASEAN adopted the ASEAN+ approach to further pursue external economic cooperation on top of the intra-ASEAN economic integration. For instance, ASEAN has been in "the driver's seat" in both the East Asia Summit and RCEP. This central role and leadership, however, have been a challenging position to maintain, "given ASEAN's own institutional weaknesses and difficulties in arriving in common positions among ten quite divergent members" (Elms & Nguyen, 2019, p. 10). For example, ASEAN FTA[14] does not have a common external tariff. This structural factor significantly influences the outcomes of negotiations between ASEAN and its +1 partners,

"The ASEAN Plus One treaties have essentially been 10 bilateral agreements rather than a single multilateral pact" (Ravenhill, 2016). The negotiation basis of RCEP is the five separate ASEAN+1 FTAs, which could partly explain the slow pace to reach a common ground for a mega economic trade bloc. Moreover, ASEAN lacks capacity: market size-related and financial resources. ASEAN may be too small to support the construction of a multilateral cooperation framework. ASEAN provides at best a very "softcore" of East Asian regionalism (Webber, 2010, p. 323).

APEC is criticized as "a perfect excuse for a chat" as it is too informal to be effective (Pang, 2011, p. 48). For example, APEC has no binding commitments or treaty obligations. APEC takes a voluntary liberalization approach to members and a non-discriminatory approach to non-members. The decision-making mechanisms are not subject to a regional authority but collective decision-making by individual sovereign nation-states. As a result of the intergovernmental nature of rule-making, a Secretariat is confined to secretarial activities, which involve "ineffective procedures for monitoring, and no mechanisms for resolving disputes among members" (Ravenhill, 2001, p. 185). With open regionalism and pro-liberalization agenda, APEC did not aim to deliver and as a result, have not delivered a sense of community. CP/TPP and RCEP are binding arrangements for Asia-Pacific economic cooperation but complement the role of APEC.

Regional institutions fall into three categories: Southeast Asia, East Asia proper, and Asia-Pacific. Regional institutions under these three categories are naturally overlapping and competing with each other. It is uncertain what the "region" is: whether East Asia, Asia-Pacific, or various other compositions. Multiple and co-existent levels and forms of regional cooperation and integration (sub-regional, trans-regional) make it hard to define regional boundaries.

1.1.2.3 And Now CP/TPP and RCEP

More recently, the category of Asia-Pacific, rather than Southeast Asia or East Asia proper, attracted more attention among East Asian countries. The mega-regional trade agreements—CP/TPP and RCEP—have grown out of this context. Both CP/TPP and RCEP posited themselves as "writing rules for global trade" and have shown very limited interest in preparing a new vision for regional integration. CP/TPP is said to aim to "be a template for 21st-century trade deals". RCEP is said to multilateralize the five ASEAN+1 FTAs and "further develop and deepen the integrated production base".[15]

CP/TPP and RCEP are supported by two different groups of economies and represent two different blueprints for future trade and investment rules across the Asia-Pacific region. The United States and Japan took the lead in TPP and CP/TPP to build a new international economic order and advance their industrial and trade interests (Cartwright, 2017). Both the United States and Japan intentionally outsourced their domestic manufacturing industry and became particularly competitive in services. They thus needed to protect their intellectual property ownership and investment overseas, and allow market access for their service industries. Therefore, CP/TPP rules were to establish consistent rules for global investment and secure a level playing field for investors. A sizable portion of the agreement touches on topics that relate directly to investment law, such as protection of intellectual property, competition policy, and the investor-state dispute settlement (ISDS).

In contrast, China and most ASEAN developing economies long backed the RCEP as a chance to shape the rules of regional production networks. Given the highly integrated supply chains for manufacturing products that span multiple East Asian economies, one of the most important benefits of RCEP is the harmonization of rules of origins (ROOs). ROOs ensure the consistent set of rules needed to qualify for tariff reductions, which could improve the utilization of preferential tariff rates and further deepen the integration of industrial chains within the region (Elms, 2020; Jiang & Yu, 2021). The underlying industrial structures explain why RCEP does not address services trade, intellectual property, or labor and environmental rules to the same extent as CP/TPP does.

To summarize, RCEP and CP/TPP contend with each other not only in the scope of membership but also over the level of engagement with trade and investment rules.[16] As discussed above, while CP/TPP goes deep into behind-the-border measures, RCEP focuses on traditional trade tariffs. These two competing mega-regional frameworks are trying to shape different rules for transborder trade, investment, and manufacturing organization.

1.2 Puzzles

As discussed in previous sections, regionalism in East Asia is characterized by a lack of purely East Asian economic community and contending institutional frameworks, which shows that regionalism in East Asia is weak. East Asia constitutes one of the most dynamic regions in the world economy, and its weak regionalism has caused heated discussions among International Relations (IR) scholars and economists over the reasons behind this phenomenon.

In the existing IR literature, liberal institutionalism is the mainstream theory used by scholars to explain weak regionalism in East Asia. This theory departs from state-led approach followed in Europe to regional cooperation and assumes that the power of institutions influences economic behavior and the movement of international economic activities. This state-led approach has led to global efforts to develop institutions for economic integration in the past decades. Scholars who believe in liberal institutionalism attribute weak regionalism to the inabilities or unwillingness of East Asian states to cooperate in building a region-wide institutional framework.

Greatly influenced by this liberal institutionalism, IR scholars from other schools have tried to blend this institution-centered analytical framework and their own theoretical approaches together to offer an integrative explanation to the problem in East Asian regionalism. For instance, realist scholars argue that great power politics has prevented East Asia from establishing a sophisticated institutional framework of regionalism.[17] Constructivist studies point to the lack of a common regional identity as an obstacle for East Asia to embrace the EU model of institution-building[18] (Acharya 2009). While noting these blended explanations from the realist and constructivist perspectives, the liberal institutional explanation—institutions matter but East Asia fails to find the right institution—nevertheless dominates in the IR discipline to explain weak regionalism in East Asia.

Differing from scholars of liberal institutionalism, some economists proposed the market force approach, which argues that the problem in East Asian regionalism is caused by market dynamics, rather than institutional ineptness. Market force explanation, in contrast, adopts a bottom-up approach. It argues that the economic realities of East Asia are different from the EU case: market-driven regionalization happened before regional institutional building in East Asia. Therefore, weak regionalism does not result from institutional building, but from the working of market forces such as trade, investment, and transborder production networks. Market force theory pays attention to the material forces at the firm level, at the investor level, and at the manufacturer level. The target of these private entities is to seek profit, production efficiency, and markets. They go global and do not have collective regional economic interests. But market forces are not national and are not able to explain the inter-state or intergovernmental exercise of regionalism. The market force approach thus fails to connect the economic realities with national institutional preferences, and in the end, institutional selections.

Similar to the market force explanation, my structural theory looks into the underlying material forces and economic realities behind institutional ineptness. But my structural theory is distinguished from the market force explanation. Rather than the business interests of individual firms proposed by market force theory, my structural theory cares about the relative power and strength of a state in its relation to others. My structural theory thus is more concerned about the structure—the distribution of production capabilities and interests among individual states in the world economic system. I will work out whether the different positions of nations in the international economic structures contributed to the complexity and high tension in their institutional preferences in regional economic organization and hence the weakness of East Asian regionalism.

By investigating the structural causes of weak regionalism in East Asia, this book attempts to address three puzzles. The first investigates the weak institutions of regional economic integration in East Asia. In contrast to the strong regionalism developed in the EU, this East Asian way of regionalism challenges the conventional ways of how we assess regionalism. It is not surprising that assessments about regionalism in East Asia are mostly pessimistic: "light regionalism" (Capannelli & Tan, 2012; Jetschke, 2009), "fragile regionalism" (Capannelli & Tan, 2012), "frustrated regionalism" (Nair, 2009), "nascent regionalism" (Evans, 2005), or "discursive regionalism" (Camroux, 2012). These judgments convey a similar idea—East Asian regionalism has been considered by many as weak, if not a failure in an institutional architecture for an economic community. As discussed earlier in Section 1.1.2, I use the word "weak" to define the unique patterns of regionalism in East Asia.

Is this weakness as problematic as most scholars claim? Considering the unique patterns and bottom-up experience of East Asian regionalism, it is, therefore, necessary to develop a bottom-up analytical framework beyond EU-centrism and liberal institutionalism. Challenging the traditional pessimistic paradigm, I aim to demonstrate that weak regionalism sometimes can be a strength in uniting East Asian states to cooperate. For instance, in contrast to an inward-looking regional bloc, open regionalism has enhanced East Asia's extra-regional connectivity with its principal trade partners such as the United States. These weak institutional frameworks have actually provided an open and inclusive platform to safeguard the region's globally oriented economic interests. Therefore, this book aims to answer the following questions: as a latecomer to regionalism, does East Asia want what has been achieved in the EU and NAFTA whole-heartedly? If states do not want political institutions with supranational qualities, is it a failure? What are the advantages and disadvantages of weak regionalism for East Asian economies to collaborate within and engage with global partners?

The second puzzle concerns a key innovation of my research which deals with international economic structures both theoretically and empirically. By replanting the structuralist framework of Kenneth Waltz, this book will clarify the conceptual differences between market forces and structural forces: market forces (commercial interests) are much more fungible, fluid, and subordinate to the states, while structural forces (distribution of capabilities) are system-wide conditions which create constraints and opportunities that shape the behavior of the nation-states. Moreover, empirically, by using the global value chain analysis, I will construct key sets of international economic structures where the positions of the nations can be observed and analyzed.

The third puzzle my research attempts to examine is why East Asian regionalism is weak with a special focus on structural forces as an overlooked influencing factor. Several studies have tried to search all possible influencing factors, blend different theoretical approaches together, and offer an integrative explanation of East Asian regionalism (Dent, 2016; Yoshimatsu, 2008; Cai, 2010). These multiple reasons include, but are not limited to, the geopolitics of great power competition and the so-called polarity, the socio-political and legal (in)compatibility among the nations, the international power differentials, and the varied development models. While acknowledging other factors at play, this book does not aim to provide a comprehensive list of all potent influencing factors. The research logic of this book, on the surface, is to explain the weak regionalism of East Asia, but the fundamental thinking is to investigate the logical relationship between the structural forces and states' institutional behavior in East Asian regionalism. How are states' institutional preferences formed? How might structural forces play a role in this process? How effective is my structural explanation to the varying attitudes of East

Asian states toward regionalism? To answer these questions, this research will zoom into the structural positioning of states in the global economy and link the positioning to their institutional preferences.

1.3 Book Outline

This book is comprised of eight chapters. Chapter 1 is the introduction. In Chapter 2, I put forward a structural theory to complement liberal institutionalism and market force theory, with a view to explaining weak regionalism in East Asia. The first section presents the liberal institutionalist explanations, suggesting that East Asian states had little experience in international institutional building and lacked a shared regional identity to support a regional economic community. Nonetheless, liberal institutional explanations do not take trade and production relationships into consideration, which is an important dimension of IR between East Asian economies. The second section is devoted to market force theory, which argues that regionalism in East Asia is driven very much by market forces including trade, investment, manufacturing, and marketing. Accordingly, supporters of market force theory believe that it is market forces rather than institutions that result in weak regionalism. However, I hold that market force theorists fail to establish the cause-and-effect relationship between the efficiency-seeking market forces and national institutional preferences. The last section deals with my structural theory which assumes a potential causal link between international economic structures and the nations' contending institutional preferences in East Asian regionalism. This contention is believed to be behind the inability of the states to agree on an optimal institutional arrangement in East Asian regionalism, hence the weakness of East Asian regionalism.

Chapter 3 illustrates how I model the international economic structures empirically to assess the structural effects on the national preferences of nations in East Asian regionalism. The first section introduces the global value chains (GVCs) approach and the Inter-Country Input-Output time-series data to depict the international economic structures. The GVCs approach provides a useful perspective to observe the distribution of production capabilities: who produces what and for whom. The second section explains why and how I transform input-output data into indicators for GVCs analysis of global, regional, and sectoral structures. More specifically, I explain the use of (1) complex network approach and regional concentration index to test the effects of the global economic structure on East Asia as a production unit; (2) mixed global and regional connectivity to test the effects of the regional economic structures on the interest and capability of nations to agree on an institutional framework for an East Asian economic community; and (3) self-sufficiency rates and agriculture-manufacturing-services Ratios to test the effects of different types of sectoral economic structures in the region on the divergence and contentiousness of the states' institutional preferences for either CP/TPP or RCEP in more recent years. The last section presents my three hypotheses, each of which corresponds to an empirical chapter.

Chapters 4, 5, and 6 are the empirical chapters in which I test the three hypotheses. Each chapter is devoted to assessing the effects of international economic structures on the states' institutional preferences in East Asian regionalism, and each focuses on a particular dimension of the theory. Chapter 4 will test the first hypothesis and investigate the effects of global economic structures, i.e., the distribution of value chains in Europe, North America, and East Asia. The second hypothesis will be investigated in Chapter 5. I will look at the effects of regional economic structures in this chapter. Chapter 6 will examine the last hypothesis and analyze the effects of sectoral economic structures on the states' preferences over CP/TPP and RCEP. In this chapter, I specifically explain why and how I use self-sufficiency rates and agriculture-manufacturing-services ratios of the national economies to explain their split position in joining CP/TPP and/or RCEP.

Chapter 7 discusses the major findings of this book. The first section revisits the structural theory and my three hypotheses. The second section summarizes the key findings from each of the empirical chapters. The last section concludes whether and to what extent the empirical evidence supports the theoretical expectations and confirms the structural theory of East Asian regionalism.

The final chapter, Chapter 8, presents the book's scholarly contributions. The project and findings are important in three aspects. First, the study adds to the scholarship on East Asian regionalism by complementing the liberal institutionalist and market force explanations of weak regionalism. Second, it enriches the use of structural and institutional analysis of international political economy. Third, my research provides a better understanding of the development of the world economic system over the two dominant frameworks: Wallerstein's core-periphery theory and the theory of multilateral institutionalism of the past 40 years.

Notes

1 The US-Mexico-Canada Agreement (USMCA) replaced NAFTA on 1 July 2020. This book only focuses on NAFTA.

2 In this book, China refers to mainland China.

3 ASEAN was established in 1967, during the polarized atmosphere of the Cold War. The grouping was aimed at promoting stability in the region. Over time, the group expanded to include its current ten members. The aims of ASEAN also extended from promoting security into advancing the economic interests of the region as a whole, including economic and trade growth.

4 Australia; Brunei Darussalam; Canada; Chile; People's Republic of China; Hong Kong, China; Indonesia; Japan; Republic of Korea; Malaysia; Mexico; New Zealand; Papua New Guinea; Peru; The Philippines; The Russian Federation; Singapore; Chinese Taipei (Taiwan); Thailand; the United States of America; Vietnam.

5 The original name was TPP, which consisted of 12 member economies including the United States. But on its first day in office, 23 January 2017, the Trump administration withdrew. After the withdrawal of the United States, Japan took the lead. The remaining economies moved forward with a slightly modified agreement and renamed it as CP/TPP, also known as TPP 11. TPP 11 countries have left the door open for the United States to re-join.

6 WTO replaced the GATT on 1 January 1995.
7 CMIM is a multilateral currency swap arrangement launched by the ASEAN+3 members.
8 ABMI is to develop local currency bond markets as an alternative source of funding to foreign-currency-denominated bank loans to minimize the currency and maturity mismatches that had made the region vulnerable to the sudden reversal of capital inflows (ADB, 2017).
9 Reported reasons for not using FTAs: The most significant reason being a lack of information on FTAs (45%), followed by low margin of preference (26%), delays and administration costs associated with rules of origin (25%), existence of export processing zones and the Information Technology Agreement (11 %), and nontariff barriers (9%) (see Kawai & Wignaraja 2008).
10 The Doha Round of WTO negotiations – formally, the Doha Development Agenda – was launched in November 2001. The work program covered about 20 areas of trade, including agriculture, services trade, market access for nonagricultural products, and certain intellectual property issues.
11 In his State of the Union address in 2015, US President Obama explained the purpose of the TPP to be rule-making by the United States: "China wants to write the rules for the world's fastest-growing region. That would put our workers and our businesses at a disadvantage. Why would we let that happen? We should write those rules" (The White House, 2015).
12 For example, the then Malaysian Prime Minister. See "Malaysia's Mahathir proposes common East Asia currency pegged to gold", https://www.reuters.com/article/us-malaysia-currency/malaysias-mahathir-proposes-common-east-asia-currency-pegged-to-gold-idUSKCN1T00FX.
13 East Asia Summit, established in 2011, is also known as ASEAN+8 or a mini-APEC for its inclusion of the United States and Russia on the basis of the ASEAN+6 framework.
14 The primary goal of ASEAN FTA is to increase the region's competitive advantage as a production base geared for the world market.
15 ERIA (2012, p. 4) states that "it is natural to design RCEP so as to further develop and deepen integrated production base, resulting in accelerating the economic growth because the establishment of production and distribution network among a larger number of countries makes the networks more vigorous and efficient".
16 According to Baldwin (2011), the 21st-century trade demands more complex international trade rules. The heart of the 21st-century trade is an intertwining of (1) trade in goods; (2) international investment in production facilities, training, technology, and long-term business relationships; and (3) the use of infrastructure services to coordinate the dispersed production, especially services such as telecoms, internet, express parcel delivery, air cargo, trade-related finance, customs clearance services, and so on.
17 Accordingly, the strategic uncertainties on the Korean Peninsula, the long-term distrust between China and Japan, and the unsolved territorial disputes have been the obstacles to sustainable regional cooperation in Northeast Asia (Rozman, 2004; Calder & Ye, 2010). Across the Asia Pacific, the "hub and spokes" security alliances allowed the United States to exert more American influences than unite the countries in Asia (Cha, 2018).
18 Constructivists argue that the continued impact of history on regional cooperation and integration (e.g., the bitter experiences of colonialization, the atrocity of World War II, and the ideological division of the Cold War) and the economic realities (diverse development models and disparate economic levels among the nations) have both played a part in constraining the formation of a common regional identity.

2 Structural Forces and East Asian Regionalism

As summarized in Chapter 1, there are three patterns defining the weakness of East Asian regionalism: (1) ambiguity in the purpose of East Asian regionalism; (2) the inability of a single and region-wide organization for the economic community in East Asia to develop; and (3) a proliferation of competing institutional initiatives. Why is East Asian regionalism weak? This puzzle has led international relations (IR) scholars and economists to develop various theories to explain it.

Existing IR literature on East Asian regionalism generally provides three conflicting theoretical perspectives: neorealism, constructivism, and liberal institutionalism. Among these three theories, liberal institutionalism is the most influential analytical framework. But to provide a broad overview of IR theories, I will present all three explanatory frameworks on East Asian regionalism in a general introductory manner. According to neorealists, great power geopolitics have been the obstacle to sustainable regional cooperation in East Asia (Rozman, 2004; Calder & Ye, 2010). The "hub and spokes" security alliances allowed the US to exert more American influences than unite the countries in East Asia (Cha, 2018). Moreover, the long-term distrust between the two regional hegemonies, China and Japan, has further impeded the political will to create a formal institutional arrangement among East Asian states. Constructivists argue that due to the continued impact of history and varied economic models, East Asian states lack a common regional identity to develop strong regionalism (Acharya, 2009). Accordingly, the bitter history of colonialization, World War II (WWII), and the Cold War divided East Asian states into different camps. More recently, the divergent economic models and development stages further hindered these states from generating a sense of regional identity. While the former two theories attribute weak regionalism to factors such as geopolitics of great power competition, incompatible identities, liberal institutionalism delves more deeply into the origins of East Asian regionalism. Liberal institutionalists believe that regional economic integration can be advanced through optimal institutional design. They emphasize institutional dynamics as a significant factor influencing regionalism. They argue that East Asia has not yet found the right regional institution, which

DOI: 10.4324/9781032613321-2

would enable East Asian states to cooperate and achieve economic integration. In other words, East Asian regionalism is weak because states are not cooperating and have different opinions on regional boundaries and regional authority.

Differing from IR approaches, some economists argue that institution-building alone, in and of itself, cannot produce well-functioning arrangements for states to cooperate in the regional economy. Rather than focusing on institutional dynamics, these economists (or market force theorists) focus on market forces and their different productional activities strategies in trade, investment, manufacturing, and marketing. Accordingly, when there is a sufficiently regionally oriented market power basis, regional institutions may work well. Conversely, when market power is globally interconnected (in the case of East Asia), weak regionalism is more favorable. However, market force explanations lack a coherent theory to analyze how market forces drive nations to seek different institutional arrangements, which, in turn, caused weak regionalism in East Asia. Market force explanation are generally narratives of market forces and their institutional consequences. It is hard to connect the market force dynamics with the specific institutional preferences of nations in East Asian regionalism.

In light of what I believe to be the inadequacies of existing explanations, I propose a complementary theoretical framework based on the theory of international economic structure (IES).[1] Economic structural forces partly overlap with the aforementioned market forces but are fundamentally different. While the market force theory focuses on industrial activities and interests of the private sector, IES is the relative strength of the national industrial interest and capability of states in the IES. I argue that a particular pattern in the distribution of economic capabilities of states has systemic effects on their preferences over institutional arrangements for an international economic order. It is the varying and rapidly changing positions of national economies in the IES that determine states' different and evolving preferences for a particular regional framework. In the structural theory I propose here, industrial diffusion and distribution of productional capabilities have added significant substance and dynamism to the power structure in the region. It is the economic structure and the different economic interests of each economy and their change over time that have led states to favor different institutional arrangements for transborder economic relations in the region. This contention among different national preferences contributed to weak regionalism in East Asia.

This chapter is structured as follows: Sections 2.1 and 2.2 consider the two popular explanations presented by IR scholars and economists for weak regionalism: the liberal institutional theory and market force theory. While existing explanations offer some intellectual insights into the problem in East Asian regionalism, they are insufficient for a more effective explanation of the weakness. In Section 2.3, I discuss in full detail the structural theory proposed here and how it can better explain weak regionalism in East Asia.

2.1 Liberal Institutional Explanations

2.1.1 Liberal Institutional Theory

Before discussing how liberal institutionalists explain regionalism and the case of East Asia, I start with a discussion of the influential theory in IR theory in the 1980s through 2010s: liberal institutionalism. Liberal institutionalism differs from other common IR theories such as realism by virtue of the fact that it rejects the realist assumption that international politics is a power struggle. Instead, it emphasizes the ability of international institutions to encourage states to cooperate. The past decades have seen the dominant influence of liberal institutionalism among academics, politicians, policymakers, and analysts. A high level of optimism over the great capacity of international institutions for a liberal institutional economic order prevailed.

Liberal institutionalism attempts to construct a broad view of the role of international institutions. Over time, it has undergone four stages of development: functionalism during the first half of the 20th century, neofunctionalism in the 1950s and 1960s, international regimes theory in the 1970s and 1980s, and neoliberal institutionalism supported by New Institutionalism in the 1990s. These different streams of liberal institutionalism define institutions variously as organizations, regimes, norms, and formal rules. Despite different interpretations of institutions, all strands of liberal institutionalism share a profound view that international institutions matter and can motivate states to cooperate.

2.1.1.1 Functionalism: Traditional Concepts of Institutions as Organizations

Functionalism is an early approach to liberal institutionalism. Proponents of functionalism hoped that a system of international organizations could provide collective security to replace the need for self-help inherent in the security dilemma. The functional idea originated from the liberal tradition of Wilsonian idealism. Woodrow Wilson, US president (1913–1921), believed that institutions possessed the capacity to overcome the problem of anarchy and convert the "jungle" of power politics into a "zoo" of rules (Heywood, 2014, p. 68). In 1918, he articulated the famous Fourteen Points,[2] which paid great attention to the creation of international organizations. He envisioned a League of Nations as an international organization to reconstruct the post-World War I (WWI) international order to ensure and maintain world peace. Under the great influence of Wilsonian idealism, international organizations, which were perceived as universal organizations serving diverse functions, became important platforms and mechanisms for order building in the post-WWI world.

Institutions here refer to traditional forms of order building and policy organization: state institutions, organizations, and agencies (Hall & Taylor, 1996). They largely focused on formal organizations, concrete entities with a physical presence—names, headquarters, and so on (Martin & Simmons, 1998).

A typical definition of international institution suggests "a formal arrangement transcending national boundaries that provides for the establishment of institutional machinery to facilitate cooperation among members in the security, economic, social, or related fields" (Plano & Olton, 1979, p. 288). The United Nations (UN), General Agreement on Tariffs and Trade (GATT), and International Monetary Fund (IMF) are primary examples of such international organizations. Functions of these international organizations are performed by specialized agencies of the UN such as the World Health Organization (WHO), Universal Postal Union (UPU), International Civil Aviation Organization (ICAO), and so on. With a great focus on the technical functions performed by international organizations, this branch of liberal institutionalism is also labeled as functionalism.

Functionalism was a dominant theoretical force supporting the building of universal organizations in the aftermath of WWII. While WWII dealt a serious blow to Wilsonian idealism, nations' interests and enthusiasm in the role of international organizations persisted after WWII. In the eyes of the American administrations led by Roosevelt (1933–1945) and Truman (1945–1953), the UN not only created an opportunity for the US to remedy the problem of its foreign policy during WWI but also helped the US to assume its responsibility as the new great power in post-WWII world affairs while protecting itself against the evil of the old world order of imperialism and colonialism. In international trade, institutions such as GATT—the precursor of World Trade Organization (WTO)—were built to shape the post-WWII international economic order by providing a set of global rules. For instance, the principle of non-discrimination is exemplified in the most favored nation (MFN) status of GATT and WTO. It implies that any benefit received by one state must be available to all. This global multilateralism prevents political rivalries and alignments from interfering with economic exchange. To sum up, functionalism has facilitated the growth of organizations as well as enhancing the influence these entities can exercise (Klabbers, 2014).

2.1.1.2 Neofunctionalism: Functional Mechanisms of the International Organization for Regional Economic Integration

In the 1950s and early 1960s, neofunctionalism, as an explanation of growing regional economic integration agreements in Europe, emerged as an updated version of the original theory of functionalism. Neofunctionalism considers institutions as functional mechanisms, processes, and arrangements for regional economic integration. According to Ernst Haas, the principal theorist of neofunctionalism, the process of regional economic integration is driven by spillover from one field into others (1958, 1961). The process of spillover refers to the tendency of regional groups to expand the scope of their issue areas and how cooperation over low politics gradually produces cooperation over high politics. Along this line, Balassa (1961) outlined a grand design of regional economic integration agreements that consist of five steps in sequence

Table 2.1 Balassa's Model of Institutionalization of Regional Economic Integration

Agreements of integration	*Key features*
Free Trade Area	Removal of tariff barriers between members with variable external barriers against outsiders
Customs Union	As above, with a common external tariff
Common Market	As above, with free movements of labor and capital
Economic Union	As above, with policy and further institutional harmonization to ensure the rationality of specialization, trade, and factor flows
Complete economic integration	As above, with complete harmonization of macro-economic, social policies, and common currency system

(see Table 2.1) in a process of regional integration from a free trade area to a customs union, a common market, an economic union, and finally to a regional economic community of complete economic integration. Accordingly, the process of regional economic integration begins with the lowering and removal of trade barriers and ends with an economic and political union, moving from economic cooperation to supranational integration.

Neofunctionalism reflects the great experience of regional integration in post-War Europe. An exemplary practice of this five-step theory was the construction of the European Union (EU), where a strong institutional setup stimulated the continuous development of the integration process (Molle, 2017, p. 60). The beginning of European cooperation was the European Coal and Steel Community in the early 1950s. It then moved on to the European Economic Community (EEC), or "Common Market" for broader economic integration in the late 1950s, and further evolved into an organization spanning policy areas, from climate, environment to external relations and security, justice, and migration. A name change from the EEC to the EU in 1993 reflected the spillover effect (EU, n.d.). In Europe, after centuries of conflicts and wars, countries came together to create a new style of governing. European unification during the second half of the 20th century was not complete. However, it demonstrated the willingness to overcome what realists see as the tendency of individual states toward anarchy. In summary, neofunctionalism has provided the theoretical infrastructure for the institutions of regional economic integration. The logic of institutionalization of regional integration had a great influence on the development of economic regionalism in East Asia.

2.1.1.3 International Regimes Theory: Regimes as Institutional Arrangements for International Order

Liberal institutionalism underwent a significant change in the late 1970s, with the development of regimes theory. Regime theorists argue that regimes not only consist of formal organizations and agreements but also a looser set of norms, principles, and procedures that shape states' expectations and guide their behavior (Bradford, 2007). The definitions of international regimes are intentionally broader than formal organizations and agreements. Krasner, for instance, defines international regimes as "principles, norms, rules and decision-making procedures around which actor expectations converge in a given issue-area" (1982, p. 185).[3] Similarly, Keohane refers to the governing arrangements as international regimes, which include procedures, rules, or institutions for certain kinds of activity (Keohane & Nye, 1989, p. 5). Unlike functionalism and neofunctionalism which regard WTO as solely an entity, regime theorists regard such organizations as a part of a larger trade regime that encompasses rules, norms, and principles in addition to the procedures and the organizational capacity that the WTO provides for the regime.

Regime theory incorporates realism and liberalism. Realists believe that patterns of outcomes in IR reflect the distribution of power among states. Liberalists disagree and argue that international institutions are central in shaping the behavior of states, facilitating interstate cooperation, and influencing the outcomes of interstate interaction. Regime theory, on the one hand, acknowledges the realist assumptions of an anarchic international system and the self-interests of states. In this sense, it differs from previous waves of liberal institutionalism. However, regime theory insists that regimes are central in facilitating international cooperation. Unlike realists, regime theorists maintain that self-interested states can still achieve cooperation despite anarchy.[4] They hold that states engage in international cooperation in pursuit of absolute gains and they are thus considerably more optimistic about the prospects for international cooperation. Often regime theorists cite cooperation in trade, human rights, and collective security, among other issues. The International Atomic Energy Agency (IAEA), for instance, is an international organization that forms part of a more broadly understood nuclear non-proliferation regime, which again belongs to a broader collective security regime (Non-Proliferation Treaty [1968]). These are instances of the roles of international regimes. Regime theorists propose a process model to elaborate the overall cause-and-effect relationship between power structure and pattern of outcomes in interstate interactions (shown in thick arrows in Figure 2.1).

Regime theorists regard international regimes as an intervening variable between the power structure and the process of political and economic bargaining (Keohane & Nye, 1989, p. 21; Krasner, 1982). Accordingly, power structure refers to the distribution of capabilities among states in the international system indicated by variables such as the relative economic size, relative levels of military spending, and so on. The bargaining process is a process of interstate bargaining that results in "constitutional contracts" and specifies the contents of regimes (Young, 1991, p. 282). For instance, public servants are trained as experts and negotiators in "translating the possession of material resources into bargaining leverage" (1991, p. 288). A negotiated regime arises from "a conscious process of bargaining in which the parties engage in extended efforts to hammer out mutually agreeable provisions to incorporate into an explicit agreement" (Levy et al., 1995, p. 281). In other words, regime theorists

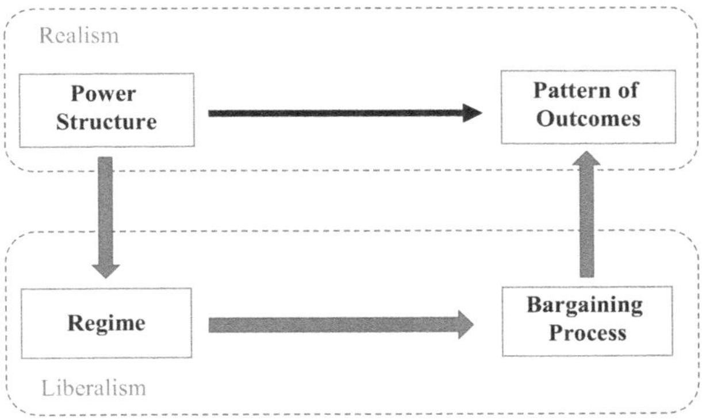

Figure 2.1 Keohane and Nye's Framework of the Theory of International Regime.
Source: Author's compilation based on the conceptual framework of Keohane & Nye (1989, p. 21).

focus on the role of regimes in the bargaining process and argue that regimes influence and, to some extent, determine the process of political and economic bargaining.

Keohane further explored the roles of international regimes systematically in his work *After Hegemony: Cooperation and Discord in the World Political Economy* (1984). He argues that international regimes can increase the likelihood of cooperation by (1) providing information about the behavior of others by monitoring the behavior of members and reporting on compliance, (2) reducing transaction costs, and (3) generating an expectation of cooperation among members (Keohane, 1984, p. xi). According to international regimes theory, institutions are not weak substitutes for world government but rather devices for facilitating decentralized cooperation among egoistic actors.

2.1.1.4 Neoliberal Institutionalism: Institutions as Rules

From the 1980s, liberal institutionalism moved to focus on the role of international institutions in facilitating cooperation among states on the basic premise of neoliberal institutionalism that became increasingly popular and influential then. This is the same premise in the theory of international regimes that regimes are central in facilitating international cooperation and influencing the behavior of states. The terms "regime" and "institution" have been used more or less interchangeably. Robert Keohane has been closely associated with this development of neoliberal institutionalism. He views institutions not merely as formal organizations but more broadly as "persistent and connected sets of rules (formal and informal) that prescribe behavioral roles, constrain activity, and shape expectations" (Keohane, 1989, pp. 3–5). More specifically, neoliberal institutionalists assume institutions to have three forms: (1) formal intergovernmental or cross-national non-governmental organizations, for example, the UN system and numerous non-governmental organizations (NGOs);

(2) international regimes, for example, the Bretton Woods Monetary System; and (3) conventions, for example, traditional diplomatic immunity.

In common with the regime theory, neoliberal institutionalism accepts much of the realist view that states are largely rational and unitary actors in an anarchical system. But neoliberal institutionalism departs from realism in its belief that institutions matter. It presumes that institutions provide benefits for interstate cooperation, especially in the procurement of public goods or the avoidance of negative externalities. In other words, state behavior is constrained and affected by variations in the degree of institutionalization across different areas of international and regional politics (Keohane, 1984; Mansfield & Milner, 1997). States create institutions to achieve their goals. Institutions influence states' behavior and the outcome of interstate interactions. Thus, neoliberal institutionalism believes that rational states devise international institutions to facilitate interstate cooperation for the benefit of self-interested nation-states.

Neoliberal institutionalism has enriched the regime theory with an analytical approach drawn from the New Institutional Economics (NIE). Douglass North is the founder of the NIE. He pioneered an institutionalist definition of institutions and a framework for analyzing the role of institutions in economic performance and change. For North, institutions are formal rules, informal constraints, and enforcement mechanisms. Formal rules refer to "political (and judicial) rules, economic rules, and contracts" [5] (North, 1990, p. 47). Informal constraints are "codes of conduct, norms of behavior, and conventions" (North, 1990, p. 36). These include reputation, broadly accepted standards of conduct, and conventions that emerge from repetitive interactions. The enforcement mechanisms ensure the effective and low-cost enforcement of formal rules and informal constraints (North, 1990, p. 57). This complex set of formal rules, informal constraints, and enforcement mechanisms create an institutional environment that induces credible commitment and reduces transaction costs in economic activities. As he stated in his Nobel Prize lecture, "Institutions form the incentive structure of a society and the political and economic institutions, in consequence, are the underlying determinant of economic performance" (North, 1994).

In many ways, neoliberal institutionalists' view of cooperation is reminiscent of that of the NIE scholars. Neoliberal institutionalists argue that states cooperate because they see international cooperation benefiting them, enhancing their security, and strengthening trust in the anarchic international environment. Institutions provide information, reduce transaction costs, deter defection, and reduce uncertainty in state actions and interaction (Keohane, 1984). Sovereign states build institutional arrangements to facilitate the flow of information and consultations between countries and enhance governments' ability to monitor other countries' compliance with their commitments.

The neoliberal institutionalist notion of institutions as rules advanced our understanding of the role of international institutions in international cooperation and order building. Here we use WTO rules as an example to illustrate how institutions shape state behavior and reduce uncertainty and risk in international cooperation. First, trade policy review is an exercise, mandated in the WTO agreements, in which member countries' trade and related policies are examined and evaluated at regular intervals. It is a key instrument allowing members to better understand each other's trade policies. This, in turn, facilitates the compliance of commitments and thereby alleviates uncertainty. Second, WTO is a multilateral framework. When an institutional framework is agreed upon at the WTO level, states can rely on the institution's established procedures and principles to guide negotiations. In this way, states can avoid the costs of creating new rules each time a new agreement is negotiated.

In summary, liberal institutionalism supports the idea that states cooperate because of institutions. Depending on the different schools of liberal institutionalism, there are four types of institutions: international organizations; mechanisms, processes, and arrangements for regional economic integration; international regimes; and international rules and norms. Functionalism perceives institutions as functional international organizations, which govern the behavior of member states and their interaction. Neofunctionalism sees institutions as mechanisms, processes, and arrangements that shape the integrative activities of the states for a regional economic community. The regime theory treats institutions as a broad institutional environment that structures state behaviors and their interactions. The neoliberal institutional school regards institutions as the rules of the game and determinants of state behaviors and international order. Despite the variations in the definitions of institutions, broader or narrower, all branches of liberal institutionalism challenge the basic premise of realism on the anarchic nature of IR and consequent pattern of state behavior and interaction. Liberal institutionalists generally regard institutions as the primary forces that drive interstate activities, shape the international behavior of states, and structure their interaction and exchange. They contend that institutions rule and "trump" everything else in determining economic development (Rodrik et al., 2004, p. 131). The four strands of liberal institutionalism all trust that successful regionalism requires the right institutional arrangements, and logically the key problem of weak regionalism in East Asia must be that states did not have sufficient and effective institutional capabilities and resources for building a regional economic community.

2.1.2 Liberal Institutional Explanations of Regionalism in East Asia

Unlike in Europe, where a partial transfer of sovereignty and a strong institutional framework have been achieved, East Asian states have not yielded anything on sovereignty. National identity is much stronger than regional identity. As a result of a statist thinking about sovereignty, East Asian regionalism is for the benefit of the nation-state and not for the region itself (He, 2004, p. 120).

Specifically, neofunctionalism attributes weak regionalism in East Asia to the prevalence of considerations of sovereignty and ideas of non-interference among East Asian states. Neofunctionalism sees integration as a process generating spillover effects, that is, integration necessarily begins from the technical and non-controversial policy areas and subsequently spills over into areas of "high politics". However, East Asian governments have been reluctant to cooperate in areas of high politics that threaten national sovereignty. For instance, in her study on regional functional cooperation in the economic and financial sector, Helen Nesadurai (2009) assesses three key financial cooperation projects in East Asia: the Chiang Mai Initiative Multilateralization (CMIM), the Asian Bond Market Initiative (ABMI), and the regional bond funds. She finds that depoliticized financial cooperation has worked well in terms of knowledge production and sharing activities. But low political engagement and a lack of regional authority have limited the functional spillovers to new areas of policy coordination such as currency and exchange rate matters. She thus concludes that concerns with maintaining policy autonomy and the confidentiality of sensitive financial information have "derailed" constructive discussions of further financial cooperation within East Asia (Nesadurai, 2009, p. 22).

Furthermore, neofunctionalism perceives East Asia as an imitator of the EU model and considers that East Asia has not found the right institution yet. As Breslin, Higgott, and Rosamond (2002, p. 13) argue, to be a "proper" form of regionalism, a degree of EU-style institutionalism needs to be in place. The neofunctionalist theory is often cited to argue that, as a result of political spillover of economic interdependence, East Asian regionalism is inevitable in time and will resemble Europe's model of regional integration. Influenced by neofunctionalist advice, ASEAN has been following the legalistic approach and exploring EU-style regional integration. For instance, in keeping with the European community-building practice, ASEAN countries established the so-called "ASEAN Community" which is comprised of three pillars, namely the political-security community, the economic community, and the socio-cultural community. However, in terms of the level of institutionalization, ASEAN has not really adopted the highly legalistic and bureaucratic approach of the EU model. One fundamental difference is that the member states of ASEAN adhere to the principle of non-interference in members' internal affairs. European regional integration became less of "a paradigmatic case of regionalism" and more like "a benchmark for particular institutionalized paths of regionalism" (Breslin et al., 2002; Dieter, 2006; Katzenstein, 1997, pp. 1–44).

In explaining weak regionalism, the regime theory has tried to look at East Asia from an EU perspective, and this has led many to consider the absence of formal multilateral institutions in East Asia puzzling. Most of the literature on international regimes has centered on European/Western, hegemonic, and natural resource regimes. Much of the controversy over East Asian weak regionalism stems from the conflict between the Western-led conventional agreements and looser processes of consensus-building in East Asia. For instance, Robert Gilpin contrasted regional integration as "politically motivated and institutionalized" in Western Europe and "primarily economic and less institutionalized" in East Asia (Gilpin, 1993, p. 33). The Western-led conventional agreements require massive political commitments by governments to legally bind themselves and reform current regulations and practices. However, East Asia has adopted consensus-seeking gradualism. It has taken a different path from that of the EU, with its large and powerful bureaucracy and the pooling of national sovereignties in a central body. East Asia's cautious, incremental progress is evident in its leadership's determination to avoid strong institutionalization. For instance, Acharya and Johnston's study speaks of the "ASEAN Way" of institution-building, which is based on informality, flexibility, consensus, and non-confrontation (2007, p. 245). In contrast to institutional designs across other regions, they point out that ASEAN states "have deliberately and carefully designed their institutions to be informal" (Amitav Acharya & Johnston, 2007, p. 246). These informal and weak mechanisms have created a multilayered web of political and economic ties across the region.

For neoliberal institutionalists, weak regionalism in East Asia is an unsolved puzzle. There is a huge gap between the pattern of regionalism anticipated in the theory of neoliberal institutionalism and the actual outcomes in the regionalism in East Asia. The former is a result-oriented integration based on laws and formal institutions, while the latter is process-oriented which features consensus-building and a low level of institutionalization. The East Asian institutional architecture is thus perceived as "institution-light" or "under-institutionalized" in the design, resources provision, delegated powers, the extent of legalization, and the efficacy of its existing arrangements for integration (Capannelli & Kawai, 2014; Johnston, 2012; Khong & Helen, 2007). Neoliberal institutionalists tend to attribute weak regionalism to factors that impede interstate cooperation such as domestic political systems, the absence of undisputed leadership (Capannelli & Kawai, 2014), great power geopolitics (Beeson, 2006), the role of culture and identities (Yu, 2003), power transition, and uncertainty about future benefits or concerns with asymmetric future benefits[6] (Lipson, 1991). They argue that it is due to these hindering factors that the institutions of East Asian regionalism are not working as designed or intended.

2.1.3 A Critique of Liberal Institutional Explanations

As discussed above, all four branches of liberal institutionalism explain weak regionalism in East Asia with a heavy reliance on comparison of the East Asian experience with the European integration experience. They argue that East Asian regionalism is not as successful as that of Europe because East Asian countries did not borrow an "EU-style" setup such as a supranational authority and a clear-cut membership for an economic community. Remarkably different from Europe's emphasis on the transfer of sovereignty, East Asia does not have a regional authority to provide a solution to the problems of interstate cooperation. Also, in contrast to the European way of closed regionalism, open regionalism in East Asia stipulates that initiatives for regional economic integration are not necessarily limited to a specified number of members within the region. Therefore, liberal institutionalists attribute weak regionalism to the institutional design such as a lack of regional authority and contested regional boundaries.

Any study seeking to define the patterns of East Asian weak regionalism must answer a fundamental question: what purpose is East Asian regionalism to serve? Or what has it achieved? There has been no such grand design in the style of the EU for regionalism in East Asia. East Asian policymakers voted no with their feet on the EU-style institutionalization and led the region to move in a different direction. Researchers of East Asian regionalism have also questioned the usefulness—"one size fits all"—of the Eurocentric theory. They assert that imitating the EU's legalistic and centralized model of cooperation may not necessarily achieve what is intended in East Asia (Møller, 2008; Yeo, 2010). They play down the importance of the institutions by arguing that institutionalization is not the end-goal of cooperation but simply a mechanism through which cooperation occurs.

Realists argue that all branches of liberal institutionalism accord excessive attention to the institution-building process and fail to see the real dynamics that shape the outcome in East Asian regionalism. For instance, Stein (2008, p. 206) reviews the liberal institutional theory and points out the over-emphasis on the role of institutions. According to Stein, an institution is an intermediate variable that may only have "marginal" or even "epiphenomenal" effects on state behavior. A flaw of liberal institutionalism is that it ignores factors such as state interests and capacities when explaining institution-building. A more vigorous attack is presented by Mearsheimer, who, quite mercilessly, criticizes liberal institutional theory and points out the endogeneity problem as "the false promise of international institutions" (Mearsheimer, 1994). The endogeneity problem refers to situations in which international institutions are correlated with state interest and capacity. Realists argue that rather than institutions, state power is the more fundamental factor accounting for state behavior.

More recently, this problem has been acknowledged even among the scholars of liberal institutionalism. The endogeneity problem in liberal institutional explanations has led to more urgent attention being given to fundamental factors, such as power and interests. Keohane and Martin (2003, p. 97) admit that insofar as the theory of institutional origins and functions is accepted, the independent explanatory power of institutional theory seems to disappear. Keohane (2012, p. 135) reminds liberal institutionalists to learn a core lesson of realism—"Institutions rest on power and changes in power generate changes in institutions". In other words, the liberal institutional theory is at its most robust when institutions are also explained by state interests and capacities.

Given the problems in liberal institutional explanations, some scholars apply a realist perspective and develop market force theory to explain East Asian weak regionalism. One critical question being debated between liberal institutionalists and market force theorists is whether the region-building process should follow a "top-down" or a "bottom-up" approach (Richard Higgott, 2016; Hoshiro, 2019; Pempel, 2005). The top-down approach refers to the government-to-government formation of institutions, while a bottom-up approach focuses on the process of rationalization powered by forces of trans-border market expansion, trade, production networking, and investment flow in the private sector. As

As illustrated in Figure 2.2, the difference between the two approaches lies in the directionality of the cause-and-effect relationship between regional institutions and market forces.

As discussed earlier, liberal institutionalism relies heavily on institutional design to shape market forces and economic activities. It adopts a top-down approach. Conversely, a core assumption of market force theorists is the bottom-up logic that the "regionness" of East Asia is first established by market-driven regionalization and later made through regionalism of institution-building. For instance, Capannelli and Kawai (2014) expound that "in the absence of common institutions and specific mechanisms to promote regionalism, market forces have induced closer economic integration through the establishment of production networks in industries such as electronics, home appliances, and automobiles".

Similarly, Richard Higgott (2016, pp. 2–4) argues that the bottom-up lens is more useful to explain the case of East Asia, as follows:

> Asian trans-regional institutionalization is developing a bottom-up set of norms and practices that differ from the top-down processes that fashioned the post-World War II global order…The less formalized, but state-driven, nature of regional institutionalization in Asia is facilitating the growth of multilateral practices at the regional and inter-regional level which challenge the norms and practices that have for so long operated in the global institutions.

Indeed, in the case of East Asia, the regionalization of market forces predated the construction of regional institutions.

Market force scholars use different words to define this distinctiveness, such as "from market-based to institution-based" (Haddad, 2007), or "from informal to formal", "from de facto to de jure economic integration" (Hiratsuka & Kimura, 2008; Kimura, 2008), or "networked regionalism" versus "institutional

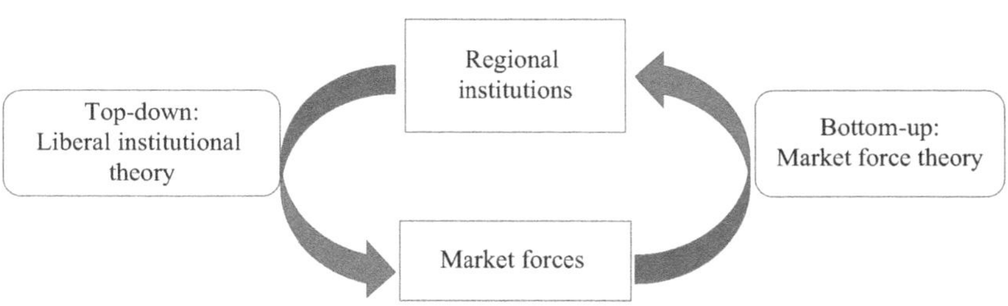

Figure 2.2 Top-Down and Bottom-Up Approaches in East Asian Regionalism.

regionalism" (Yeo, 2010).[7] Regardless of these different definitions, market force theorists support a bottom-up view of East Asian regionalism as they believe that it is the market forces that drive nations to seek different institutional arrangements. Moreover, I argue that market force theory complements liberal institutionalism's explanations by providing compelling insights into the underlying market forces behind institutions. Accordingly, if there is no regionally oriented common ground in market power and interests, even the optimal institutional designs, as advocated by liberal institutionalists, will fail to build a regional economic community.

2.2 Market Force Explanations

There is substantial work on the role of market forces in East Asian regionalism. Market force theorists assess market forces in different categories: trade, Foreign Direct Investment (FDI), and transborder production networks (TPNs). Table 2.2 compares the ways of assessing these three sets of market forces.

Among these three, trade and FDI accounts traditionally dominate because there are readily available national data and they are indicators of the power of "the two engines of globalization" (Jin, 2012). Trade accounts measure transborder flows of products and services. FDI accounts cover the transborder movement of industrial capital. TPNs demonstrate a system in the industrial organization of capital, technology, management skills, and other production resources.

Differing from trade accounts focusing on the flows of commodities and FDI on capital, the TPNs approach is the most comprehensive, because it records the sources and destinations of all production resources and outputs. However, due to the difficulty in quantifying the magnitude of TPNs, empirical studies on TPNs have not been well developed until recently. These three approaches, each of which has its pros and cons, attempt to shed light on how market forces drive transborder productional activities and institutionalize a transborder economic order in East Asia.

To help understand market force explanations, the following section is divided into four parts. The first three subsections look at analyses of the three sets of market forces—trade, FDI, and transborder production networks—and

Table 2.2 Assessing Market Forces

Approaches	*Measurement*	*Data availability*	*Appropriateness as the proxy*
Trade	Products and services	Easy	Low
FDI	Industrial capital	Easy	Low
TPNs	All production resources such as capital, technology, management skills	Difficult	High

show how they form a set of explanations of East Asian regionalism. The final subsection puts forward a critique of the market force explanations, highlighting their lack of a strong theoretical framework in linking these forces to East Asian regionalism.

2.2.1 *Trade Accounts: Transborder Flows of Products and Services*

Trade economists use trade accounts to explain the power of market forces. Given its easy availability, using international trade data is the most popular approach in evaluating regional economic integration. There are three major approaches to the empirical description of trading patterns in East Asia: (1) intra-regional trade, (2) inter-regional trade, and (3) global trade networks.

2.2.1.1 *Intra-Regional Trade*

Many academic studies have focused primarily on intra-regional trade relations in East Asia (Chen, 2008; Drysdale & Garnaut, 1993; Frankel and Wei, 1997; Kwan, 2001; Petri, 1993). As defined by ADB, intra-regional trade share is the percentage of trade with intra-regional partners to the total trade of a country/region.[8] By applying this approach, Figure 2.3 presents a parallel comparison of trade partnerships in the EU, NAFTA, ASEAN+3, ASEAN, and

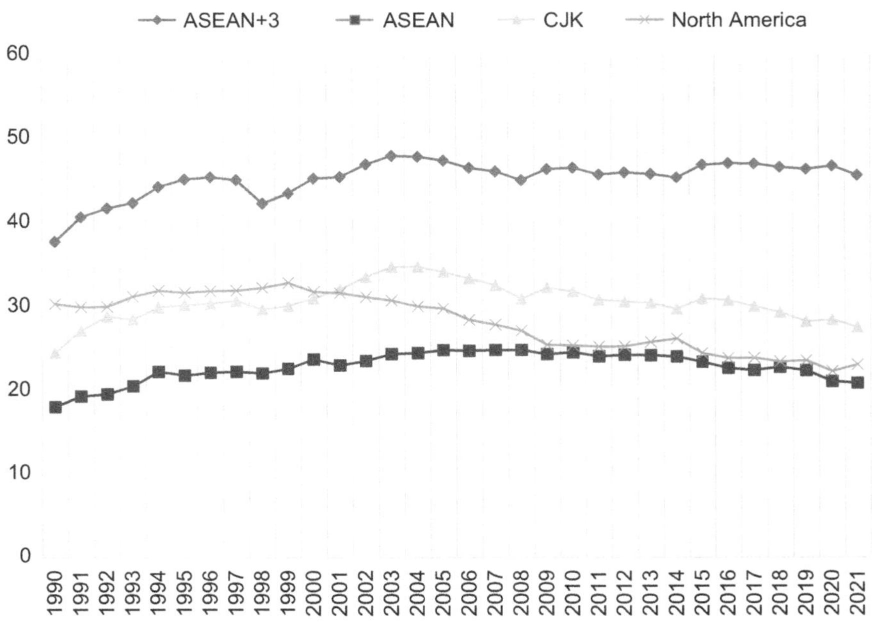

Figure 2.3 Intra-Regional Trade Ratios in Different Regional Frameworks.

Source: Asia Regional Integration Center (2019).

China-Japan-South Korea (CJK). From 1990 to 2017, the intra-regional trade share within ASEAN+3 grew substantially, increasing from 38% to 47%. In regional comparisons, the level of intra-regional trade within ASEAN+3 was mostly higher than that of North America and rapidly approaching that of the EU.

Based on the empirical data above, intra-regional trade researchers argue that East Asia has developed a solid regional material basis to support regionalism. They believe that the East Asian economy is increasingly regionally concentrated and requires therefore institutional efforts to support its development. Accordingly, they cite non-economic factors as obstacles to region-building in East Asia, such as divergent interests between developing economies and advanced economies (Stubbs, 2002), and domestic interests and pressure groups (Aggarwal & Urata, 2013; Katada & Solís, 2010; Yoshimatsu, 2005). For these intra-regional trade analysts, market forces in East Asia are increasingly regionally oriented, a reality that requires strong regionalism, but the region fails to provide regionalism due to non-economic factors.

2.2.1.2 Inter-Regional Trade

In contrast to the intra-regional trade school, the second group of trade economists argues that it is important to pay attention to both the intra- and inter-regional trade linkages. They hold that East Asia has not only been regionally interdependent but also globally connected. The inter-regional connectedness between East Asia and other regions in the world, particularly with Europe and North America, has its historical roots (Ando and Kimura, 2013b; Ando & Kimura, 2014). In their early stages of industrial development, most East Asian economies adopted a strategy of processing export-led growth, which involves domestic firms obtaining parts and components across East Asia, processing them domestically, and exporting the value-added goods to the global markets. As a legacy of processing export-led growth,[9] intra-regional and inter-regional trade linkages form a triangle when plotted on a map, thus the "triangular trade" pattern. Figure 2.4 demonstrates the two arms of the triangular trade in the East Asian economy.

In the first arm of intra-regional linkages, China and ASEAN's developing economies heavily rely on intermediate inputs from Japan and newly industrialized economies (NIEs) such as South Korea and Taiwan. In the second arm of inter-regional linkages, China and ASEAN economies (excluding Singapore) are manufacturing bases and export platforms, sending final goods to external markets such as the US and the rest of the world (ROW). Trade economists, such as Fujita (2007), have identified this typical voyage of a "made in East Asia" final product as triangular trade.

In explaining weak regionalism in East Asia, these scholars find two obstacles to East Asian regionalism. The first one is the intensifying competition within the region. For years, China has been securing a position of monopoly in Factory Asia, putting the "Made in China" label on a vast array of

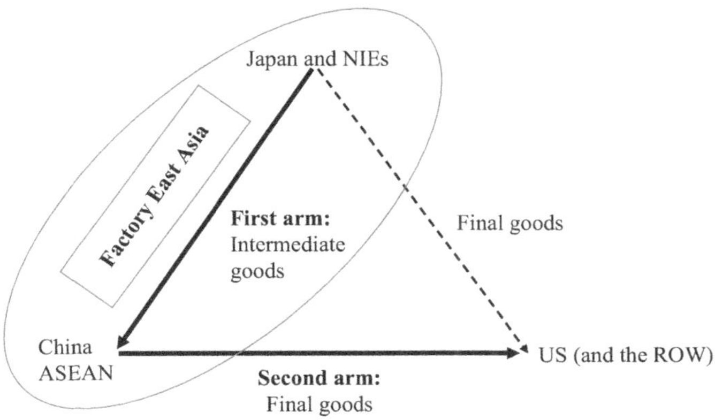

Figure 2.4 Triangular Trade Partnerships across the Asia-Pacific Region.
Source: Adapted from Fujita (2007, p. 72).

manufacturing goods. However, ASEAN economies, including Malaysia, Thailand, Vietnam, and Indonesia, are boosting their growth to become an attractive manufacturing hub. According to Wong and Chan (2003), China and ASEAN economies are more competitive than complementary, given that they share similar characteristics in the export structure. Major export items range from labor-intensive products (e.g., textiles and apparel) to capital and technology-intensive ones (e.g., electronics). As a result of increasing competition in manufacturing activities, East Asian economies have developed conflicting attitudes toward building a regional trading bloc.

The second obstacle is the heavy dependence on global markets. Triangular trade reflects Factory East Asia's dependence on extra-regional markets to digest its production capacity. Regional production and trade networks are developed to produce final goods destined for consumption outside the region, mostly in the US and the EU (Mikic, 2011, p. 310). Taking China's export destinations as an example, China's final goods exports are heavily concentrated in extra-regional markets (Athukorala, 2010, pp. 282–283). The share of Chinese exports to OECD countries (excluding Japan and South Korea) in its total export increased from 29.3% to 50.1% between 1992 and 2004. Due to the dependence on extra-regional markets, open regionalism, rather than a regional bloc, is perceived by these scholars as a pragmatic approach to serve market interests. In sum, inter-regional trade academics attach great importance to the role of extra-regional powers and believe that this dependence on extra-regional forces has significantly hindered the development of East Asian regionalism.

2.2.1.3 *Global Trade Networks*

By combining intra-regional and inter-regional trade accounts, the third group of trade economists uses the network method to map global trade structures.

By comparing trade structures across different regions, they argue that they can offer a potentially more powerful explanation of the weakness of East Asian regionalism.

According to their comparative research, the trade structure in East Asia has shown two distinct characteristics. First, intense intra-regional component trade is a characteristic feature of East Asian economies. In comparison with Europe and North America, component trade has played a more significant role in trade expansion in East Asia as seen in various systems of measurements and analysis[10] (Athukorala & Yamashita, 2006). At the single-economy level, for example, the portions of component trade in Singapore, Malaysia, and the Philippines account for over half their total trade in manufactured goods (Dent, 2016, p. 50). The high portions of their component trade reflect the highly developed transborder production-sharing model and the resulting regional trade integration in East Asia.

Second, East Asian trade networks are more hierarchical and imbalanced than the EU model. By comparing the volume of bidirectional trade flows, we can easily tell the structural difference between Factory East Asia and Factory Europe. For example, Figure 2.5 presents the global trade structure of the year 2009. The width of the arrows represents the volume of value-added trade.

Ferrarini and Hummels (2014, p. 3) describe their analysis of Factory East Asia as part of the structure:

> At the top, countries such as Japan—and the US from outside the region—inject value-added through the provision of key components and services to the PRC, the hub downstream, as well as through Malaysia, Thailand, and to a lesser extent the other Association of Southeast Asian Nations economies, as well as India.

They observe that the US and Japan are the most important value-added suppliers to China. In return, China has much less value-added to provide. This vertical and imbalanced trade structure in Factory East Asia contrasts sharply with the EU model. In Factory Europe, Germany not only works as the absorption hub but also as the supply hub. The width of bidirectional flows in Europe is very close, which reflects more horizontal and balanced trade relations.

In explaining weak regionalism, proponents of global trade networks question the usefulness of a regional bloc if East Asia's trade regionalization remains functionally dependent on external economies. On the contrary, they contend that weak regionalism might be more economically desirable. First, they argue that as component trade prevails in East Asia, the high intra-regional trade ratio may not accurately estimate the level of regional trade integration (Dent, 2016, pp. 50–51). The actual level of regional trade integration is believed to be lower than suggested by the intra-regional trade ratio because components move across borders several times before the production process is completed. This can cause the problem of multiple counting and thus overestimation in intra-regional trade ratio (Johnson & Noguera, 2012;

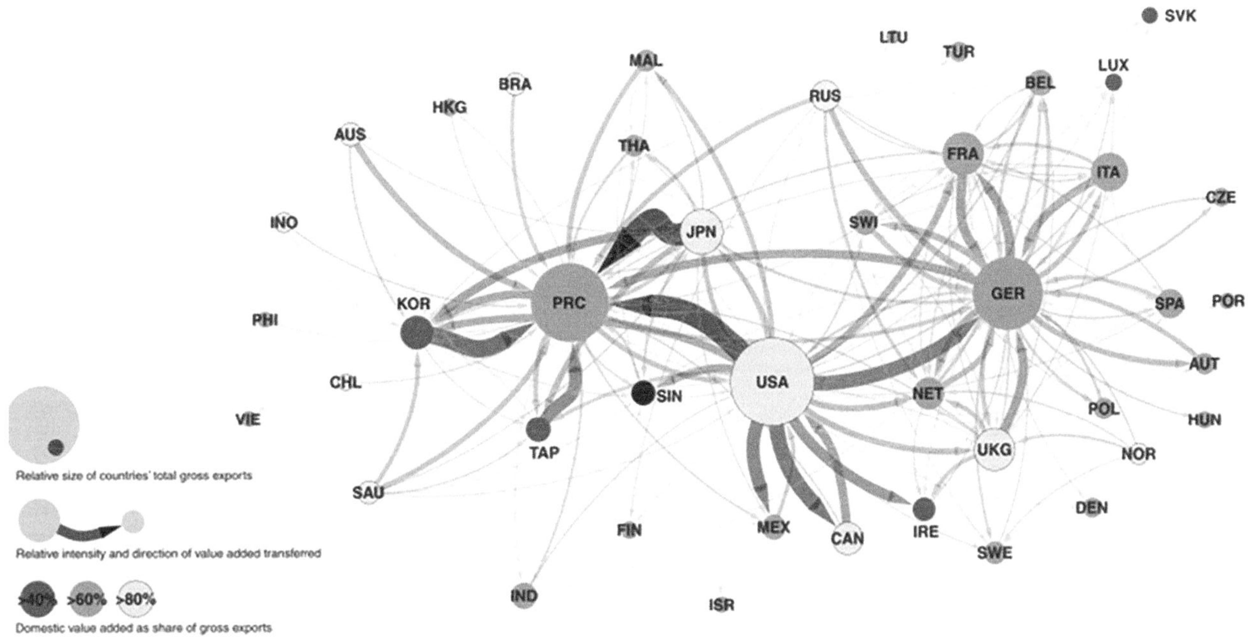

Figure 2.5 Global Trade Structure (2009).

Source: Ferrarini & Hummels (2014, p. 2).

Kwon & Ryou, 2015; OECD, 2013). Second, researchers of trade networks interpret the vertical and imbalanced trade structure in East Asia as caused by heavy external dependence (Ferrarini, 2013; Ferrarini & Hummels, 2014; Kasahara, 2013). Vertical processing trade patterns in East Asian regional production networks rely heavily on component provision from extra-regional partners, such as the US. These researchers argue that East Asia's dependence on the global economy hinders its movement toward a regional economic and political bloc (Gilpin, 1995, p. 8).

To summarize, trade relations range from intra-regional, to inter-regional, to global. Given the complexity of trade networks in East Asia, each of the three sets of trade partnerships presents a different input to trade integration. Intra-regional trade gives some support for trade regionalization, while inter-regional and global trade are less supportive. These conflicting dynamics lead to a belief that trade accounts alone cannot provide an adequate understanding of market forces. Complementing trade accounts, FDI accounts offer a way of observing another aspect of regional economic integration and tracking the transborder movement of industrial capital—a critical force in regional economic integration.

2.2.2 FDI Accounts: Transborder Movement of Industrial Capital

Trade and FDI flows are "two engines" of globalization. While trade accounts record transborder flows of products and services, FDI accounts focus on the transborder movement of industrial capital. International industrial capital flows when foreign investors, usually multinational corporates (MNCs) based in one economy, establish operations under their managerial control in another economy. For example, Japanese MNCs have been actively expanding their overseas production in developing economies in East Asia taking advantage of favorable local conditions (e.g., cheaper labor cost). Host economies also benefit from foreign investment with incoming industrial capital, technologies, and managerial know-how. These play a crucial role in local economic growth. FDI provides a win-win situation for both the home economy and host economies.

There are a large number of studies investigating the complementary relationship between FDI and trade in the region (Fukao et al., 2003; Kojima, 1973; Nishitateno, 2013; Thorbecke & Salike, 2013). For instance, according to Kojima (1973), the push forces for outward FDI are the cross-border differences in production factor costs (especially labor) and other location advantages. Multinational firms have motivations to invest in and transfer production to lower-wage countries by exporting sophisticated parts, components, and technology for assembly. Urata (2001) defines this complementary relationship between FDI and trade in East Asia as an "FDI-trade nexus" and explains how this nexus works in developing TPNs.

To complement insights from trade accounts, I explain the measurement of market forces from the perspective of FDI. To do this, I begin with an analysis of the patterns of FDI in East Asia by destinations, sources, motivations, and industry composition. Based on this analysis, I discuss the implications of the FDI patterns for weak regionalism in East Asia.

2.2.2.1 *Patterns of FDI in East Asia*

Unlike the domination of intra-regional mutual FDI in the EU, one-way vertical FDI is a noteworthy characteristic in East Asia. East Asia is one of the world's top recipients of FDI. FDI inflows in East Asia have been fundamental for economic growth in the region. ASEAN and China both have a high dependency on FDI for their export-led growth. In their early stages of economic development, both ASEAN and China were major destinations of FDI (Ku, 2010, p. 202; Puah et al., 2007). ASEAN's and China's inward FDI stock in 2018 reached $2.4 trillion and $ 1.6 trillion, respectively, accounting for 7.4% and 4.9% in global FDI stock.

Figure 2.6 compares FDI inflows to ASEAN and China from 1971 to 2018. In the period, ASEAN and China recorded a tremendous upward movement of FDI inflows from below $1 billion to over $140 billion. FDI flows to ASEAN and China rose to all-time highs of $156 billion and $141 billion, respectively, in 2018.

In terms of the sources of the FDI inflows, the patterns are different in the periods before and after the 1997 financial crisis (Kawai & Urata, 1998; Urata, 2002). In the pre-crisis period, Japan was the dominant source country. Most FDI inflow in East Asia was from within the region. From a Japanese

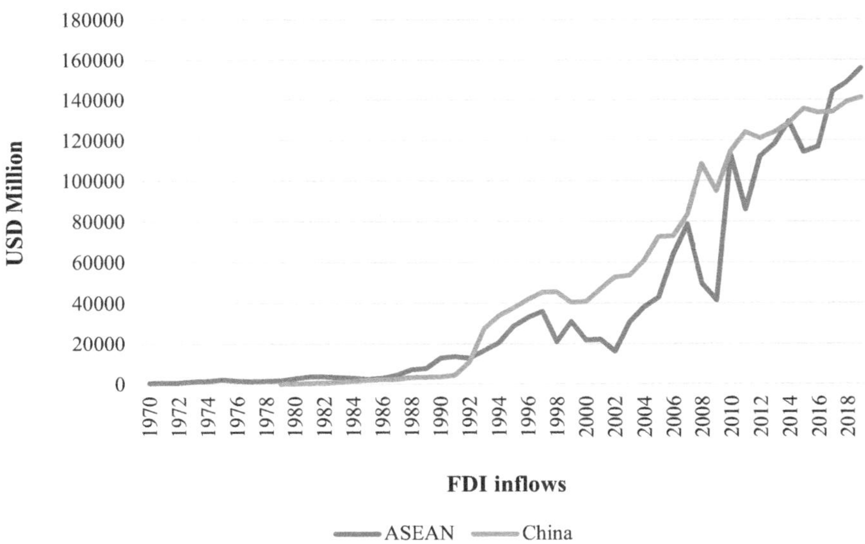

Figure 2.6 FDI Inflows to ASEAN and China (1971–2018).

Source: Author's compilation using data of UNCTAD.

perspective, regional destinations are attractive because of geographical proximity, cheap labor, and considerable long-run economic potential in emerging economies. Japanese MNCs expand their production networks via exporting sophisticated parts, components, and technology to host economies in East Asia. By the mid-1980s, Japan's FDI first concentrated on the NIEs such as South Korea, Taiwan, Hong Kong, and Singapore. It then expanded to ASEAN-4 in the late 1980s. The geographical distribution finally included China and other developing ASEAN economies, especially Vietnam, in the 1990s.

In the post-crisis period, sources of FDI inflows in East Asia became more diversified and globalized. With the active participation by extra-regional industrial capital, Japan, the US, and the EU became the leaders in providing FDI to East Asia. Japanese FDI diminished significantly due to the nation's prolonged recession. In contrast, American and European firms started to undertake FDI actively in East Asia in the 1990s. They took advantage of the opportunities arising from the inactive FDI from Japan and the 1997 financial crisis (Lipsey, 2006; Thangavelu, Rajan, and Parinduri, 2008). For example, American MNCs, such as electronic giants Dell, Hewlett-Packard, and Apple, came with a growing preference for subcontracting manufacturing in East Asia as their manufacturing hub. Western European companies also became increasingly aware of the growing importance of their region's economic relations with East Asia (Dent, 1997). European players invested actively in the fields of automobiles, electronics, heavy electrical machinery, and financial services. For instance, in electronics, Nokia (Finland), Ericsson (Sweden), and Siemens (Germany) succeeded in establishing their Asian production bases (Masaki & Kawate, 1998).

Besides the sources and destinations of FDI, some researchers investigate the different motivations that drive FDI.[11] They find that a substantial proportion of intra-regional FDI in East Asia is less market-seeking and more efficiency-seeking than FDI from extra-regional sources (Athukorala, 2009; Baldwin & Okubo, 2014). One example of market-seeking FDI is that Japanese MNCs produce "Made in China" products and sell them locally. Investors use multinational production to avoid trade costs. On the other hand, efficiency-seeking FDI is commonly known as export-oriented FDI.[12] For example, Japanese MNCs produce "Made in China" products and export these goods to the US. This efficiency-seeking FDI rises because of production fragmentation and cost differences in different economies.

When it comes to FDI in East Asia, the discussion is focused almost exclusively on efficiency-seeking investment for its great contributions to export-led industrialization in developing countries of the region (Ishida, 2012; Ito & Krueger, 2000; Li, 2013; Tonby et al., 2014). Both China and ASEAN have become the major manufacturing hubs. China's attractiveness to foreign investors as a production hub is obvious. Every fluctuation in its manufacturing output and cost levels makes headlines around the world. Likewise, foreign investors also have a growing awareness of ASEAN's value as a base of operations, where economies at vastly different stages of development share immense growth potential.

The industry composition of FDI has also attracted much scholarly attention. The examination of sectoral distribution reveals that a significantly large portion of FDI in East Asia has been undertaken in the manufacturing sector, especially textiles, electronics, and automobiles (Marukawa, 2002). FDI in the textile industry has economic significance for late industrializing countries in East Asia. It is widely perceived as one of the simplest and easiest industrialization routes (Akamatsu, 1962; Rasiah & Ofreneo, 2009; World Bank, 1993). The electronics sector, where parts and final goods are both highly tradable, is another example of sectoral preference.[13] The production fragmentation strategy adopted by MNCs is to allocate production blocks across East Asia. The growing automobile industry also offers opportunities for investment in manufacturing. Automobile manufacturing and production have skyrocketed most notably in China, Thailand, Indonesia, Vietnam, and Malaysia. Automakers have gradually expanded their local procurements in host countries (Nishitateno, 2013; Sasuga, 2013). Strong evidence shows that FDI in the manufacturing sector is an important contributor to economic growth and development in the host economies (Wang, 2009). East Asia stands to benefit from developing into a globally attractive FDI destination and a primary manufacturing hub of the world.

2.2.2.2 Explaining Weak Regionalism

FDI researchers argue that FDI patterns in destinations, sources, motivations, and composition are closely relevant to weak regionalism in East Asia. Two noteworthy characteristics of the FDI patterns have been used to explain weak regionalism. One is the increasing participation of global industrial capital. The other is the competition between ASEAN and China in attracting FDI. FDI researchers argue that this external dependence together with the internal competition demotivated states in East Asian regionalism for a regional economic community.

First, the long-term dependence on industrial capital from outsiders has made the idea of an exclusive East Asian regionalism problematic. FDI sourcing patterns in East Asia have shifted from the Japanese leadership to a more globalized one. The involvement of extra-regional industrial capital helps East Asia integrate with the global economy while weakening the material basis of a coherent regional economy.

Second, ASEAN and China have been competing to become global manufacturing hubs, especially in textiles, electronics, and automobiles. ASEAN and China both have a high dependency on FDI for their export-led growth. FDI is pursued to fuel the industrialization process of East Asian developing economies. A major concern of ASEAN economies from the early 1990s was the crowding-out effect of China's rise as a major host to FDI, including Japanese FDI (Athukorala, 2009). To attract FDI inflows, there has been a high degree of competition involved, which has made ASEAN economies anxious about China's rise. This China anxiety partially explains the resistance of some ASEAN economies to the idea of an East Asian economic community. Instead, ASEAN economies have initiated the ASEAN economic community among themselves. They attempt to build an ASEAN-centered arrangement and create a single market and production base.

In sum, few have discussed the patterns of the flows of industrial capital in East Asia to show how market forces researchers analyze the power of market forces in this particular area and how this is linked to the problem of East Asian regionalism. Like trade, FDI is believed to be another important variable adding new dynamics to regional economic transactions. In particular, researchers have worked carefully to consider the shift in the sources and destinations of FDI. Traditionally, Japanese MNCs undertook export-oriented FDI in ASEAN and China. More recently, American and European MNCs also increased their presence in East Asia for the cost-minimization of production. FDI economists thus ascribe weak regionalism to these increasing extra-regional FDI sources coupled with intense competition between the two major regional FDI recipients, ASEAN and China.

2.2.3 Transborder Production Networks

As in the cases of trade and FDI, the market force theory believes that the patterns of TPNs have shaped East Asia as an economic region. TPNs are connected systems among firms across national borders. They are called production networks because they are based on the division of labor in production. TPNs are formally defined as "the way resources, capital, technology, and know-how flow across borders" (Borrus, Ernst, and Haggard, 2000, pp. 1–2). TPNs are arrangements that link production units in different countries to supply components, materials, and management for the final assembly of a particular product.

While admitting that national accounts of trade and investment data do give some indication of market force explanations, the TPNs scholars argue that national accounts alone provide an incomplete picture of regional economic transactions in East Asia.[14] Bernard and Ravenhill point out the limits of the national accounts in their representative work *Beyond Product Cycles and Flying Geese: Regionalization, Hierarchy, and the Industrialization of East Asia*. They argue that

> The national economy is held to be the appropriate unit of analysis and the nature of production is ascertained by examining the flow of goods and capital between countries…This state centric view sees political economy as a tightly coupled process between the rise and fall of products and the rise of national economies.
>
> (Bernard & Ravenhill, 1995, pp. 183–184)

In other words, it is the networks among firms woven by networks of production, exchange, and distribution that now constitute the basic organizational unit of manufacturing activity. The internationalization of production gives rise to transborder flows of production factors such as goods and services (trade) and industrial capital (FDI). TPNs scholars contend that it is the networks that matter. Accordingly, trade and FDI accounts are at best important components in the development of international production networks in East Asia. It is the TPNs that determine the patterns of trade and FDI (Athukorala, 2011; Athukorala & Yamashita, 2006; Fukao et al., 2003; Kawai, 2005; Wang et al., 2009). The value of choosing the production networks, rather than national accounts, as the unit of analysis, is that they better capture the complexities and dynamics of regional industrial organization.

2.2.3.1 Patterns of East Asian TPNs

In the case of East Asia, three stages can easily be identified in the evolution of TPNs: flying geese pattern; regional production networks; and global production networks (see Table 2.3). Each stage features a unique pattern of TPNs, which closely mirrors the changes in the division of labor in East Asia.

The first stage from the 1950s to the mid-1980s features a flying geese pattern.[15] As illustrated in Figure 2.7, the flying geese pattern focuses on two dimensions: (x) the inter-industry dimension; and (y) the international division of labor. The x-axis suggests the sequential development of industries in a particular economy.

Generally, an economy starts from light manufacturing (e.g., garments) to heavy industries (steel) and sequentially moves up the product ladder to more sophisticated sectors (popular TV, video, HDTV). The y-axis concerns the sequential pattern of industrialization of East Asian economies. East Asian economies are said to follow one another in a developmental trajectory. From the mid-1950s through the early 1970s, Japan was the leading industrial power in the region. During the 1970s and 1980s, the NIEs, namely, Hong Kong, Singapore, South Korea, and Taiwan, replicated the development experience of Japan.[16] Similarly, industrial transformation recurred in ASEAN-4 (namely, Indonesia, Malaysia, Philippines, and Thailand) and China, and more recently

Table 2.3 The Development of East Asian Transborder Production Networks

Periods	*Patterns of TPNs*	*Division of labor*	*Trade pattern*	*FDI source*	*Key participants*
1950s–1985	Flying Geese	Horizontal	Intra-regional	Japan-led	Japan, NIEs
1985–1990s	Regional production networks	Vertical	Intra-regional & inter-regional		Japan, NIEs, ASEAN-4
1990s–2015	Globalized production networks	Vertical specialization	Global trade networks	Globalized	Japan, NIEs, ASEAN-4, China, US, Vietnam

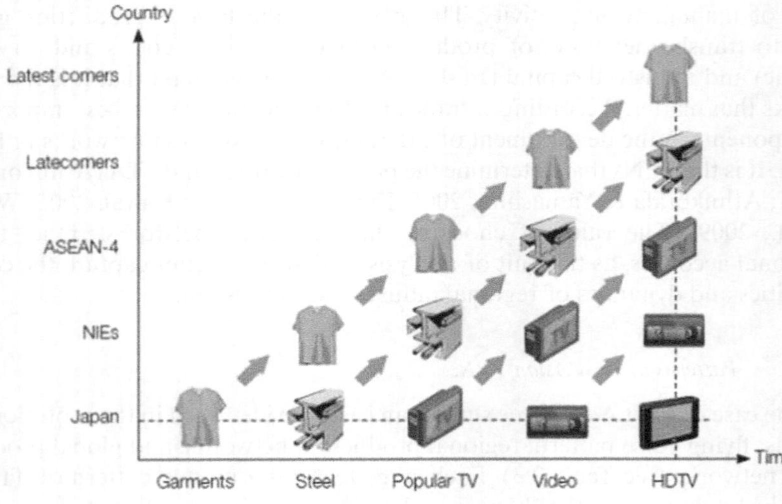

Figure 2.7 Structural Transformation of East Asian Economies.
Figure credit: Okita (1985, p. 21).

in countries in upper continental Southeast Asia such as Vietnam, Cambodia, Laos, and Myanmar.

The second stage from the mid-1980s to 1990s features the development of Japan-led regional production networks. The signing of the Plaza Accord (1985) marked a watershed in the development of TPNs. The rapid and steep appreciation of the Yen became a catalyst to Japan's outward investment in ASEAN-4, a regional group that includes Malaysia, Thailand, the Philippines, and Indonesia. During the four-year period from 1986 to 1989, growth in Japanese investment in ASEAN was spectacular, with the sectoral focus moving quickly from textiles and metals to the production of electrical machinery (Bernard & Ravenhill, 1995, pp. 181–182). The spatial expansion of such networks connected ASEAN with production in Northeast Asia.

The integration of ASEAN with regionalized manufacturing activity in several industries was one of the most prominent shifts in the late 1980s and early 1990s. Economically, the level of development of East Asia varies greatly. In regional production networks, Japan was in the first tier, with NIEs in the second tier, and ASEAN-4 in the third tier. This regional heterogeneity provided sources of integration. As Borrus and his fellows (2000, p. 12) observe, "the region's economic development occurred in phases that created unusually heterogeneous production capabilities and thus a high-degree of intra-regional complementarity".

A vertical intra-industry division of labor, particularly in manufacturing, strengthened the Japanese-led and exclusionist regional production networks in East Asia. Yamamura and Hatch (1997) suggest that the transplantation of many standard Japanese business practices in East Asia is based on the concept of *keiretsu*. Keiretsu refers to an industrial structure based on powerful corporate groupings, which allows Japanese MNCs to develop a complex web of production networks across the region. In this Japanese-led regional industrial system, East Asian economies were integrated as subcontractors and component suppliers to the Japanese industrial core. Some scholars thus name the Japan-led regional production networks as "regionalization of the Japanese economy" or a new Japanese-led "East Asian co-prosperity sphere" (Gilpin, 1995, p. 6). Some critics argue that Japanese-led regional production networks give non-Asian competitors an unfair disadvantage in economic competition. American and European MNCs had a very hard time breaking into the regional production networks in Japan's power embrace.

The third stage in the 1990s to the mid-2000s highlights a globalized scale of the regional production networks. Particularly, the US has become the most important external force in shaping regional economic order (Sum, 2002). The rise of global production networks (GPNs)[17] indicated the significant change in the geographical scope of transborder production from a regionally oriented to globally interconnected East Asian economy.

In the case of Japan, the structural focus of its TPNs has shifted from a regional focus to global expansion. By the mid-1980s, East Asia was in Japan's domination because of its deepening economic presence in the region (Yamamura & Hatch, 1997). The traditional flying geese model of economic interactions between Japan and East Asia worked as a unifying force of regionalization (Ozawa, 2003). Japanese MNCs built TPNs in East Asia in automobiles, auto parts, electronics, machinery, and other important industries. They maintain exceptionally tight control over their network members—both formally affiliated manufacturers and more informally related suppliers—throughout the region. This production alliance is named the "keiretsu-ization" of East Asian manufacturing industries (Yamamura & Hatch, 1997). As a result, non-Japanese foreign firms wishing to enter markets faced extreme difficulties.

In this context, the US desired to assure that East Asian production networks and markets were open to all. The US started to counter Japan's emerging and deepening production alliances in East Asia. Under the political and economic power of the US, Japanese-led Asian production networks were reshaped. On the one hand, Japan opened up Japanese-led production networks in East Asia.[18] That FDI surge was soon followed by the arrival of MNCs from Japan and the US, some from Europe, and their construction of cross-border production chains into what became fondly known as Factory Asia. On the other hand, Japan increased its investment in North America after NAFTA was enacted in 1994. Further into the 1990s, the perceived economic threat posed by Japan receded, globalization accelerated, and multinational supply chains proliferated. Japanese and US economic interests in the Asia-Pacific region have become substantially aligned.

The shift in the structural focus of Japanese-led production networks had a great impact on its attitude toward regionalism. Japan finally decided to support the idea of the Asia-Pacific, rather than East Asia in the late 1980s. The Japan-US economic alliance was widely recognized as the propeller and cornerstone of their joint leadership in the Asia-Pacific region. The shared economic structural interests underlaid the Japan-US strategic partnership on East Asian regionalism, particularly in promoting the APEC agenda and the TPP agenda later.

Similarly, in the case of China, the evolving economic structure and its changing position within the structure greatly impacted its preference in East Asian regionalism. In the early stage of China's economic rise in the 1980s and early 1990s, China's focus was on greater China. As Weidenbaum puts it,

> This strategic area contains substantial amounts of technology and manufacturing capability (Taiwan), outstanding entrepreneurial, marketing, and services acumen (Hong Kong), a fine communications network (Singapore), a tremendous pool of financial capital (all three), and very large endowments of land, resources, and labor (mainland China)
>
> (1996, p. 80)

With the implementation of China's market-oriented reforms and opening-up policy, Greater China emerged as a new epicenter for industry, commerce, and finance. Enthusiasm toward forming a Greater China FTA ran high. Negotiations of bilateral trade agreements between China, Taiwan, and Hong Kong were launched. These included the Closer Economic Partnership Arrangement (CEPA) between Hong Kong, Macao, and mainland China, the Economic Cooperation Framework Agreement (ECFA) between Taiwan and mainland China. The long-term goal of these trade agreements, as noted by Chinese officials and academics, is to integrate the economies of Hong Kong, Macao, and Taiwan and then establish the long-proposed "Greater China Economic Circle" (Liu, 2003; Pan, 2003).

However, the hopes for a Greater China FTA and the Greater China Economic Circle faded when mainland China embarked upon its "Going Global" strategy aiming to integrate with the global economy. The importance of Hong Kong and Taiwan as sources of FDI diminished somewhat in the 1990s as multinationals from Europe, Japan, and the US entered mainland China directly (Tseng & Zebregs, 2002, p. 4). China is not only one of the world's largest FDI recipients but it also began to undertake aggressive outward foreign direct investment (OFDI) on a global scale. The global expansion of China's industrial capital and production relations requires new institutional frameworks to support, facilitate, and protect. The Belt and Road Initiative (BRI) is seen as designed to create interconnected hub-and-spoke production networks centered on the hub of China (Cai, 2017).

2.2.3.2 How TPNs Discussion Explains Weak Regionalism

Two critical points emerge from the discussion above on the evolution of TPNs that are useful for us in understanding how the market force researchers relate this to East Asian regionalism. First, it is commonly believed that the globalization of regional production networks is the root cause of weak regionalism in East Asia. By the 1990s, the market-driven regionalization, for example, the formation of Japan-led East Asian production networks and supply chains, required a supporting regional institutional framework (Baldwin, 2008; Kawai and Wignaraja, 2010). However, from the late 1990s, driven by the forces of globalization, the structural focus of East Asian TPNs further shifted from regionally concentrated to globally networked. An ADB study in 2012 explains this regionally integrated and globally connected East Asian economy as follows:

> The region's diversity, development pattern, and global links have generated a unique Asian model of regionalism—dynamic, open, multi-track, and multispeed—which enhances prosperity not only in the region but also in the rest of the world. Asia's open regionalism underscores the importance of strengthening trade, investment, and capital flows within the region while maintaining strong ties with, and remaining open to, the rest of the world. It aims to build a regionally integrated and globally connected Asia.
>
> (ADB, 2012, pp. 61–62)

This study suggests that East Asian production networks call for institutions of regional integration, but at the same time, challenge regional institutions, which exclude non-East Asian economic powers. In other words, open and weak regionalism, which can better serve the market forces of the region, is not necessarily a bad thing.

Second, TPNs scholars often see obstacles to the institutionalization of regional cooperation in East Asia driven by their shared export-oriented development patterns and converging comparative advantages. Initially, the TPNs promoted a multitier division of labor that helped to form an economic region in East Asia. Economies at different levels of development were tied together by growing production linkages among the Japanese MNCs, their overseas affiliates, and local partners. However, East Asian economies have adopted an export-oriented growth model and become involved in global competition (Song, 2012). East Asian countries have become more competing with one another than cooperating, for example, China and Japan. Given the converging comparative advantages and intensifying competition, it is impractical for East Asian states to focus on building a regional economic community because their TPNs interests and connections do not support such an inward-looking and closer regional entity.

2.2.4 Gaps in the Market Force Explanations

We have looked at representative works of the market force approach to explain East Asian weak regionalism. Market force theory argues that regionalism in

East Asia is driven very much by the economic interests and forces in trade, FDI, and TPNs. The cause of failure in East Asian regionalism is found not in institutions, but in the working of market forces. Market forces may initially concentrate in East Asia, but their destinations are not confined to the region. They go global in seeking efficiency, as evidenced in the surge of trans-regional flows of products, parts, materials, capital, and people. East Asia has developed a distinct approach in regionalism emphasizing openness and broad connectivity that regional economic frameworks are compatible with global trade liberalization.

However, the problem with the market force explanations is that it lacks an effective theoretical framework to explain how market forces drive nations to seek different institutional arrangements. In their challenge to institutional explanations, market force analysts downplay the role of institutions and consider the outcomes in East Asian regionalism simply as the effects of market forces. Market force explanations thus are narratives of these market forces and their institutional consequences. For example, in their analysis of TPNs, the complexities of global and regional connectedness are usually interpreted as the root cause of the overlapping regional institutions in East Asia. This interpretation lacks an effective theoretical framework to establish the logical link between market dynamics and contending preferences in regional institutional arrangements.

This is where I develop my thinking for a more effective theoretical framework to explain the problem of East Asian regionalism. My structural theory is not necessarily an alternative to but rather a further development of the two sets of explanations. On the one hand, I agree with liberal institutionalists that institutions can play an instrumental role in promoting interstate cooperation. But I argue that institutions not only shape interstate interaction but are themselves shaped by more profound forces in IR. On the other hand, I favor market force explanations that East Asian regionalism is largely a productional forces-driven process by traders, investors, and manufacturers to seek institutional support at intergovernmental levels. To better illustrate how material productional forces contribute to the pattern of East Asian regionalism, in the next section I will consider the logic of IES that connects these material and productional forces and the institutional preferences and the practices of states in East Asian regionalism and the hypotheses arising from this theoretical framework that will guide empirical research for this book on the problem of East Asian regionalism.

2.3 A Structural Theory of East Asian Regionalism

In this section, I discuss how this research project theorizes what caused the high tension and the contention in the institutional preferences of states in East Asian regionalism, which, as we have shown in Chapter 1, contributed significantly to the problem or weakness in East Asian regionalism.

To establish such a structural theoretical framework, the remainder of this section proceeds in three parts. In part one, I first discuss the concept of IES.

In part two, I illustrate the theoretical logic that connects the structural forces and institutional preferences. Finally, in part three, I present how I model IESs in this research project and ways of assessing the effects of the IES on the institutional preferences of the states in East Asian regionalism.

2.3.1 *International Economic Structure*

I first look at the concept of IES itself. What do we mean when we speak about an IES? And how do we demonstrate its effects? Ever since Kenneth Waltz's *Theory of International Politics*, international structure has been widely accepted as a useful framework to analyze state action and interaction in international politics. Waltz defines an international structure as a system-wide distribution of capabilities of states in an "anarchic" international system (1979, p. 93). The distribution of capabilities forms a material structure in interstate relations. The anarchic condition means that there are no other forces that can effectively motivate or constrain states except the structural force. A state's position in the international structure is therefore important. The relative position in a particular pattern of distribution of capabilities determines how states define their interests, calculate their actions, and behave in interaction with others. According to Waltz, the capabilities vary across states in the following areas: the size of population and territory, resource endowment, economic capability, military strength, and political stability and competence. But he has never offered a precise definition of the compatibilities and assigned indicators for empirical assessment of the distribution and hence the positions of states.

Accordingly, the IES is defined as the system-wide distribution of economic capabilities and interests of the states, and it reflects the relative power and strength of a state in their relation to others. An IES is unique in the distribution of economic power. It can be multipolar and competitive or hegemonic and hierarchical. Each state has a distinct position in relation to others. Change in the economic capacity and interests of a state or states leads to shifts in the structure.

Developing Waltz's theoretical framework a step further, Immanuel Wallerstein has pioneered a framework to describe the international economic system in structural terms. In his celebrated book, *The Modern World System*, Wallerstein focuses on three hegemonic powers in the capitalist world economy—Holland, Great Britain, and the US (Wallerstein, 1980). As Figure 2.8 illustrates, he discovers that a core nation or a hegemony is defined by simultaneously productive, commercial, and financial superiorities over other nations. These three superiorities overlap in time, but they are successive. The productive superiority out of the three is "the only solid base on which to stay ahead in the capitalist world economy" (Wallerstein, 1980, p. 48). The productive efficiency in the agro-industrial sectors leads to the commercial primacy in world trade, which leads, in turn, to the control of the financial sector of banking and investment. These three sets of capabilities—productive, commercial, and financial—have dictated the pattern of the core and periphery structure of the

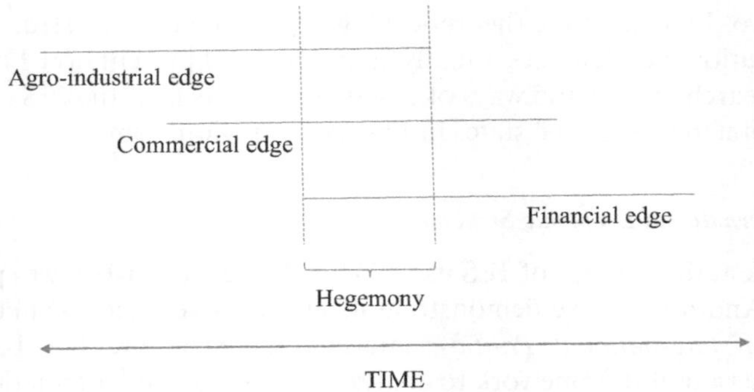

Figure 2.8 Wallerstein's Model of the Sources of the Structural Position of Core Nation/Hegemonic Power.

Source: Wallerstein (1984, p. 40).

capital world system in the past 500 years of European industrial growth and global expansion.

Whereas his 1980 book focuses on the historical development of the modern world economy, in a later book—*The Politics of the World Economy* (1984)—Wallerstein explores the relations between core nations and periphery areas. In his world system theory, Wallerstein conceptualizes the world economy in a structure of core and periphery areas.[19] Accordingly, "core processes in core areas—and more and more of the processes that require less skilled and more extensive manpower that is easiest to keep at a low-income level in other areas—peripheral processes in peripheral areas" (Wallerstein, 1984, pp. 4–5). Wallerstein argues that in the contemporary capitalist world economy, as production is increasingly organized in transborder commodity chains, the pattern of a spatial hierarchy of the production processes leads to economic polarization between core countries and periphery countries.

Lake (1984) further brings into play empirical material for an enhanced concept of IES. According to him, IESs can be hegemonic, hierarchic, or multipolar. A state's position in the power distribution is critical to understand the effects of the IES. Lake identifies states in terms of six categories measured by their relative size and relative productivity.[20] Of the six categories, a hegemonic leader is the most powerful state because of its greatest size and productivity in a structure at the time. Lake defines an IES as the hierarchic distribution of trade and production capabilities of states dominated by hegemonic power. Moreover, Lake focuses on the dynamism of IES as the hegemonic power rises and declines. As shown in Figure 2.9, Lake captures the transformation of the IES with the rise of powers into hegemony and the subsequent decline from hegemony. These form a transition from one type of IES to another.

Lake's work provides an innovative way to empirically define the positions of states and their shift over time, and a way of virtually describing the distribution of state capabilities in the international system at a given time.

Lake's work also demonstrates that an IES is dynamic as the power positions of states constantly shift. With these shifts, the character of the IES also changes, for example, from the Great Britain-led hegemonic hierarchic structure in the 1870–1938 period to the US-led hegemonic structure in the 1950–1977 period.

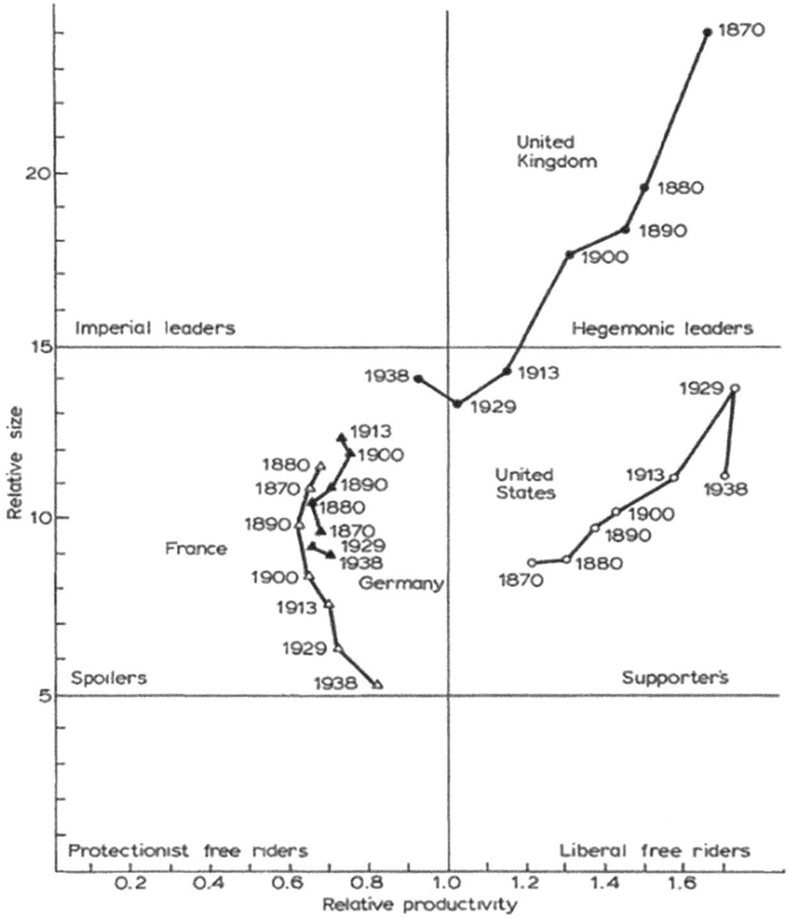

Figure 2.9 Lake's Capturing of the Evolution of International Economic Structure. (a) Pax Britannica: 1870–1938; (b) Pax Americana: 1950–1977.

Notes: Different positions of the states at different times in the respective distribution of national capabilities, as measured by relative size and relative productivity. Relative size is measured by a nation's proportion of trade, while relative productivity is measured by national output per man-hour relative to the average national output per man-hour in the other middle and large-sized nations.

Figure credit: Lake (1984, p. 159, 163).

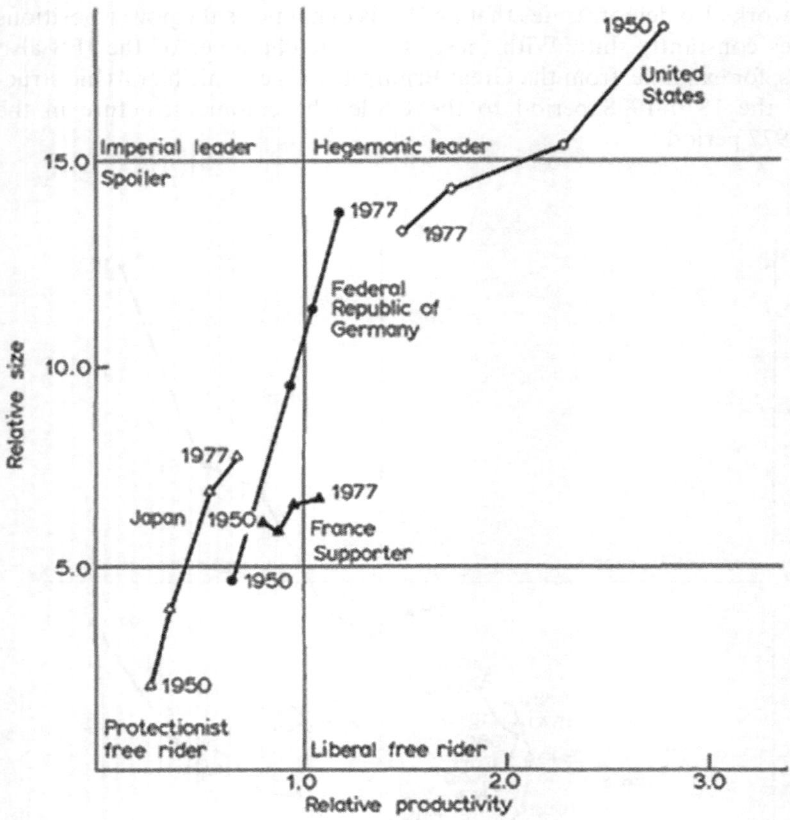

Figure 2.9 Continued

Along this line, Huang interprets IES very much in the original spirit of Waltz and Lake. He agrees with Waltz and Lake that IESs are measurable and observable (Huang, 2019). As Figure 2.10 shows, Huang depicts the pattern of the global distribution of national wealth and economic capabilities where East Asia is a primary area of origin of economic interests and capabilities.

In studies empirically depicting IESs, national accounts such as GDP size, trade volume, and productivity have been used. Huang (2020) discusses the use of production networks data to model an IES. He argues that although the distribution of GDP is a simple and good index to measure the distribution of economic capabilities, it misses the economic interactions and complex interdependence between nations. In an era of transborder production networking, industrial parts supply capital, technology, and know-how flow transnationally. In such an interdependent world economic system, nations not only compete for national GDP growth but also cooperate to participate in transborder

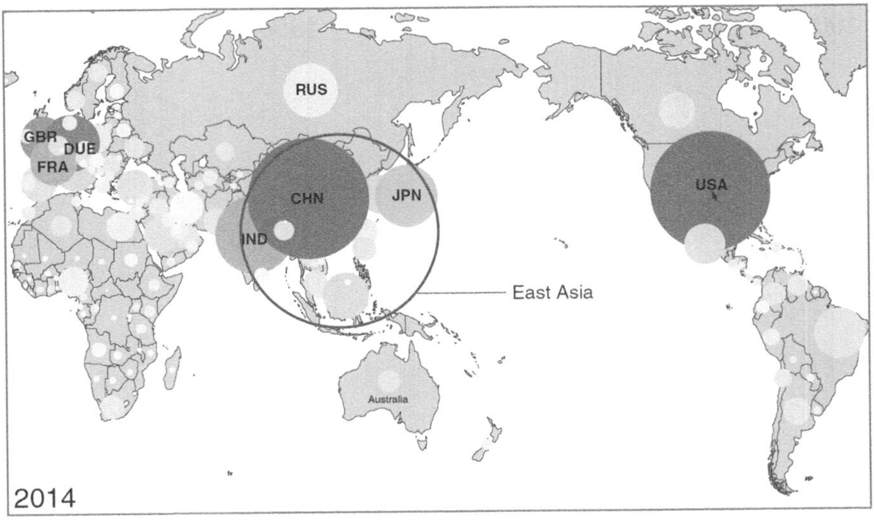

Figure 2.10 Huang's Depiction of the Global Distribution of National Economic Capabilities, 2014.

Figure credit: Huang (2019, p. 254), real GDP of states geo-economically located with size measured in 2011 USD.

production. The IES thus should be thicker than the GDP ranking and is increasingly shaped by industrial activities and relations across borders.

Huang adds a new set of indicators—transborder production networks—for the analysis and assessment of the effects of an IES. He maintains that integrative transborder industrial, capital, and trade dynamics help form a region-wide division of labor. Huang uses work by IDE-JETRO and WTO (2011) as a model for an analysis of the structure of production networks. Built on the sophisticated indicators of connectedness, the IDE-JETRO model, as shown in Figure 2.11, maps the evolution of the structure of production networks in East Asia and its shift in the mid-1980s through the mid-2000s.

The pattern of regional distribution of trade capabilities shifted from a unipolar and Japan-led structure in 1985 and 1990 to a bipolar US-Japan centered structure in 1995, a tripolar China-Japan-US centered structure in 2000, and a multipolar structure in 2005. Notably, in 1985, only four participants came into the picture: Japan, Malaysia, Singapore, and Indonesia. It was Japan, the leader in the flying geese model, who dominated the supply chains. Then in 1990, the number of participants rose. Japan extended its production networks to the new followers: Thailand, South Korea, and Taiwan. Since Japan signed the Plaza Accord in 1985, the strong Yen drove Japanese enterprises to increase overseas production in neighboring economies. In 1995, the US became involved. Malaysia and Singapore worked as the bridge that linked the two industrial powers. In 2000, one year before it

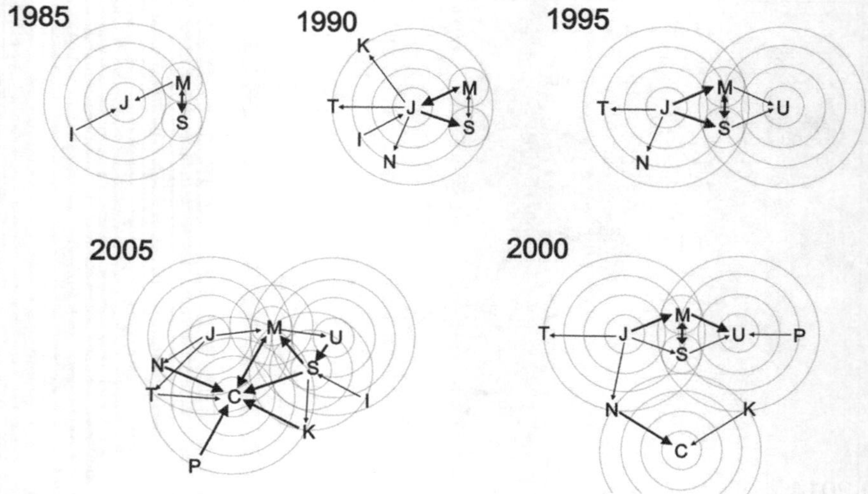

Figure 2.11 IDE-JETRO's Depiction of the Structure of Production Networks in East Asia and Its Shift, 1985–2005.

Notes: C-China; I-Indonesia; J-Japan; K-South Korea; M-Malaysia; N-Taiwan; P-Philippines; S-Singapore; T-Thailand; U-United States.

Graph credit: IDE-JETRO & WTO (2011, p. 75).

was accepted into the WTO, China built up the production networks with strong connectedness to both Taiwan and South Korea. The tripolar structure among the US, Japan, and China became visible. In 2005, China started to play a pivotal role in building regional production networks. According to Huang, over time, regional production relations in East Asia have been dominated by one or several industrial powers. These hierarchical structures involve unequal exchange and competing national interests that have profoundly influenced the development of the international economic and trade relations of East Asia.

In brief, the aforementioned discussions and analysis of IESs focus on an essential dimension of IESs: the distribution of economic capabilities. An IES is unique in the interstate distribution of economic powers and influences. It can be multipolar and competitive or unipolar and hierarchic. Each state has a position in the economic structure in relation to others. Changes in the economic capacity and interests of a state or states lead to changes in the power relations among these states.

2.3.1.1 IES: The Structure of Value Chains

This book will employ the framework of IES to model the structure of TPNs. I use the framework here very much in the original spirit of Kenneth Waltz, taking the IES to be the distribution of economic interests and capabilities of the states. I will focus on the distribution of a particular set of economic interests and capabilities, value-added in transborder production contributed by different states. Very similar to TPNs, global value chains (GVCs) or supply chains refer to the transnational fragmentation of production. These concern contributions by different states to the total value of a product, the production of which is fragmented in different countries. GVC analysis is used in this book to build IESs. In the following discussions, I will use these concepts interchangeably: production networks, value chains, and supply chains.[21]

A starting point for understanding the structure of value chains is the notions of value-added and value chain, as developed by international business researchers. They focus on the strategies of both firms and states in the global economy. In its most basic form, value-added is the difference between the value of goods and the cost of materials or supplies that are used in producing them. A value chain is a sequential set of additions of value to the product in the whole process of its production, by which "technology is combined with material and labor inputs, and then processed inputs are assembled, marketed, and distributed" (Kogut, 1985, p. 15). If a value chain is fragmented across national borders, it is called a transborder or global value chain. Different amounts of value-added in the process in different states form a structure of the transborder value chains. For instance, the global value chain of Nutella can be identified in the structure of an internationally fragmented value chain on a single product (see Figure 2.12).

Figure 2.12 The Global Value Chain of Nutella.

Graph credit: OECD (2012, p. 17).

There is a core-periphery structure in the GVCs of Nutella:

> The food processing company Ferrero International is headquartered in Italy and has nine factories producing Nutella: five are located in Europe, one in Russia, one in North America, two in South America, and one in Australia. Some inputs are locally supplied, for example, the packaging or some of the ingredients, like skimmed milk. There are however ingredients that are globally supplied: hazelnuts come from Turkey, palm oil from Malaysia, cocoa from Nigeria, sugar mainly from Brazil (but also from Europe), and the vanilla flavor from China (the manufacturer of vanillin is a French company that also produces in France). Nutella is then sold in 75 countries through sales offices (that are more numerous than those few represented in the figure).
>
> (OECD, 2012, p. 17)

The GVC description shows that the world economic system is hierarchically organized into blocs and that countries play different roles (e.g., headquarter economy, factory economy). This value-added accounting of production networks reveals the relations between production units, provides a new empirical way to model and analyze IES and assess its effects.

Similarly, the GVCs of Huawei is another example of how GVC analysis describes and analyzes an IES and provides a better understanding of its character and effects. Figure 2.13 demonstrates the suppliers exposed to Huawei across the globe.

The Financial Times quoted Goldman Sachs as saying,

> Across Huawei's vast supply chain, which stretches from China and Chinese Taipei to Japan, the US, and Finland, the impact of the US indictment sent share prices sliding as investors fretted over the future of the Chinese Telecoms equipment giant and whether it would now be hit with an export ban.
>
> (Fildes & Lucas, 2019)

The GVCs of Huawei are indicative of the periphery position of China's electronics industry, which relies heavily on the US, Japanese, Taiwanese, and South Korean suppliers for key components. Despite years of strategic investment, China has been (so far) unable to master the production of its products in value ownership and contribution.

From the examples above, we learn that GVC builds and sustains a vast and unequal international division of labor splitting the world into headquarter and factory economies. The structure of value chains is hierarchic. The position of countries in GVCs affects the value countries are able to capture in the transnational production and distribution of production (Kostoska et al., 2020). Most of the value is created in activities upstream, for example, innovation, research and development (R&D), design, and downstream, for example,

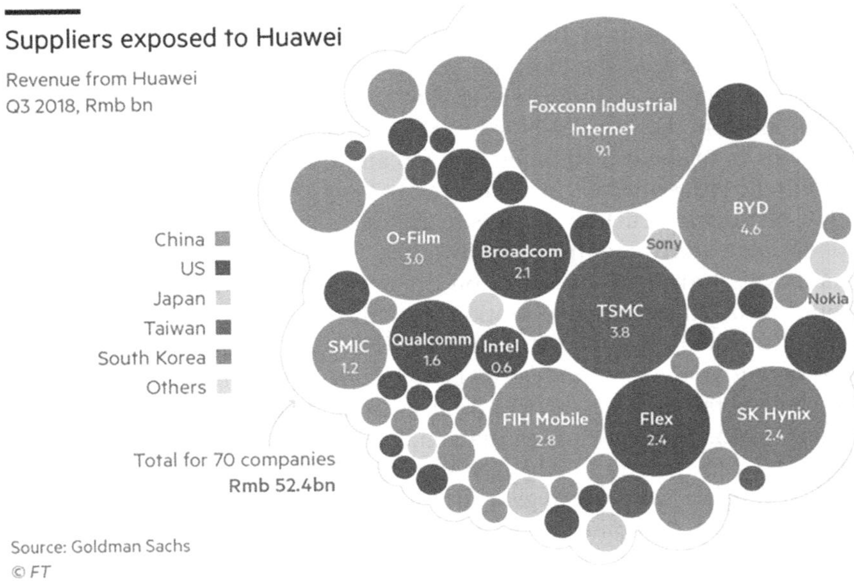

Figure 2.13 The Global Value Chains of Huawei.

Graph credit: Fildes & Lucas (2019).

marketing, branding, logistics, while typically only limited value is created in the actual manufacturing/assembly stage. These activities for example, assembling and processing, take place in "factory" economies of developing countries, while intellectual work, for example, R&D and design, takes place in the "headquarter" in capital-rich nations. It all seems to make perfect sense that in most developing countries exports have risen substantially without a comparable increase in domestic value-added, but production-linked gains typically expected in export-led growth dwindling.

Product-level stories such as Huawei and Nutella are only the tip of the iceberg. Empirical studies at the industry level had not been undertaken until the 2010s. The development of research on GVCs accounting as well as the release of Inter-Country Input-Output (ICIO) tables has opened up insights into the structure of value chains at the industry level. These tables enable shifts in the focus of GVC from micro case studies to macro and quantitative analysis. As will be discussed in Chapter 3, where I discuss data and methodology, the analysis of value chains at the industry and country levels provides system-wide quantitative results for research on IESs.

2.3.1.2 Using GVC Analysis to Analyze IES in East Asia

The hierarchic structure of value chains has been particularly relevant to the industrial development of East Asia. In the second half of the 20th century,

Japan-led industrial diffusion in East Asia led to the flying geese pattern of industrial development in the region. A core-periphery structure developed in the relations between the "leading goose", that is, Japan and the rest. The regional economic structure can be seen to have only a single core (Japan). This is different from the cases of North America and Europe where income levels of nations in regional integration (the US and Canada in the former and the EU15 in the latter) are very similar.

The hierarchic structure remains in the relations between the lead country and the networked countries in East Asia in the 21st century, despite the dynamics of transborder production organization of industrial production. Facilitated by efficient transportation and advanced communication technology, the regional economic structure of East Asia has transformed from a single core to a multicore industrial belt. The multiple cores, which have their own agglomeration forces, spread from Japan and South Korea in the northeastern corner, passing through mainland East Asia including China, Hong Kong, and Taiwan, and to ASEAN-4 in Southeast Asia. A vast and unequal division of labor splits the region into headquarter economies in Northeast Asia and factory economies in Southeast Asia.

There are three patterns to observe in the IES in East Asia. First, the economic rise of East Asia has significantly reshaped the world economic structure. As Huang has argued: "East Asia's economic rise has shifted the worldwide distribution of industrial, financial, and trading interests, relations, and capabilities to East Asia" (2019, p. 146). While the newly emerging industrial powers will seek to build a worldwide division of labor, how East Asian states engage and develop relations with those in the other regions is of critical importance. This book will compare the global distribution of value chains to see the structural relations among the three regions—Europe, North America, and East Asia. Each region is assumed to be a productional unit in the discussion of regional concentration of economic interests and capabilities in the world economic structure. Their positions in the world economic structure can be described and analyzed using data and methods in GVC analysis. This analysis is important for us to understand the effects of the world economic structure on the material basis for East Asia to be a legitimate unit for a regional economic community.

Second, in different stages of economic development and different waves of East Asian industrialization, countries in the region developed into different types of economies with different economic positions in the regional economic structure. Some moved up to the top of the structure and became global hubs and hegemonic powers in the region, while others are in the lower streams of the value chains and the lower ladders of the structural hierarchy. The scale and focus of their economies differ significantly in terms of global/regional connectivity. East Asian economies are extremely susceptible to the pressures of economic regionalization and globalization. Table 2.4 shows the two paths in the convergence of the effects of globalization and regionalization on the international economic order in East Asia in the 1980s and 1990s.

Table 2.4 Effects of Globalization and Regionalization on East Asia: 1980s and 1990s

Paths	*Structural contexts*	*Actors*	*Involved strategies of re-territorialization*	*Examples*
Regional-globalization	Embedded exportism	Local-national-regional actors and their networks	New (sub)-regional division of labor	Growth triangles, "flying geese"
Global-regionalization	Global neoliberalism	Global hegemony (the US)	Trade/investment liberalization and regional market access	APEC's "open regionalism"

Table credit: Sum (2002, p. 59).

In the 1980s, East Asia was under mixed pressures of regionalization and globalization. Driven by the Japan-led flying geese dynamics, regionally oriented market forces dominated the organization of TPNs. East Asian economies developed highly integrated regional production networks which resulted in a triangular trade pattern. However, East Asia was not the purpose or the destination of these market forces. In search of a more efficient form of trans-border organization, market forces went global in the 1990s. Global production forces came into play in the region. The US adopted an open regionalism approach. Institutionally, it initiated the APEC project to promote trade and investment liberalization and regional market access in East Asia. The US-led economic forces significantly reshaped the economic structure of East Asia. The aforementioned IDE-JETRO and WTO study shows that by 1995, the Japan-led production networks in East Asia evolved into a structure of Japan-US industrial complex in GVCs (2011, p. 74). From the 1990s, the US became the most significant external force in the shaping of the regional economic order. The second dimension of my empirical research in this book will be devoted to analyzing the regional economic structure and its effects on East Asia regionalism. Each national economy in East Asian regionalism is regarded as a productional unit. I focus on the position of each economy in the regional economic structure, using their rates of participation in regional value chains involving regional productions only and GVCs involving also extra-regional partner countries.

In addition to structural analysis at the global and regional levels, the effects of IESs on East Asian regionalism can also be analyzed at the industry level in the particular pattern of the nation's economic structure. There is extreme heterogeneity in sectoral economic structures across East Asian economies. Their developmental stages are different and so are their agriculture-manufacturing-services ratios. Sectoral economic structures, in terms of the relative weight of the three sectors in the GDP of the nation, shift from being agriculture-dominated to manufacturing-oriented and to services-led in the process of the nation's industrialization and economic development. This change in the agriculture-manufacturing-services ratios further results in a shift in employment opportunities from low productivity, low-wage agricultural jobs to higher productivity, higher-wage manufacturing jobs, and then jobs in the service sectors such as financial intermediation, communications, and transport. The share of agriculture in national GDP and employment fell while that of manufacturing and services increased. East Asian-developed economies have already matured and developed services-oriented economic structures, while others are newly emerging in the past two decades or so and still possess agriculture and/or manufacturing-oriented industrial structures. These structural conditions are intentionally connected and an important material basis of the IESs. Analyzing these conditions shall reveal how states in East Asian regionalism are positioned in the regional and global structures, and these conditions influence diverging institutional preferences of the states in East Asian regionalism.

In brief, this research will apply the framework of IES and the GVC analysis to model IESs in East Asian regionalism and analyze their effects on the institutional preferences of the states. The causal logic underlying the framework needs further discussion and explanation before we set to use the theory to hypothesize the three sets of relations this research to investigate. The analytical framework of the structural theory proposed here can be translated into a graphic model as shown in Figure 2.14.

In the world economic structure at the global level, each regional economy is treated as a basic production unit, for example, Factory East Asia, Factory North America, and Factory Europe. The world economic structure is the distribution of productive capabilities of all states in the world. We want to see whether there are concentrations of world productional capabilities in the three areas where a high concentration rate is expected in the theory of economic regionalism. The position of each region in the structure is measured by the total value-added by the region in the GVCs. By comparing how regionally

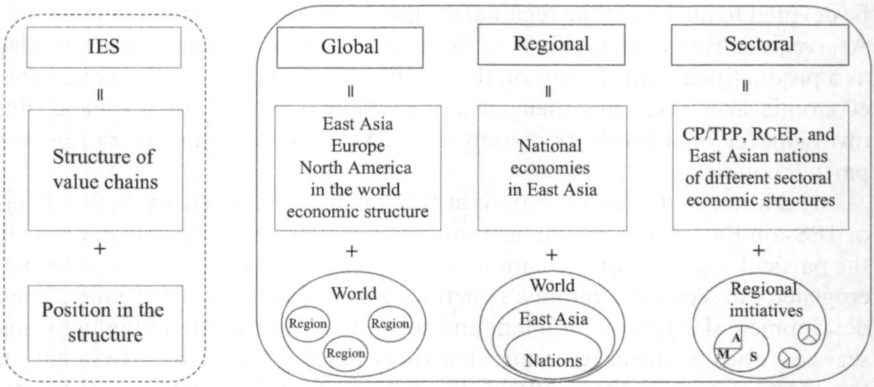

Figure 2.14 A Framework of Modeling and Analyzing International Economic Structures.

concentrated and globally interconnected each factory is, we can determine if there is a regionally concentrated economic structure to support a regional institution-building project.

In the regional economic structure in East Asia, each nation is regarded as a stand-alone production unit, for example, Factory China and Factory Japan. The IES is measured by the distribution of capabilities among states in East Asian regionalism. The position of each national economy in the structure is determined by the total value-added by the nation in value chains operating in East Asia. We want to know whether the value-added activities are more regionally focused or more globally oriented. This is suspected to have a great impact on the divergence in nations' interests and preferences for different institutional arrangements for transborder economic activities in the region. By comparing how much regionally concentrated and globally interconnected each national economy is, we can understand the underlying structural dynamics that have driven nations to seek various types of institutional arrangements for a regional economic community.

At the sectoral level of IES, each national economy has a different structure with different weights of the agriculture, manufacturing, and services sectors in its total GDP. This variety in development stages is believed to have formed an economic structure in the region along the line of a division of labor between advanced economies, developing economies, and those in between. Through investigation of this dimension in this book, we want to know how these different structural dynamics influenced the nations' preference over competing initiatives in East Asian regionalism.

Together, these three areas of research focus explain what the structural forces are in the structural theory. Discussions of the IES here provide analytical and empirical substance to the structural theory. I turn to discussions of how structural forces relate to institutional preferences and selections in the next section.

2.3.2 How Structural Forces Relate to Institutional Preferences and Selections

From the discussions above, we have learned that a major feature of the structural theory is distinguishing the distribution of power which is a structural-level variable as opposed to power itself which is a state-level variable. States are confined to the unit level and treated as "black boxes", with fixed preferences for wealth, security, or power. When explaining policy outcomes, looking at the structural-level variables parsimoniously explain why "dissimilar units behave in similar ways". However, when considering the policy-making process, due to the inadequate elaboration on state behavior, the structuralist framework cannot fully address how structural forces are "translated" into the institutional preferences of states.

To solve the explanatory gap of the structural theory, here I engage with liberalism to establish the theoretical logic that links IESs to states' policy decisions. Unlike purely economic analyses, liberal scholars highlight the impact of institutional factors. For instance, Mattli (1999b) contends that demand by market players is not enough for integration to succeed. He presents regional integration as a two-step process and outlines a distinct division of labor between market players as "demanding" and political leaders as "supplying" transnational policy coordination. On the demand side, market players like big businesses are incentivized to lobby for regional rules, regulations, and policies that reduce economic and political uncertainty, as well as a wide range of financial risks relating to cross-border trade and investment. On the supply side, there are conditions under which political leaders are willing and able to accommodate demands by market players for institutional arrangements. Willingness depends on the payoff of integration to political leaders, while ability rests on the presence of an undisputed leader among the group of countries seeking closer ties.

This division of labor between market players and political leaders is an echo of the distinction between regionalization and regionalism. As discussed earlier, Breslin and Higgott (2000, p. 344) define regionalization as bottom-up integration processes that derive "from markets, from private trade and investment flows, and from the policies and decisions of companies". Regionalism, on the other hand, is a top-down process that "requires governments to sanction the relaxation of barriers to trade and investment or, more proactively, to facilitate the provision of incentives to investment and trade sponsorship" (Breslin & Higgott, 2000, p. 346). This distinction between regionalization and regionalism reinforces the division of labor between market players as "demanding" and political leaders as "supplying" deepening regional integration (Castle et al., 2016).

Another representative liberal scholar, Andrew Moravcsik, also suggests that we need to "take preferences seriously" (Moravcsik, 1997). By that, he means that we need to look at where the preferences of states come from and then predict international behavior. Built on the European integration process, he constructs a framework for the study of international cooperation (see Table 2.5), which includes three phases: national preference formation, interstate bargaining, and institutional choice (Moravcsik, 1998).

The first stage concerns national preference formation. Based on major decisions in the European integration process, Moravcsik argues that it is economic interests that dominate when national preferences of member states are formed. The second stage, interstate bargaining, seeks to explain the efficiency and distributional outcomes of EU negotiations. The design of and membership in institutions remain political choices that are the result of political contestation. According to Moravcsik, asymmetrical interdependence has the most explanatory power to determine the outcomes of interstate bargaining. The third stage, institutional choice, explores the reasons why states choose to delegate or pool decision-making in international institutions. Moravcsik contends that states delegate and pool sovereignty to get more credible commitments. Such a three-phase framework of international cooperation reveals how structural forces relate to institutional choices.

Table 2.5 International Cooperation: Andrew Moravcsik's Framework

Stages	*National preference formation*	*Interstate bargaining*	*Institutional choice*
Explanatory variable at each stage	Economic interests	Asymmetrical interdependence	More credible commitment
Observed outcomes	Underlying national preferences	Agreements on substance	Choice to delegate or pool decision-making in international institutions

Source: Moravcsik (1998, p. 24).

This book mainly considers the first stage of national preference formation. Although I acknowledge the role of political processes (i.e., the second stage of interstate bargaining) on institutional choices and policy outcomes, this study highlights the importance of the underlying economic interests (i.e., IES). In other words, I will focus on structural forces as an essential underpinning of policy choices that shape institutional outcomes and contribute to explaining East Asian regionalism.

2.3.3 *Theorizing the Effects of International Economic Structures*

Now I use the framework discussed above to specify the IESs and the logic behind their effects on the problem in East Asian regionalism. I organize this discussion in three groups of questions that form the basis for the three hypotheses to develop in Chapter 3 for the organization of empirical investigation and analysis in this book.

More specifically, with the aid of Figure 2.15, I discuss my theoretical thinking about the causal relationship between (1) the global economic structure and the material basis of East Asia as an economic community, (2) the regional economic structure and the interests and capabilities of states for regional institutional arrangements governing transnational economic activities and relations in East Asia, and (3) the group of nations of similar sectoral economic structures and the nations' preferences and choice over competing sets of institutional arrangements in East Asian regionalism.

Figure 2.15 is an extended diagram of Figure 2.14, with the three sets of structural forces, their effects on the three aspects of the weakness in East Asian regionalism logically linked. I explain these three sets of relationships.

First, I focus on the global economic structure and the concentration of global productional interests and capabilities in Europe, North America, and East Asia. Along with North America and Europe, East Asia is believed to be one of the regions where transnational production interests and forces concentrate in the global economic structure landscape. However, in contrast to the successful experiences of state-led regionalism in the EU and NAFTA, East Asia has been ambiguous what their various projects and initiatives of

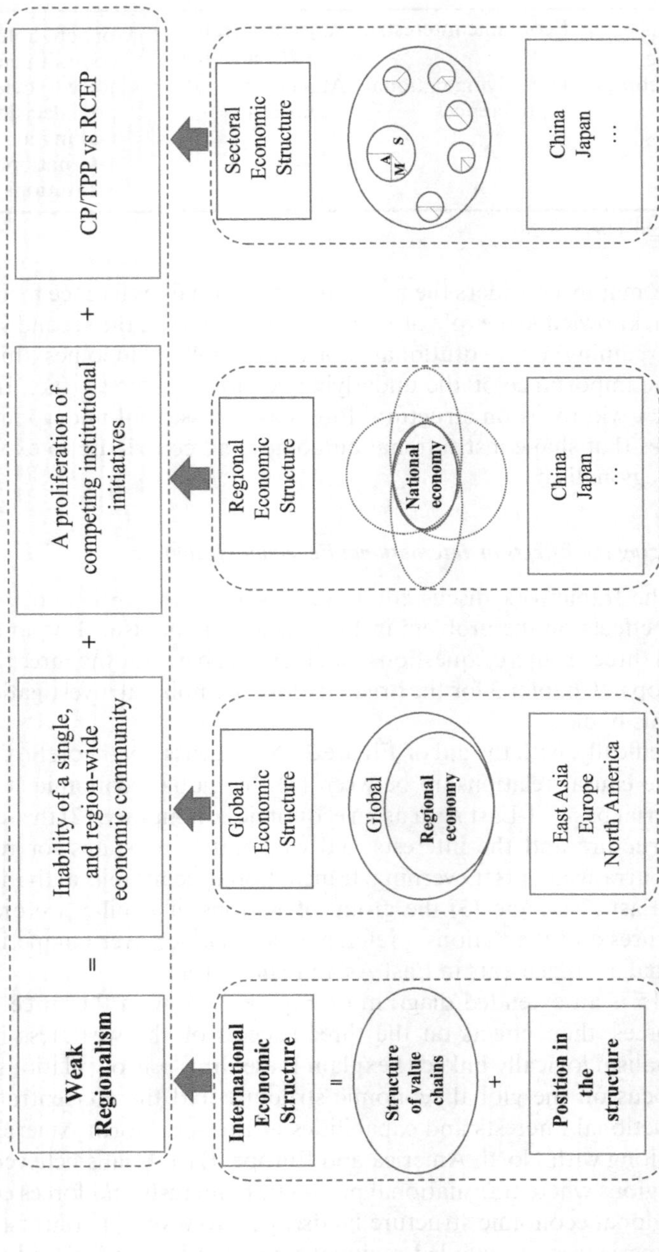

Figure 2.15 Theorizing the Effects of the International Economic Structure on East Asian Regionalism.

regionalism intended to achieve: economic integration for a regional economic community or economic cooperation for trade and production networks and has been slower if any in making progress toward a regional economic community. I suspect, on the basis of the logic of my structural theory, that this was because of the lack of a solid material basis to support an institutional arrangement for an integrative economic community. My hypothetical question about the first proposed relationships is whether there are significant concentrations of transnational production interests and capabilities in Europe, North America, and East Asia in the past 40 years of rapid development of regionalism in the three regions and whether the level of concentration was lower in East Asia than in Europe or North America.

Second, I focus on the regional economic structure and institutional preferences of nations in regional institutions. The position of each economy in the regional economic structure is determined by its participation in regional value chains (RVCs)—involving regional partners only and GVCs—involving also extra-regional partner countries. I suspect that the conflicting influence of regional and global productional forces led nations to prefer different types of and multiple regional arrangements in East Asia. Japan's shift from its early focus on East Asia to the Asia-Pacific and China's early focus on greater China, which shifted to the Asia-Pacific and a global focus with its BRI, are good examples of this. In both the cases of Japan and China, there is an East Asian focus in the regionalization arising from waves of East Asian industrial growth, but East Asia has not been the destination or the purpose of these market forces that are led by Japan, China, Singapore, or South Korea. They are always searching for a more efficient form of transborder organization. They are global. So my theoretical question directed at this proposed relationship is to what extent transnational production interests and capabilities that influence the nations' preferences for regional institutions come from within the nation, from within the region, or from outside the region. Or how the production interests and capabilities in East Asia are structured, and how this particular structure influenced the institutional interests and preferences of nations for regional institutional arrangements.

Finally, I ask questions about the relationship between the grouping of countries in the region on similar national sectoral economic structures and their preferences and practice over two competing sets of institutional arrangements in East Asia, CP/TPP, and RCEP. I suspect that sectoral economic structure, in terms of varied shares of agriculture, manufacturing, and services sectors in total national productional output, influenced the interests and attitudes of the nations toward different and competing regional institutional arrangements presented in CP/TPP and RCEP.

Countries with different sectoral economic structures tend to have different institutional preferences. Japan and Singapore, for example, might have a services-oriented economy which can explain their strong support and leadership for CP/TPP. China and ASEAN-developing countries, on the other hand, might have a manufacturing-oriented economy. This might be a factor for their support and leadership for RCEP. Therefore, my theoretical question on this proposed relationship is whether there is a pattern of grouping of countries of similar sectoral economic structures and how their structural positions relate to their divergent institutional preferences and practices in East Asian regionalism.

These questions together suggest that the underlying logic of my structural theory that forces of the IESs of different geographical and functional scopes influence the interests and capabilities of nations in East Asian regionalism. The tension and conflict in these interests and capabilities are believed to be behind the lack of development for a single region-wide institutional arrangement, proliferation of mega initiatives and projects of regional institutions, and the emergence of two overlapping sets of mega multilateral arrangements in East Asian regionalism. The remainder of this book is empirical investigation and analysis to test the hypothesized relationships, starting from research design and empirical material organization in Chapter 3.

Notes

1 I acknowledge that a variety of factors (e.g., the prevalence of great power politics, the lack of regional identity, institutional ineptness, and the global dispersion of market forces) have played a role in shaping the weakness of East Asian regionalism. However, in this book, I will focus on structural forces as an overlooked factor that can contribute to explaining East Asian regionalism.

2 The Fourteen Points was a statement of principles for peace that was initiated on 8 January 1918 by President Woodrow Wilson. It was to be used for peace negotiations in order to end World War I. For the content of Fourteen Points, see https://avalon.law.yale.edu/20th_century/wilson14.asp.

3 Krasner further distinguishes principles and norms from rules and decision-making procedures. He argues that changes in principles and norms are changes of the regime itself, while changes in rules and decision-making procedures are changes within regimes. For instance, in the area of international trade, the most-favored-nation (MFN) treatment—treating all nations equally without discrimination—is one of the norms of the liberal international order. However, WTO allows members to conclude regional trade agreements (RTA) as a special exception under certain conditions. Hence, RTA is a rule which violates but does not challenge the basic norm of MFN treatment.

4 Regime theory's theoretical appeal was strengthened after the end of the Cold War (1947–91) when some of the realists' predictions failed to materialize. Many realists had argued that the European integration was largely a result of the US -Soviet Union bipolarity and predicted that the European regime would wane as a result of the collapse of one of the super powers and the subsequent withdrawal of the US from Europe. As this did not happen, regime theories claimed that institutionalized cooperation can indeed be sustained in the absence of a hegemony.

5 Specifically, according to North, "Political rules broadly define the hierarchical structure of the polity, its basic decision structure, and the explicit characteristics of agenda control. Economic rules define property rights, that is the bundle of rights over the use and the income to be derived from property and the ability to alienate an asset or a resource. Contracts contain the provisions specific to a particular agreement in exchange" (1990, p. 47).

6 Compared with the EU, East Asia has a less equally distributed and stable power structure. East Asia is one of the most dynamic and fastest growing regions in the

world. The dynamics of international relations in East Asia are undergoing broad and fundamental changes. This asymmetry in interdependence and the changing power structure are not ideal conditions for building stable cooperation.

7 Due to their similarities, here I only take one of them—"networked regionalism" versus "institutional regionalism"—as an example to illustrate the distinctiveness of East Asian regionalism. Yeo (2010) contends that the region-building process in Asia operates on a logic different from institutional regionalism in Europe. He contextualizes region-building in Asia as a networked regionalism which features openness (instead of regional bloc) and issue-based leadership (instead of central leadership).

8 It is computed as the dollar value of total trade of country/region *i* with country/region *j* expressed as a percentage share of the dollar value of total trade of country/region *i* with the world. A higher share indicates a higher degree of integration between partner countries/regions (available at: http://aric.adb.org/integrationindicators/technotes).

9 If the national economy is the unit of analysis, processing export places both ends of a production process (raw material and final goods) outside the nation's customs territory. In 1988, then Chinese Premier Zhao Ziyang described the strategy as "Liang Tou Zai Wai" (两头在外), which means "two ends abroad". Since then, this term has been widely used in Chinese academic literature to describe the processing export-led growth.

10 These include UN Broad Economic Classification (BEC) and Trade in Value Added (TiVA). See Athukorala (2011), Ferrarini (2013), and Ueki (2011), for BEC product classification, and see Ferrarini and Hummels (2014), for the production of TiVA indicators.

11 One way to differentiate is by an investor's motivations by using a framework established by British economist John Dunning. According to Dunning (1980), there are four kinds of investor's motivations: natural resource-seeking, market-seeking, strategic asset-seeking, and efficiency-seeking investment. This last category—efficiency-seeking FDI—refers to the FDI that comes into a country seeking to benefit from factors that enable it to compete in international markets.

12 Export-oriented FDI occurs when the majority of the output in the host economy is not absorbed in local markets but exported to the investing economy or other economies.

13 According to the report of OECD (2018b), over 2012–2016, greenfield FDI in ICT and electronics manufacturing as a share of the manufacturing total exceeded 10% in Vietnam (26.5%), China (22.3%), Malaysia (20.4%), and the Philippines (12.4%).

14 See Bernard and Ravenhill (1995, pp. 185–187) for an example of the electronics industry that shows how production linkages in East Asia are more complex than the trade and investment data conventionally used to describe them.

15 For detailed discussions on the historical evolution of the flying geese pattern as well as its interpretations, see Akamatsu (1962), Cumings (1984), Bernard and Ravenhill (1995), and Kasahara (2013). Common reference to the flying geese is to a pattern of industrial diffusion from Japan to late industrializing countries in East Asia (Cumings, 1984).

16 The economic rise of these economies is regarded as "a process that is tightly linked to the emergence, maturation, and decline of particular industrial sectors" (Bernard & Ravenhill, 1995, p. 171).

17 Global production networks refer to "the globally organized nexus of interconnected functions and operations by firms and non-firm institutions through which goods and services are produced and distributed" (Coe et al., 2008, p. 471).

18 For more details on the opening up of Japanese production networks, see Ernst and Ravenhill (2000).

19 Wallerstein argues that the "world-economy" should be distinguished from that of "world economy" or international economy. The latter concept presumes that there are a series of separate economies which are national in scope. These national economies trade with each other, the sum of these interaction and exchange being called the world economy. In contrast, the concept "world-economy" is not a coming together of national economies, instead, it assumes that there exists an economy wherever there is an ongoing extensive and relatively complete social division of labor (Wallerstein, 1984, p. 13).

20 See Lake (1984, pp. 150–151). The three categories of states of high relative productivity are hegemonic leaders, supporters, and liberal free riders. The other three categories of states of low relative productivity are imperial leaders, spoilers, and protectionist free riders.

21 Global value chains are not really different from global production networks or global supply chains, and the debate on these concepts is beyond the scope of this research.

3 Design and Organization of Empirical Investigation and Analysis

Building on the theoretical framework developed in Chapter 2, I discuss the design of the empirical investigations, methods of testing the hypotheses, and data organization in this chapter. At the center of these empirical investigations is an analysis of how the international economic structures in East Asia shaped the anxiety, contention, and divergence of states for an institutional architecture of an East Asian economic community.

I will discuss the logic, methods, and data organization in building these international economic structures so that the effects of which can be empirically examined and assessed. I discuss the construction of key indicators with which we can determine the value of the key variables in the hypotheses developed from the structural theory for the research problem. This chapter is organized as follows. Section 3.1 transforms the structural theory and derives the analytical framework into three hypotheses that can be empirically analyzed against the evidence. Section 3.2 further discusses the global value chains (GVC) approach and explains the scholarly rationale and technical debate over the use of the GVC approach for the description and analysis of international economic structures in East Asian regionalism. Section 3.3 explains the organization and use of data for empirical description and analysis of the international economic structures. I discuss the choice of input-output tables as the main data basis, methods of data visualization for structure description, and indicators for testing the hypotheses.

3.1 How the Structural Theory Hypothesizes the Structural Effects

Building on the discussions in Chapter 2, I first transform the structural theory and analytical framework into three specific hypotheses that will guide our empirical investigation. Each hypothesis theorizes one set of effects and determines which international economic structure to analyze and which indicators to apply for analysis of the effects. The first hypothesis focuses on the effects of global economic structure. It compares the regional concentration indexes (RCIs) of value-added production in East Asia with those in Europe and North America. The second hypothesis focuses on the effects of regional economic

DOI: 10.4324/9781032613321-3

structure. It considers East Asia as a group of national economies where national interests compete for an institutional architecture for a regional economic community. It compares the levels of global/regional connectivity of the national economies for their divergent institutional preferences over regional institutions. The third hypothesis focuses on the effects of different types of sectoral economic structures on East Asian regionalism. This hypothesis is designed to see whether different sets of sectoral economic structures impact the nations' institutional preferences in the case of two mega-regional arrangements, Comprehensive and Progressive Agreement for Trans-Pacific Partnership (CP/TPP) and Regional and Comprehensive Economic Partnership (RCEP), competing for membership and legitimacy.

At the global level, Hypothesis 1 assumes that the function of a strong and highly institutionalized regional arrangement requires the support of a coherent and well-integrated regional economic structure. Conversely, without regionally concentrated production activities, institution-building alone cannot produce a strong and effective regional organization of production and distribution.

Hence, Hypothesis 1: *Weakness in East Asian regionalism was partly because of the lack of material support for an East Asian economic community. There were concentrations of global production interests and forces in Europe, North America, and East Asia. The higher the regional concentration index, the more successful the project of a regional economic community.*

Hypothesis 1 takes regions as basic production units, Factory Europe, Factory North America, and Factory East Asia (see Figure 3.1). The left part of the figure indicates the hypothesized relationship between the world

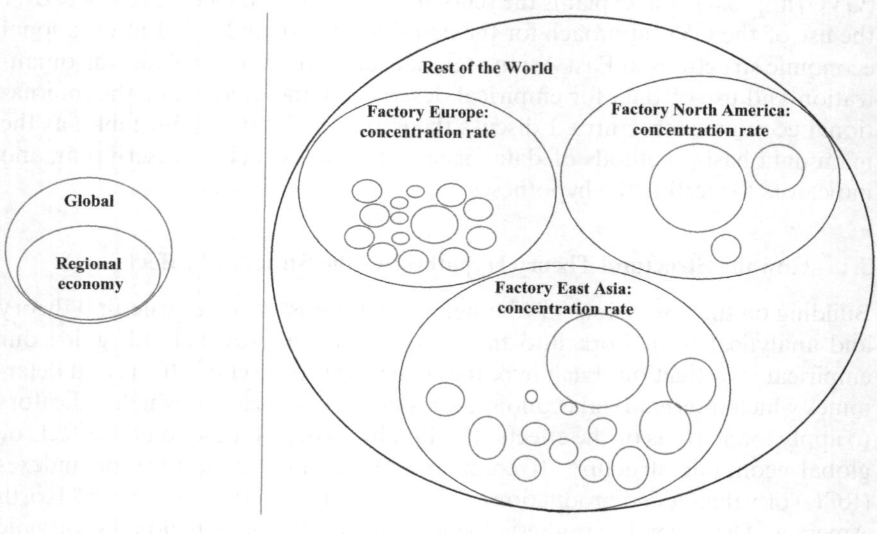

Figure 3.1 A World of Regional Factories.

economic structure and regional projects, while the right part suggests the primary indicator to investigate and analyze.

Hypothesis 1 provides an opportunity to determine whether the different levels of concentration are responsible for the project for a regional economic community, and, in the case of East Asia, whether East Asia was lower in concentration rate, which, as our theory suggests, was a reason for weakness in East Asian regionalism.

At the regional level, Hypothesis 2 assumes that the regional economic structure was partly responsible for the divergence and contention in the preferences of states for regional institutions. Hypothesis 2 theorizes that if a national economy is more regionally concentrated, it will seek an exclusivist East Asian regionalism. Otherwise, a more globally interconnected national economy will pursue outward-looking regional visions, such as Asia-Pacific or even beyond.

Therefore, Hypothesis 2: *The weakness of East Asian regionalism was partly because of the divergent positions of the nations in the regional economic structure. The more divergent in their global/regional connectivity, the stronger their desire for different institutional arrangements in East Asian regionalism. This divergence is suspected to be mostly shaped by the mixed influence of globally, regionally, nationally originated value-added in the production networks in East Asia.* Hypothesis 2 takes the national economy as the basic production unit, for example, Factory China and Factory Vietnam (see Figure 3.2).

Similar to Figure 3.1, the left part shows the hypothesized relationship and how production interests and capabilities of global and regional origins relate to

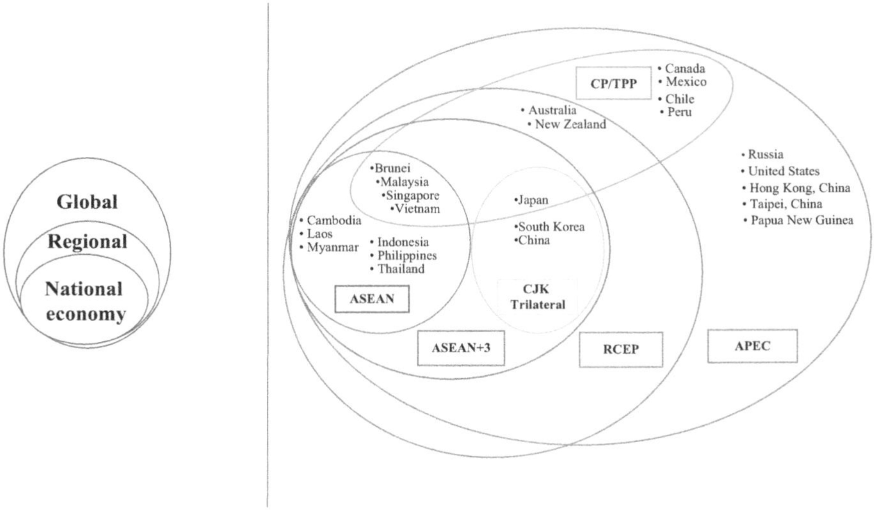

Figure 3.2 National Interests for and Engagement with Divergent Initiatives and Projects for Regional Institutions.

East Asian regionalism. The right part indicates the interests and engagement of nations' preferences over multiple regional initiatives. Hypothesis 2 reasons that East Asian regionalism is of intergovernmental multilateralism. National interests dominate their institutional options and choices for regional institutional arrangements. Each East Asian economy has different positions in the international economic structure, some more regionally integrated and others more globally oriented. These different complexities in global/regional connectivity have effects on their institutional preferences. An inward-looking East Asian bloc, ASEAN+3 (Association of Southeast Asian Nations), is only one of the various institutional options. But there are also other institutional options such as ASEAN, China-Japan-South Korea (CJK) trilateral FTA (free trade agreement), RCEP, CP/TPP, and Asia-Pacific Economic Cooperation (APEC).

At the level of sectoral economic structures, Hypothesis 3 assumes that each national economy has different sectoral structural interests as defined by self-sufficiency rate (SSR) and agriculture-manufacturing-services ratio (AMSR). The SSR reflects the economic size or production capacity. The AMSR is an indicator of the growth stage or development level of a national economy. Variations in these two indicators connect nations in East Asian regionalism into several groups, such as developed economies, developing economies, or transitional/emergent economies. Each group shares a similar developmental agenda and a similar position toward specific regional arrangements. Hypothesis 3 theorizes this relationship in two specific cases: CP/TPP and RCEP. Hypothesis 3 states that: *A services-focused economy is more interested in CP/TPP, while a more agriculture/manufacturing-oriented economy is more likely to support RCEP*.

Similar to Figures 3.1–3.3 indicates the hypothesized relations on the left side and the empirical investigations on the right side.

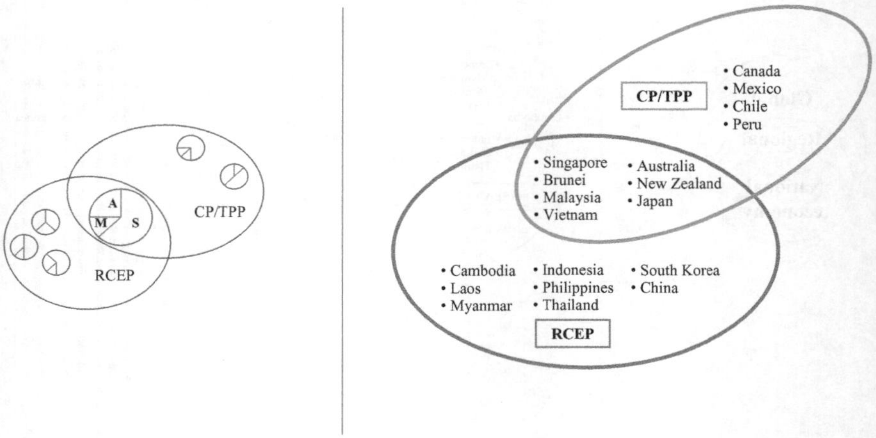

Figure 3.3 What Influences Nations' Institutional Choices: CP/TPP and/or RCEP.

To sum up, these three hypotheses are designed to investigate the effects of global, regional, and sectoral economic structures on the weakness in East Asian regionalism. Each hypothesis corresponds to one aspect of the weakness, as discussed in Chapter 1. At the level of global economic structure, we want to find out whether the regional economy of East Asia is as concentrated as that of Europe and North America. At the level of regional economic structure, the intention is to see whether there is great divergence among the nations in the levels of global/regional connectivity of these national economies. At the level of sectoral economic structures, we want to find out whether different sectoral economic structures group the nations to make different institutional choices in East Asian regionalism. These three hypotheses provide sufficient analytical and empirical space for us to test our structural theory and arrive at a more realistic explanation of the problem in East Asian regionalism.

3.2 Justifying the Use of GVC Analysis

The three hypotheses require us to build the empirical model of the international economic structures and construct three indicators for assessing the structural effects. The GVC analysis fits the requirements for empirical investigation and analysis. I start with a discussion of GVC analysis as a general method for analyzing international economic interdependence at the product level and firm level. I then discuss the use of input-output tables data for GVC analysis at the economy/sector level. Finally, I discuss how the input-output data is organized in GVC analysis for our empirical investigation and analysis.

3.2.1 Product-Level and Firm-Level Case Studies of GVCs

The visualization is a great example of using GVC analysis to form a visual description of the structure of the global value and supply chains of a single firm. The GVC approach establishes a firm-centric or product-centric focus on multinational firms "as potential agents of upgrading and development" and corporate governance (Gereffi et al., 2005; Ponte & Sturgeon, 2014).

The last few years have seen a number of product-level case studies on mapping GVCs. These include Barbie dolls (Tempest, 1996), iPod (Dedrick et al., 2010), and Boeing 787 Dreamliner (Tang et al., 2009). All these products, though labeled as made in a single country, actually involve value-added and parts supplied from different countries around the world. More and more products today are "made in the world" and comprise components from many economies across national borders.

However, these product-level and firm-level case studies provide only part of the story about production networks. The Huawei case (illustrated in Figure 2.3), for example, tells about GVCs for the firm where intermediate inputs (ICs) were directly sourced in the production networks. It does not show further, however, where the ICs used in the making of the ICs to Huawei were sourced. A macro view at the sector-economy level, which goes beyond these case studies, is necessary to measure the international fragmentation of value chains at the economy/sector level. As shown below, this requires a full set of inter-country input-output (ICIO) tables, where all bilateral exchanges of intermediate goods and services are accounted for.

3.2.2 Economy/Sector-Level Framework of GVCs Accounting

GVC accounting at the economy/sector level requires a comprehensive accounting of all transactions in the global economy between industries and final users across countries. This is facilitated by the value-added accounting framework and the ICIO tables[1] that have become available recently.

3.2.2.1 Value-Added Accounting Framework

Value-added is the capital value generated by production activities. The international fragmentation of value chains refers to that different parts of a product are produced in specialized factories in different countries around the world. Ando and Kimura explained in Figure 3.4 five production blocs in a production process, starting from research and development (R&D) activities for new products, to the production of standard/specific parts and components, and the production of final products by assembling them (Ando, 2020, p. 137). Each production block is connected by value-added in service-link costs, such as transport costs, telecommunication costs, and coordination costs, and/or headquarter (HQ) services.

To measure the contribution of each in the transborder production processes, value-added is quantified in each production block. When these production blocks are located in several different countries, a division of labor across borders as GVCs is formed, resulting in international fermentation of the

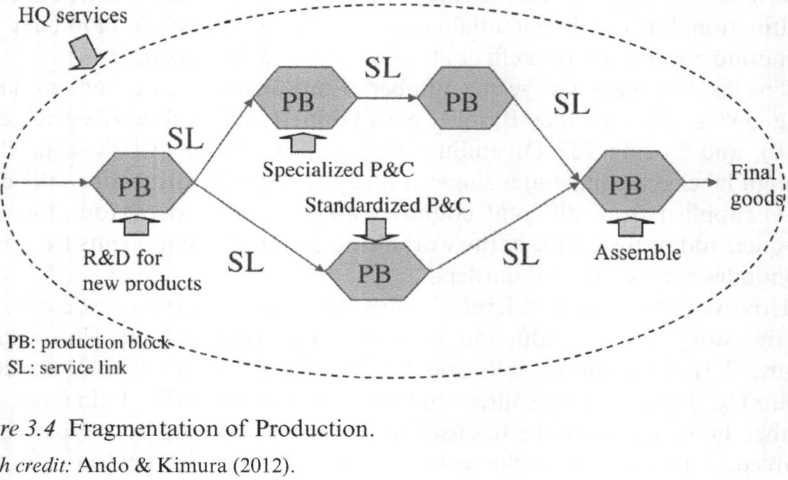

Figure 3.4 Fragmentation of Production.

Graph credit: Ando & Kimura (2012).

production process. This division of labor and fragmentation and indeed the international structure of the production forces are best captured using GVC analysis.

3.2.2.2 ICIO Tables

Value-added and parts supplied to the production of final goods are sourced from different countries around the world. However, these transborder flows of value-added are not always precisely reflected in conventional accounting frameworks of international trade and global production networks. The ICIO tables address this issue including data on all value-added by all countries in the production of goods and services. Built on the core variable of value-added, ICIO tables have been developed to capture direct production linkages between countries at the economy-sector levels.

The input-output analysis model is not something new. It was developed by Wassily Leontief, a Nobel-Prize-winning economist, in the 1930s. The core concept of the input-output tables is simple—an industry's outputs are another industry's inputs. A national input-output table shows, in chess-board format, the inter-industry transactions of goods and services in the national economy for a certain period (usually one year).

Although the national input-output accounts provide a good description of value chain linkages across industries within a given country, the problem is that they stop at the borders. National accounts lack information on how imported goods are produced and how exports are used in production abroad, and thus cannot reveal the full picture of the inter-country production linkages. This problem is fatal as "production processes are characterized by international fragmentation leading to an interdependent structure which has to be accounted for" (Dietzenbacher et al., 2013).

To meet this challenge of fully accounting value-added and parts supplied in transnational production networks, ICIO tables combine national input-output tables to produce inter-country input-output data. An ICIO table is a set of national input-output tables that are connected in bilateral international trade flows. Figure 3.5 shows a schematic outline for a World input-output table (WIOT) involving three countries.

The ICIO table provides a comprehensive representation of all transactions in the global economy between industries and final users across countries. Value is created by inter-economy/sector linkages of the world economy as a system and is distributed in the form of wages, profits, taxes, and other rewards. As explained by Timmer et al. (2015) in the user guide of ICIO tables, the columns contain information on production processes from the perspective of producers, and the rows indicate the distribution of the output of industries over user categories from the perspective of users. From the perspective of producers, the production process of a particular product requires supply from other industries as well as value-added by labor and capital. From the perspective of sellers, products can be used as intermediates by other

			Use by country-industries							Final use by countries			Total use
			Country 1			...	Country M			Country 1	...	Country M	
			Industry 1	...	Industry N	...	Industry 1	...	Industry N		...		
Supply from country-industries	Country 1	Industry 1											
		...											
		Industry N											
	......												
	Country M	Industry 1											
		...											
		Industry N											
Value added by labour and capital													
Gross output													

Figure 3.5 Schematic Outline of an ICIO Table.
Graph credit: Timmer et al. (2015, p. 577).

industries, or as final products by households and governments (consumption) or firms (stocks and gross fixed capital formation). An important accounting feature in the ICIO table is that the gross output of each industry (given in the last element of each column) is equal to the sum of all uses of the output from that industry (given in the last element of each row). ICIO tables thus allow researchers to systematically track and classify the use of each country/industry's output as an input into another country/industry's production or as final demand.

3.2.2.3 *Use of ICIO Data in Analyzing Trade and Transborder Production Networks*

The development of value-added frameworks and ICIO tables has significantly strengthened our ability to analyze structures of GVCs at the economy/sector level. Much progress has been made in new methods for GVC accounting and analysis: bilateral trade flow decomposition and final good decomposition.

Decomposition of bilateral trade flows estimates domestic and foreign contents of value-added of a bundle of exports. Jointly initiated by the Organization for Economic Cooperation and Development (OECD) and the WTO, the Trade in Value-Added (TiVA) Database has been developed.[2] It contains a wide range of indicators on the value-added components of gross exports and the level of GVC participation by economy and industry (OECD, 2013). This approach further developed methods of vertical specialization (Hummels et al., 2001) and full decomposition of gross exports (Koopman et al., 2014). Based on such analysis of value-added trade statistics, Baldwin and Lopez-Gonzalez conclude that "Supply chain trade is not global—it's regional" and "The global production network is marked by regional blocs, what could be called Factory Asia, Factory North America, and Factory Europe" (2015, p. 1718). This decomposition approach helps policymakers and academics better understand trade in the 21st century.

One limitation in value-added-based trade analysis is that it tells where value-added comes from, but not necessarily where it is ultimately absorbed. For example, if a smartphone is made in China and sold to Chinese customers, it is not exported. Trade economists do not give any consideration to this domestically consumed smartphone. This type of trade analysis is not comprehensive enough to provide full insight into the structural details of GVC distribution across economies.

In comparison to trade accounts, the system of final goods is more detailed as it considers all final goods, whether for trade or domestic demand. It derives the distribution of value-added by all economies/sectors involved in the production of a particular final good. It is a very useful empirical tool for economic research and structural analysis at the international level as it highlights inter-economy relationships covering all sectors of the economy.

3.2.2.4 My Construction of the International Economic Structure and Investigation and Analysis of Their Effects in This Book

The final good decomposition will allow me to capture the transnational distribution of value chains in East Asia and model the international economic structure and data for investigation and analysis. "Reconstructing" of GVCs at the economy/sector level can reveal the origins of value-added in final products. This will enable us to identify the national origins of the value-added in transborder production networks.

3.2.3 Decomposition of Final Goods

I again start with the structure of the transnational production network of a Huawei smartphone as a product-level example to elaborate on the method of final goods decomposition. Suppose the whole production process of the smartphone involves three tiers of production located in three different economies,[3] which are China (Huawei as the final assembler), Taiwan (Foxconn as the integrated circuits/IC manufacturer), and the US (Qualcomm as the IC designer). To map out all the value contributors in the transnational value chain, I track every value-added component via backward production linkage. Figure 3.6 demonstrates the simplified production network of a Huawei smartphone.

There are three tiers of production, displayed backward: final assembly (tier 0), IC manufacturing (tier 1), and IC design (tier 2). The final stage of assembling is completed in China (economy 1) and requires domestic inputs (capital, labor, and land) worth \$30. The rest of the value-added \$450 is embedded in the imported IC from Taiwan (economy 2). In the IC manufacturing stage, the integrated circuits are manufactured in Taiwan and require domestic intermediate goods worth \$150. Finally, the US (economy 3) contributes primary inputs worth \$300 to IC design.

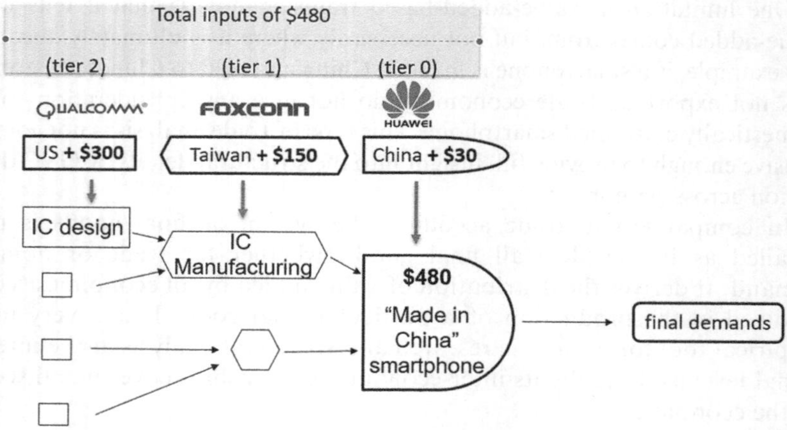

Figure 3.6 Transnational Value Chain of the Production of A Huawei Smartphone.
Source: Author's compilation based on Los et al. (2014).

Overall, in the whole production process of Huawei smartphone, the distribution of value-added is as follows: China ($30), Taiwan ($150), and the US ($300). The gross value-added is calculated as follows:

$$
\begin{aligned}
g &= g(\text{tier0}) + g(\text{tier1}) + g(\text{tier2}) \\
&= \text{China's VA} + \text{Taiwan's VA} + \text{US's VA} \\
&= \$30 + \$150 + \$300 \\
&= \$480
\end{aligned}
$$

It is in this backward way that the value-added contributions in each production stage by each economy can be identified and calculated.

The basic relationship is calculated as follows:

$$
\begin{aligned}
g &= g(\text{tier0}) + g(\text{tier1}) + g(\text{tier2}) + \ldots \\
&= \hat{V}(\mathrm{I} + \mathrm{A} + \mathrm{AA} + \ldots)\mathrm{Y} \\
&= \hat{V}(I - A)^{-1}\mathrm{Y} \\
&= \hat{V}\mathrm{BY}
\end{aligned}
$$

where **g** reveals the origins of value-added from each source economy and sector, which are ultimately attributed to produce the given economy-sector (i, j). $\hat{\boldsymbol{V}}$ is the diagonal matrix of vector v, which represents the value-added over gross output ratios from each of the economy-sector. $B = (\boldsymbol{I} - A)^{-1}$ is the well-known Leontief inverse. It ensures that value-added contributions in all tiers of suppliers are taken into consideration. **Y** is a specific final output matrix of the given economy-sector (i, j). The technical discussions of the equation can be found in Los, Timmer, and de Vries (2015).

3.3 Empirical Data Organization

Now I explain how I use the final goods decomposition approach and ICIO tables data to construct the international economic structures. I first discuss the three key indicators for ascertaining the relationships hypothesized in our structural theory. I will then explain why and how I map the structures at the economy/sector levels. In the final part, I discuss data transformation for mapping the structures and constructing the indicators.

3.3.1 *Key Indicators for Hypotheses Testing*

For testing the three hypotheses, I use three indicators for empirical evidence. All these indicators are calculated from the final goods decomposition discussed above. More specifically, I use (1) complex network method and RCI to test Hypothesis 1; (2) index of global and regional connectivity (GRC) to test Hypothesis 2; and (3) SSR and AMSR to test Hypothesis 3.

The RCI is developed by the input-output team of the Asian Development Bank. I developed the GRC myself using the final good decomposition method. The SSR and AMSR are indicators derived from skyline charts, developed by Uda (2003). I discuss the design, construction, and use of these three indicators in hypothesis testing in the following sections.

3.3.1.1 Complex Network Approach and Regional Concentration Index

To test Hypothesis 1, I use the complex network method to map or visually describe global economic structures from 1995 to 2015. Second, I compare the RCIs in three major regional production units: Factory Europe, Factory North America, and Factory East Asia, to determine the level of economic "regionness" of each of the three regions.

More specifically, I will adopt the complex network method developed by Ferrarini and Hummels (2014) to map concentrations of global production interests and capabilities in the three regions. Despite their apparent simplicity, network visualization is sufficient for exposing regional concentrations in the global economic structure (Escaith et al., 2018). Each complex network map is made up of directed edges (sourced from, contributing to) and connecting nodes (national economies). Figure 3.7 is a sample of network visualization of an international economic structure.

Figure 3.7 consists of four nodes, which represent four economies: China, Japan, South Korea, and the US. The relative size of the node represents the volume of the domestic value-added component in the economy's final products and services in the sector. The imported value-added components from the source node to the destination node are visualized through arrows indicating

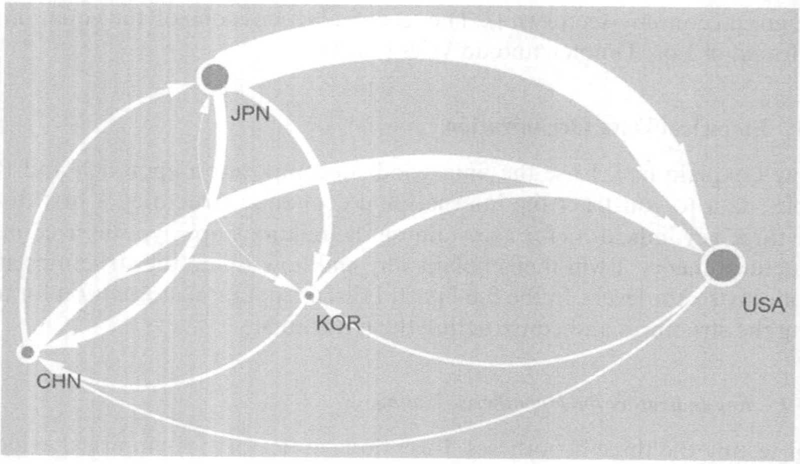

Figure 3.7 Structure of the Production Network of the Automobile Sector in 2005.

the flow direction. The relative width of the arrows is determined by the volume of value-added from the source economy to its partner economy. The complex network method enables visualization of the structural distribution of transnational production interests and capabilities of regions (as well as nations and sectors).

The RCI indicates the level of regional clustering of global productional interests and capabilities. Technically, the RCI measures the extent to which a region absorbs value-added within the region relative to that absorbed by the world. For a given region *q* and given sector *i*, the RCI is computed as:

$$RCI(b)_{(q,i)} = \frac{vby_{q,(q,i)} / vby_{*,(q,i)}}{vby_{*,(q,i)} / vby_{**}}$$

where an asterisk * denotes all traders.

RCI is a calibrated index that takes the ratio of intra-regional value-added contribution in the region's final products to the share of the region's final products in the world's final products. Element denoted *vby q, (q, i)* gives the amount of value-added originated from the region itself recorded in final products of a given region *q* and given sector *i*. Element denoted *vby**, (q, i)* indicates the amount of total value-added recorded in final products of a given region *q* and given sector *i*. Element, *vby***, represents the amount of total value-added in final products of the world economy.

Using the yearly RCIs, I compare the levels of regional concentration of production networks in Europe, North America, and East Asia. An index close to 1 means value flows in a region at about the same rate as it flows outside the region. The higher the index is, the more disproportionately a region relies on producers within itself.

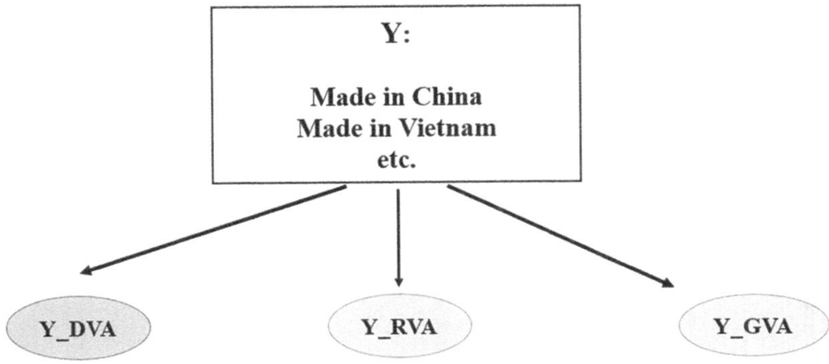

Figure 3.8 DVA-RVA-GVA Split of Final Goods.

3.3.1.2 Index of Global and Regional Connectivity

To test Hypothesis 2, I use the final goods decomposition method to break a national economy's final goods into three parts based on the origins of value-added (see Figure 3.8).

Y represents final goods labeled as made in a particular East Asian economy. Y is decomposed into three parts: domestic value-added (DVA), regional value-added (RVA), and global value-added (GVA). DVA, RVA, and GVA represent value-added sourced domestically, regionally (in East Asia), and globally (outside East Asia), respectively. The sum of the three equals the total value-added of final goods.

Based on the DVA-RVA-GVA decomposition, I further construct a two-dimensional index to describe the position of each East Asian economy in the regional economic structure. As Figure 3.9 shows, I build the GRC of each East Asian economy coordinated by two indicators: the domestic-foreign split of value-added contributions in final products and services and the regional-global split of value-added contributions within foreign value-added contributions.

More specifically, the x-axis represents the share of foreign value-added (FVA) in final products, indicating the participation rate of an economy in GVCs. Generally, the higher the FVA share, the more open and internationally integrated an economy, and the more willing the nation to invest time and energy in international institutional building. The y-axis represents the ratio of RVA over GVA. This dimension measures the focus of an economy's international economic integration, suggesting whether it welcomes regional institutional arrangements or wider ones such as trans-regional and global multilateralism. The higher the ratio, the more regionally integrated an economy is, the more motivated the nation is to build regional trade blocs.

By the point of intersection of the x-axis and y-axis is (RVA/GVA = 1, FVA/(FVA + DVA) = 10%), economies can be classified into four groups, each bounded by two half-axes. Economies in Quadrant I satisfy two conditions: first, RVA > GVA, and second, the share of FVA > 10%. On the first, the distribution of value chains is more regionally oriented than globally dispersed. On the

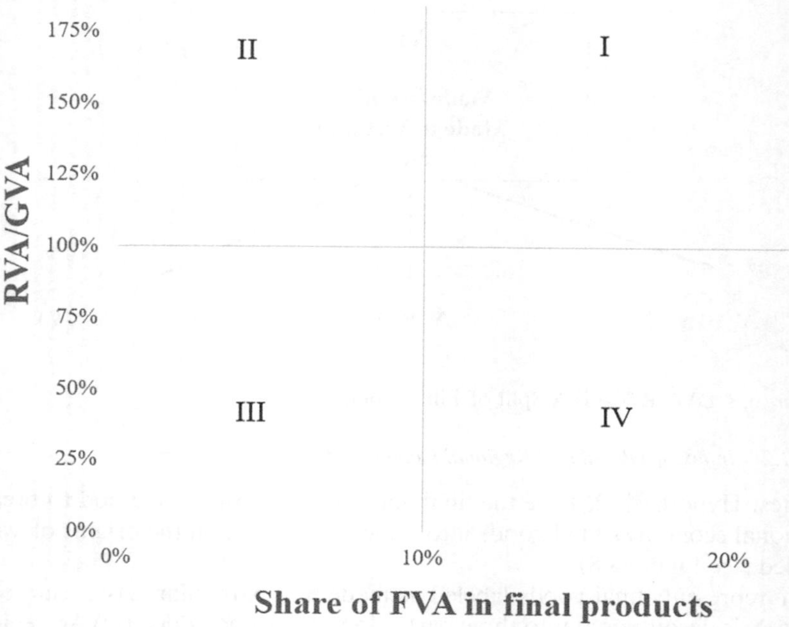

Figure 3.9 Index Positioning East Asian Economies in Regional Economic Structure.

second, the economy is open and depends substantially on foreign productional forces. Economies in this quadrant would have the motivation to welcome or even initiate an exclusivist regional arrangement. Economies in Quadrant II also rely on foreign inputs. However, for these economies, the origins of foreign inputs are more globally dispersed. Thus, they are more motivated to become involved in trans-regional and global institutional arrangements. In contrast, economies in Quadrants III and IV are more self-reliant with high DVA ratios (>90%). Since most of the value-added contributions are sourced domestically, they are less interested in global institutional arrangements.

3.3.1.3 *Self-Sufficiency Rates and Agriculture-Manufacturing-Services Ratios*

Finally, to test Hypothesis 3, I use the skyline chart method to visually describe the SSR and AMSR of an economy. Figure 3.10 is a sample of skyline chart description of the structure of a national economy discussed in an IDE-JETRO and WTO study on GVCs in East Asia (2011). Figure 3.10 shows one stacked column corresponding to the total value-added in a sector of the economy. There are two points to note in capturing information on a stacked column. First, its height is determined by the SSR. The SSR indicates if the sector has enough production capacity to satisfy the economy's domestic demand. Technically, the SSR measures the share of domestic supply-induced output in total supply, which is determined by both the demand structure and supply structure.

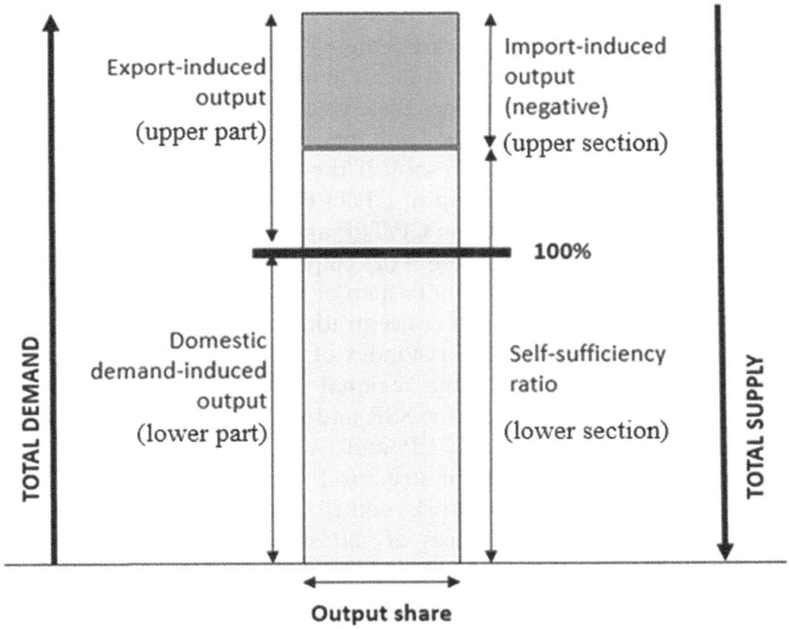

Figure 3.10 The Skyline Chart.
Graph credit: IDE-JETRO & WTO (2011, p. 62).

Let us consider the demand structure first. The total demand for a product is either induced by domestic demands such as consumption and investment or foreign demand in terms of export. At the lower part of the building, the amount of output induced by domestic demand is taken to be 100%. Above this, the building gains extra height from output induced by export demand. On the supply side, the supply of a product is either via domestic production or import. If an economy's domestic production satisfies all of the induced demand, the economy would be self-sufficient. Otherwise, the economy has to import products from overseas. So, there are two sections in the upper part of the building. The upper section shows the amount of domestic output displaced by imports. The lower section indicates the SSR of the industry. According to Leontief (1963), a mature and self-sufficient economy tends to have a flat self-sufficiency line across all buildings in a skyline chart, where full self-sufficiency is achieved when there is not too much reliance on foreign markets for demand and supply of products.

Second, the different shares of agriculture, manufacturing, and services in the total output suggest a distinct developmental stage of an economy. According to the law of Petty Clark, when the per capita income of an economy rises, the main focus of its industrial output shifts from agriculture to manufacturing, and then from manufacturing to services (Clark, 1951).[4]

In Chapter 6, I will first display the skyline charts of regional groups: CP/TPP and RCEP. As CP/TPP rules are centered around the trade in services and investment and RCEP focuses on trade in manufactured goods, I hope to find out from the skyline charts whether these two regional groups are different in their sectoral economic structures. I will then construct skyline charts on each East Asian economy. I use this to show if the sectoral economic structures of economies with dual membership in CP/TPP and RCEP are more services-oriented than those excluded from CP/TPP and involved only in RCEP.

To sum up, in testing Hypothesis 3 in Chapter 4, I use the complex network approach and RCI with ICIO data to map or visually describe the global economic structures and the levels of concentration in the three regions. In testing Hypothesis 2 in Chapter 5, I use the index of GRC to specify the position of each East Asian economy in the regional economic structure. In testing Hypothesis 3 in Chapter 6, I use the SSR and AMSR to measure sectoral economic structures of CP/TPP, RCEP, and each East Asian economy. These three hypotheses together test our structural theory that the structural forces of transnational production networks contributed to the complexity and high tension in institutional preferences of states in East Asian regionalism for regional arrangements for trade and production and hence the weakness of East Asian regionalism.

3.3.2 Case Studies of Textiles, Electronics, and Automobiles

The aggregate GVCs are of interest in themselves, but industry-level mapping can further complement the overall picture of the transnational distribution of value chains. To that end, I also select some cases for investigating the structural effects at the industry level. I select three sectors: textiles, electronics, and automobiles for two reasons. First, each of these sectors has a significant share in the total output, as shown in Figure 3.11.

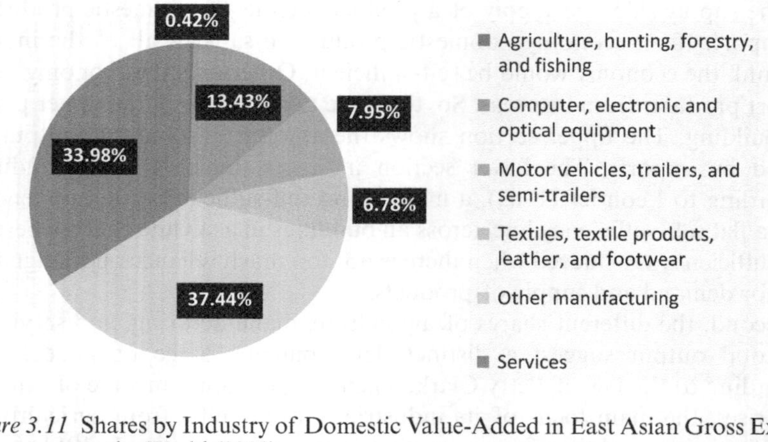

Figure 3.11 Shares by Industry of Domestic Value-Added in East Asian Gross Exports to the World (2011).

Source: Author's compilation based on OECD-WTO TiVA database.

Since the 1980s, the centrality of Factory East Asia as a global manufacturing hub in these sectors has grown significantly. In 2011, the shares of DVA in East Asian exports to the world in textiles, electronics, and automobiles industries were 6.78%, 13.43%, and 7.95% of the total DVA in all industries of these sectors.

Second, each of these sectors represents an important category of manufacturing. Following the method by McKinsey Global Institute (2012), manufacturing outputs can be divided into five different categories (see Table 3.1).

The categories of products produced in Factory Asia are more likely, but not exclusively, to fall under the first and the last two categories. Specifically, the textile sector represents labor-intensive tradables, the electronics sector represents global technologies/innovators, and the automobile sector represents global innovation for local markets. With these two considerations, I select these three sectors for the case study at the industrial level.

Table 3.1 Categories of Manufacturing

Sector	*Key Traits*	*Examples of Industries*
1 Global Innovation for Local Markets	• High research and development (R&D) intensity; with competition driven by innovation and quality • High trade intensity, but assembly and production can be regionalized • Geared towards serving customers located near factories	• Chemicals and pharmaceuticals • Transport equipment, including automotive • Machinery, electrical appliances
2 Regional Processing	• High local content requirement, and located near sources of raw materials and final demand • Highly complex and costly logistics • Low tradability • Automated production, with little R&D	• Rubber and plastics • Fabricated metals • Food and beverages • Printing and publishing
3 Energy/ Resources Intensive Commodities	• Intermediate inputs to other sectors; low tradability • Price competition with little product differentiation	• Wood products • Paper and pulp • Basic metals • Minerals-based products • Refined petroleum, coke, and nuclear products
4 Global Technologies/ Innovators	• High R&D intensity, with competition driven by R&D • Highly tradable, with very high value to weight ratio which makes it economical for the products to be manufactured far from the source of final demand	• Computers and office machinery • Semiconductors and electronics • Medicals, optional, and other precision equipment
5 Labor Intensive Tradables	• High exposure to price competition • Highly labor intensive • Globally traded, with low proximity needs for production	• Textiles, apparel, leather • Furniture, jewelry, toys, and other manufactured goods

Table credit: McKinsey Global Institute (2012, p45).

3.3.3 Data Sources, Transformation, and Indicator Construction

3.3.3.1 Data Sources

Data in final goods decomposition are sourced from the UIBE GVC Indicator Database. The UIBE GVC Indicator Database[5] is developed by the Research Institute for Global Value Chains at the University of International Business and Economics in Beijing. This database covers the most widely used GVC indicators, which are computed from the ICIO tables published by OECD, ADB, World Input-Output Database (WIOD), and other global initiatives. A sample of the ICIO tables is found in Table 3.2.

Each of the ICIO tables has different features in terms of the economies covered, sector classifications, and timespans. The WIOD is the most widely used for its data quality and updates. But WIOD only covers five East Asian economies: China, Japan, South Korea, Taiwan, and Indonesia. The Asia input-output (AIO) database is Asia-focused and covers most of the East Asian economies. But in time series, it only covers up to the year 2005. OECD-ICIO tables cover 13 East Asian economies: five Northeast Asian economies (China, Hong Kong, Taiwan, Japan, South Korea) and eight out of 10 ASEAN economies (except Laos and Myanmar). In time series, OECD-ICIO tables have two editions (released in 2016 and 2018, respectively) and together cover the period from 1995 to 2015. ADB-MRIO (the Asian Development Bank-Multiregional Input-Output) tables also cover most of the East Asian economies: five Northeast Asian economies and nine ASEAN economies (not Myanmar). It covers the years 2000, 2007 to 2019. Both OECD-ICIO and ADB-MRIO have facilitated the production and analysis of GVC-related statistics for East Asian economies.

Table 3.2 Inter-Country Input-Output Tables

ICIO tables	*Institutions*	*Economies*	*East Asian economies*	*Sectors*	*Timespans*
WIOD_2013	Consortium of European Institutions	40	5	35	1995–2011
WIOD_2016[a]		43	5	56	2000–2014
AIO[b]	IDE-JETRO	10	9	24	1985,1990,1995, 2000, 2005
OECD-ICIO 2016	OECD/WTO	63	13	34	1995–2011
OECD-ICIO 2018[c]		64	13	36	2005–2015
ADB-MRIO[d]	ADB	45	9	35	2000, 2007–2019

Source: Author's compilation based on the UIBE GVC Indicator Database, accessed on 1 January 2020.

a https://www.wiod.org/home
b https://www.ide.go.jp/English/Publish/Books/Io.html
c https://www.oecd.org/sti/ind/inter-country-input-output-tables.htm
d https://mrio.adbx.online/

Based on the considerations above, the OECD-ICIO and ADB-MRIO tables are chosen for our empirical analysis and hypothesis testing. Specifically, the calculation of the VBY decomposition of final goods is sourced from the 2016 and 2018 editions of the OECD-ICIO. The data for the years 1995 and 2000 are taken from the 2016 edition, and the data for 2005, 2010, and 2015 are based on the recently updated 2018 edition. The data for the RCIs and the regional input-output tables for CP/TPP and RCEP are sourced from ADB-MRIO.

3.3.3.2 Programs for Data Transformation, Structure Visualization, and Indicator Construction

Three software programs are used in this research to transform data, construct a visual description of the international economic structures, and establish indexes and indicators of the positions of East Asian states in these structures. They are R studio, Cytoscape, and Excel VBA.

To deal with the huge matrixes of ICIO data, R studio is used to transform data for reproducibility and easy use. OECD and ADB transmit R-compatible data to users. For data processing using R codes, I use methods from (1) Los et al. (2015) for the final goods decomposition and (2) the system codes of the UIBE GVC indexes.[6] Inspired by Ferrarini and Hummels (2014), I use Cytoscape to visualize the global economic structure and calculate the concentration rates of regions in Chapter 4. The software Cytoscape can be downloaded from the official website.[7] VBA in Excel is used to draw the skyline charts in Chapter 6. The VBA program is downloaded from the website[8] of Uda Kenjiro, the initiator of the skyline charts approach.

Notes

1 I discuss these technical matters only briefly to help understand the conceptual and practical underpinnings of GVC analysis and the input-output data. I do not extensively discuss how information from the national accounts and international trade statistics has been merged to arrive at a harmonized version of intercountry input-output tables. These technical matters omitted here have been explained in the user guide written by the World Input-Output Tables construction team (Dietzenbacher et al., 2013; Timmer et al., 2015) that accompanies the dataset used in this project.
2 https://www.oecd.org/sti/ind/measuring-trade-in-value-added.htm.
3 The real production networks of a Huawei smartphone are far more complicated than the three-economy model and involve more stages of production undertaken by more companies. But for simplicity, here I only discuss three representative stages.
4 There are a few exceptions against the law because other factors such as natural resource endowments might be at play, too. But East Asian economies generally are not blessed with such resources; therefore, the law applies to all of them.
5 http://rigvc.uibe.edu.cn/english/D_E/database_database/index.htm.
6 http://rigvc.uibe.edu.cn/english/D_E/database_database/index.htm.
7 https://cytoscape.org/.
8 https://www.ccn.yamanashi.ac.jp/~kuda/en.html.

4 East Asia in the Global Economic Structure

This chapter reports on my testing of Hypothesis 1. We construct the global economic structure of transnational production interests and capabilities, and use regional concentration index (RCI) to determine the level of concentration in Europe, North America, and East Asia. I suspect that the level of concentration of East Asia is lower than that of Europe and North America. I want to find out if that is the case by testing the hypothesis.

This chapter compares East Asia, Europe, and North America in the world economic structure. Recent research identifies the growing importance of value chains organized at the regional level that drives global value chains (GVCs) participation and contribution to a handful of industries (Bamber et al., 2014; Stollinger et al., 2018). While studies of regional value chains (RVCs) capture significant interest, what constitutes an RVC remains unclear. The main issue in this respect is that RVCs relate to transborder production between countries in the same region, whereas GVCs refer to joint production involving extra-regional countries. To what extent is the value of production in the region regional or extra-regional?

In what follows, Section 4.1 discusses how I organize comparisons of East Asia, Europe, and North America as stand-alone production units. I focus on all industries and three key industrial sectors, that is, textiles, electronics, and automobiles. Furthermore, I focus on the period between 1995 and 2015 to track changes over time.

Section 4.2 uses GVCs and RVCs data to construct global economic structures and to develop an RCI. I will first use the complex network method developed by Ferrarini and Hummels (2014) to visualize the global economic structure. Network visualization is an effective way of mapping structures of transnational value chains. Despite their apparent simplicity, network graphs are very effective for more advanced analysis of the structural relations and the pivotal role that production partners play (Escaith et al., 2018). I will also use those data to develop an RCI that shows the levels of intra-regional connectivity of industrial production in Europe, North America, and East Asia. The region's RCIs, derived from the network graphs, provide a more precise indication of the levels of regionalization. Specifically, I establish the ratio of the industrial production of East Asia that takes place among economies of the

DOI: 10.4324/9781032613321-4

same region and that with economies from outside the region. The resulting RCIs shall reveal whether East Asia has a lower level of intra-regional connectivity than Western Europe and North America as theorized in Hypothesis 1.

4.1 Organization of the Empirical Material

To construct global economic structures and determine the levels of regional concentration in East Asia, Europe, and North America. I decompose a country's final products into domestic value-added and foreign value-added in all industrial sectors and the three key industrial sectors. I do that for all countries in the world available on Inter-Country Input-Output (ICIO) tables. By decomposing the production of final goods in this manner, I capture which countries the value-added comes from. This will allow for a clear picture of the structural relations among the national productional forces and interests.

4.1.1 Regional Comparisons among East Asia, Europe, and North America

Hypothesis 1 looks at East Asia as a stand-alone production unit in the global economic structure. The benchmarking of Europe and North America[1] is used for several reasons. First, both Europe and North America have established a single and region-wide institutional architecture in their region. Looked from East Asia, the European Union (EU) and North American Free Trade Agreement (NAFTA) are the most developed experiences in regional economic integration. What drove East Asian countries in East Asian regionalism has been their concerns of being left out in the global development of regional trade blocs.

Second, Europe, North America, and East Asia are three major regions in the world for the global influential clusters of production interests and capabilities in their region. According to Baldwin and Lopez-Gonzalez (2015), international production networks and value chains are mostly regional rather than global. Most supply chain trade happens within what is called Factory Asia, Factory Europe, or Factory North America.

Third, it is a puzzle how strong the regional concentration of international production networks is within Factory East Asia compared to Factory Europe and Factory North America. Traditionally, East Asia has intensive production linkages with Europe and North America (Ando & Kimura, 2014). The increasing dominance of East Asia as an industrial base may have affected its international production ties with North America and Europe. The regional comparisons are useful for us to understand the position of East Asia as a stand-alone production unit.

4.1.2 All-Industrial-Level Analysis and Individual Industry Case Study

In constructing the global economic structure and RCIs, I investigate the pattern not only at the general level, including all industrial sectors, but also at the level of individual industrial sectors. I chose three specific industrial sectors for the latter: textiles, electronics, and automobiles. The reasons for my choice of the three industrial sectors are as follows. First, these industries are particularly important for export-oriented industrialization in East Asia. Labor-intensive manufacturing for export in these industrial sectors has been a major engine of East Asia's rise. The industries have been successful in creating extensive and dense production networks within the region.

Second, the development of these industries has been propelled by a massive inflow of foreign direct investment (FDI), resulting in the extensive growth of transnational corporation (TNC)-driven regional networks in the sectors. Because of different FDI policies in East Asian countries, these production networks work differently among individual countries in general and in the three industries in particular.

Third, each of these sectors has a unique feature in manufacturing and is in a distinct category of manufacturing in ICIO tables. The textile sector represents labor-intensive and tradable manufacturing, the electronics sector represents global technologies, and the automobile sector represents global innovation for local markets. These different features influenced the pattern of the global distribution of productional interests and capabilities in different ways.

4.1.3 Time Period Coverage

Hypothesis 1 testing covers the development of the global economic structure and regional concentration for the period from the mid-1990s and mid-2010s for two reasons. First, the period is chosen because of data available from the ICIO tables. We use data from the OCED-ICIO tables, which are available only for the period from 1995 to 2015.

More importantly, though, these two decades witnessed the rise of China as a formidable manufacturing powerhouse and the emergence of a China-centered regional production network in East Asia. The rise of China has led to the reorganization of production in East Asia. This period is also the time when regionalism spread around the world, from Europe, North America, to East Asia. This period is very significant for the research problem that is the focus of this book.

4.2 Construction of the Global Economic Structure and Regional Concentration Index

Using the input-output data and the methods in GVC analysis, we construct the global economic structure and the RCI. I first use the complex network method to visualize the networks of the global economic structure. The structure of value chains is visually presented in a network graph that shows the volume, source country, and destination country in the transnational movement of final goods. The imported value-added components from the source node to the destination node are visualized through arrows indicating the flow direction. The relative size of the nodes represents the volume of the domestic value-added component in the national economy's final products and services. The relative width of the arrows is determined by the volume of value-added from a source economy to its partner economy.

I will then use the same input-output data to construct RCI. RCI measures the extent to which a region absorbs value-added from itself relative to how much the world is absorbing value-added from this region. This index is designed to show the share of production occurring within a region. The yearly RCI further indicates the change in the level of intra-regional industrial production in Europe, North America, or East Asia over the period.

4.2.1 Global Economic Structure: Assessing Patterns of Global Distribution of Transnational Production Interests and Capabilities

The global economic structure by all industrial sectors: 1995, 2005, and 2015. Let us first look at the global economic structure with all industrial sectors. Figures 4.1, 4.2, and 4.3 are three network graphs that show the global economic structure in 1995, 2005, and 2015. The full names of country abbreviations (e.g., SGP for Singapore) are shown in Appendix 1. A core-periphery structure is visible in the network graphs. In 1995, three core economies—Germany, the US, and Japan—are seen at the center of a tightly knit web of transnational value-added distribution.

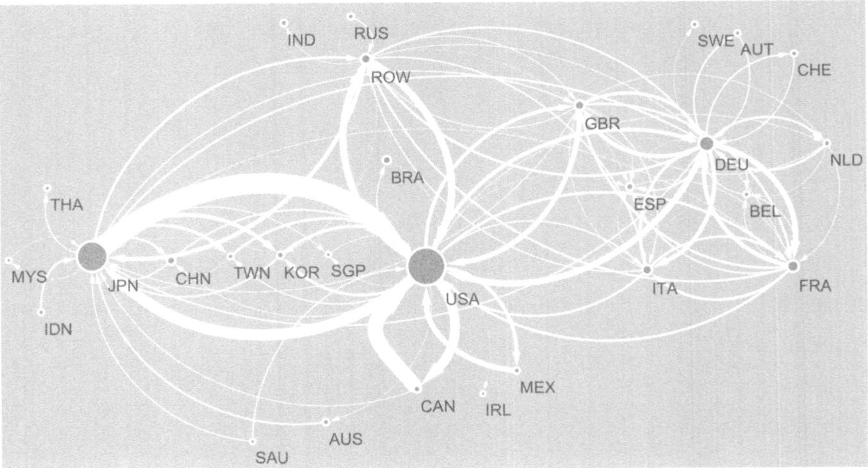

Figure 4.1 The Global Economic Structure of All Industrial Sectors, 1995.

Source: Author's calculations (All visualization figures were drawn with the help of Cytoscape, an open-source platform for complex network analysis and visualization (www.cytoscape.org). The network graph extends across all economy pairs, involving more than 3,000 connections. To avoid clutter, only the top 3% are shown in the figure. The table versions of the maps are available upon request) using Cytoscape and data from OECD-ICIO Tables.

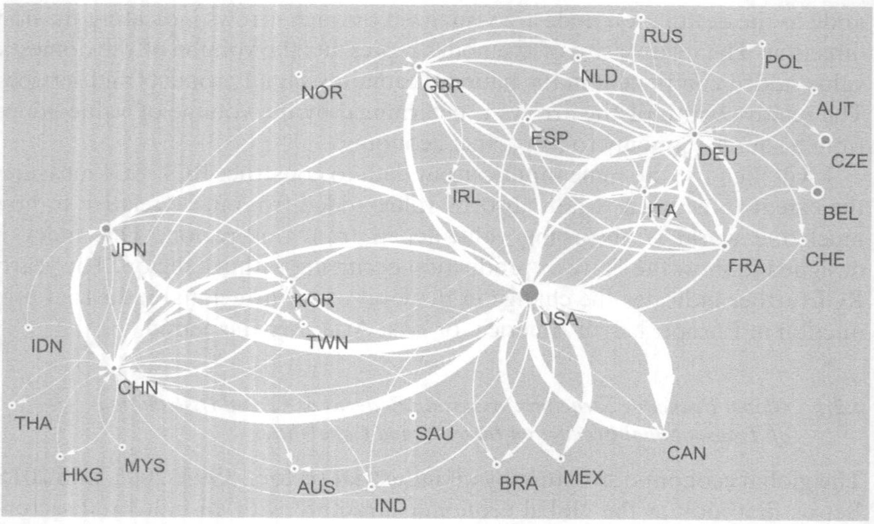

Figure 4.2 The Global Economic Structure of All Industrial Sectors, 2005.

Note: Author's compilation using Cytoscape and data from OECD-ICIO Tables.

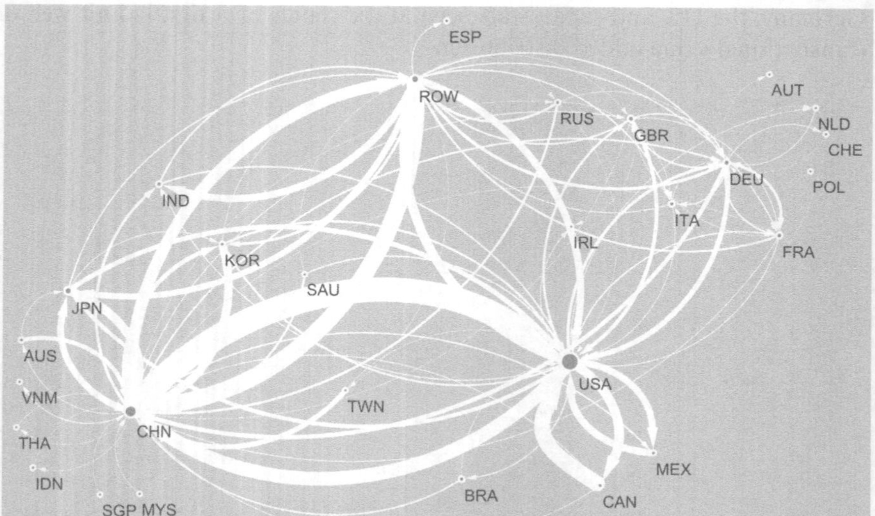

Figure 4.3 The Global Economic Structure of All Industrial Sectors, 2015.

At the regional level, Germany was positioned as the hub of the European RVCs, where horizontal integration prevails, and value-added flows in both directions between economic pairs. The North American and East Asian value chains are more hierarchical. The US dominated the regional production blocs of North America. The US and Canada had strong interdependence, which was partly due to their bilateral free trade agreement (FTA) in 1989. NAFTA in 1994 further broadened the bilateral FTA to include Mexico. Since then, Mexico started to deepen its integration into the regional production networks and grew as the most labor-intensive and low value-added segments in the region. Japan dominated production networks between East Asia and the US. Japan provided a great amount of value-added to the US in components and services and to a lesser extent indirectly via China, Taiwan, South Korea, and Singapore.

Figure 4.2 shows that the situation started to change with the rise of China in the 2000s. By 2005, the global structure shifted into a triangular pattern, whereby Japan remained the main US partner and China emerged as a close second in the regional production networks. Particularly, China's accession to World Trade Organization (WTO) in 2001 started a new era of intensive GVC participation. China's increasing production interests, capabilities, and the exponential growth of its markets generated a great surge in manufacturing investment, mostly from Japan and the US. The emergence of China affected the dominance of US-Japan economic connections in the region.

Moreover, East Asia saw a deepening structural interdependence of the regional economy. Vertical international production sharing became an essential part of each national economy in East Asia. After the 1997 Asian financial crisis, East Asian economies started to engage in multilateral cooperation among themselves in the interest of the "common good". For most of the 1990s and well into the early 2000s, these institutional efforts accompanied pervasive corporate activities to forge arrangements for an economically more integrated East Asia. The ASEAN+3 process, the Chiang Mai Initiative and its successor, Chiang Mai Initiative Multilateralization (CMIM), the East Asia Summit, and a host of minilateral and multilateral FTAs are a few examples of the rapid development of East Asian regionalism.

In regional comparison, the structure of value chains in Europe remained largely unchanged, while North America saw structural change in two aspects: (1) enhancement of intra-regional connectivity and (2) increase in the involvement of global productional forces, especially from the rest of the world (ROW, indicated in the figure).

Figure 4.3 shows how the transnational production interests and capabilities were globally structured in 2015. China-centered regional production networks pushed the US and Japan to the periphery.

In East Asia, the forces of transborder production networks (TPNs) gradually shifted from Japan to China. China was mainly a user of foreign inputs and a destination of value-added. China's production chains were used as an export platform for Japan, South Korea, and Taiwan to re-export their value-added to the ROW. China was also a supplier of intermediate goods and services used in other economies' production. There was a great increase in value-added from China to other developing economies in the region such as Vietnam where intermediates are assembled into final products.

In regional comparison, Europe still saw the dominance of Germany in the regional production networks, which were increasingly overshadowed by forces from East Asia and North America. North America retained US-centered regional production networks, while its central player, the US, was also heavily connected with China.

Overall, we see some interesting features in the global economic structure sector. First, the growth of TPNs was not limited to East Asia, and such networks evolved across regions. Factory East Asia built strong productional linkages with the US. Second, the geographical distribution of value chains changed substantially. The two decades witnessed the decline of the US-Japan economic domination and the strengthening of the US-China economic partnership. Third, transnational production networks in Europe were more balanced and horizontal, while those of North America were more vertical and unidirectional. Fourth, in terms of change over the period, the expansion of GVCs accelerated in the first decade but slowed down in the second decade. It seems that the global financial crisis of 2008 led to this slowdown. GVCs retracted and became more regional.

4.2.1.1 The Global Economic Structure by Industry: 1995, 2005, and 2015

The pattern of the transnational distribution of productional interests and capabilities varies across industrial sectors because of sectoral-specific factors such as transport cost, modularity of production processes, and rules of origin requirements. I have constructed the global economic structure of transnational production interests and capabilities in three industrial sectors to capture the structural characteristics of the distribution of these forces.

Figure 4.4 presents the global economic structure. The sector is highly labor-intensive and relatively easy for developing economies to grow. It is sensitive to price fluctuations and globally traded with low proximity needs for production. The textile sector is a "springboard" for national industrial development and is often a typical starter industry for countries to engage in export-oriented industrialization (Gereffi & Frederick, 2010, p. 2).

The geographical distribution of production in the textile sector shifted dramatically over the 20 years. This resulted in sizeable losses in transnational production interests and capabilities in Europe and North America and important gains in East Asia. The biggest change in the textile sector occurred in East Asia where new production centers grew rapidly. The relevant scholarly literature has established that the textile sector played a significant role in East Asia's export-led industrialization (Gereffi & Memedovic, 2003). Japan was a world-class exporter of textile products in the 1950s and 1960s. The newly emerging economies include South Korea, Taiwan, Hong Kong, and Singapore in the 1970s and 1980s, followed by China and several ASEAN economies (Indonesia, Thailand, Malaysia, and the Philippines) in the 1990s, and more recently, Vietnam in the 2010s.

In the structure in 1995, productional partnerships between the US and Japan, between the US and Canada, and in Europe are visible. In 2005, China emerged as a final assembly country, absorbing great value-added from Taiwan, South Korea, and Japan and then exporting final goods to the US and the ROW. By 2015, China dominated global production networks in the textile sector. Intra-regionally, it connected substantially with almost every regional member economy, for example, Vietnam, Japan, Taiwan, Indonesia, South Korea,

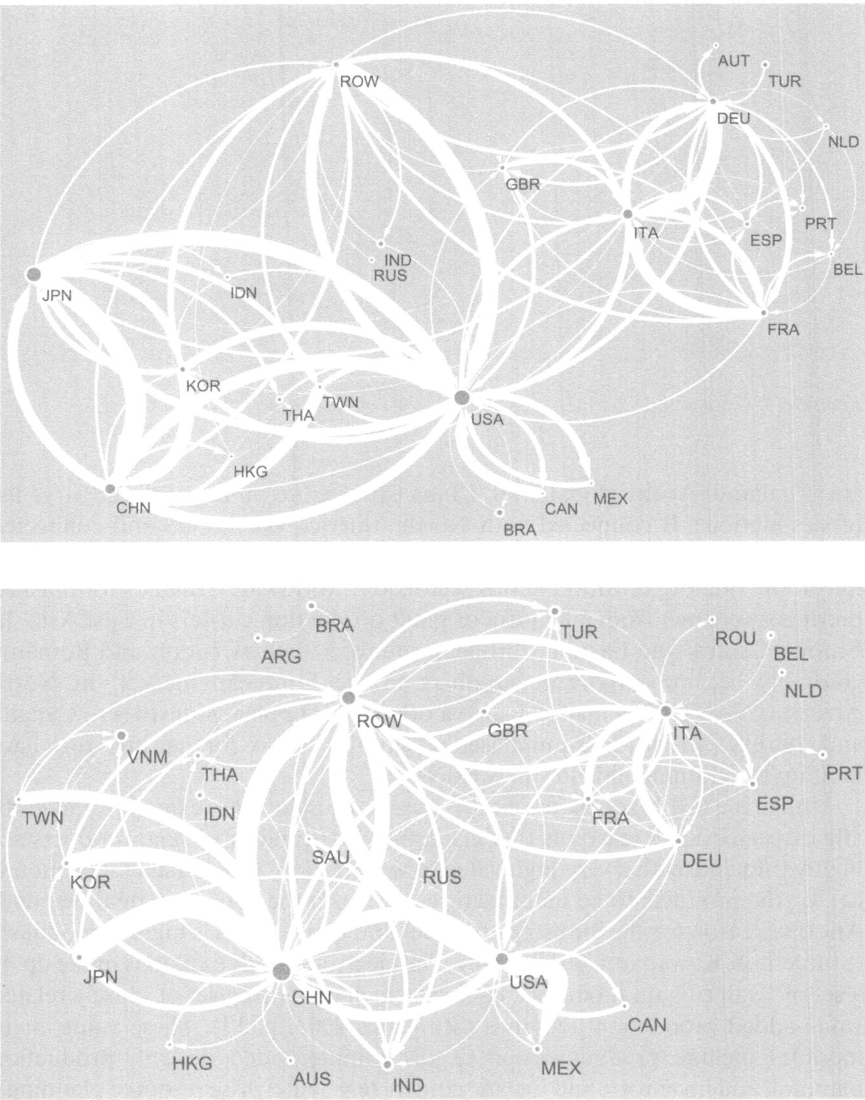

Figure 4.4 The Global Economic Structures of Textiles: 1995, 2005, and 2015.

Note: Author's compilation using Cytoscape and data from OECD-ICIO Tables.

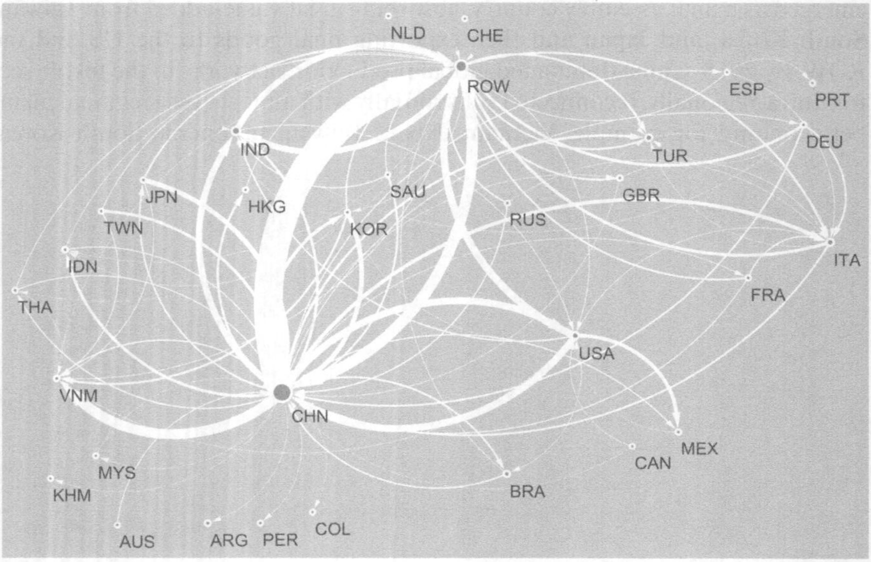

Figure 4.4 Continued

and Thailand. At the global level, China exported to an unparalleled large list of destinations. It connected with North America via the US and connected with Europe via Italy. Global sourcing of parts and materials became the norm for production organization in this sector, and worldwide demands for finished products were met from a handful of giant production clusters in East Asia. In Europe, Central and Eastern European countries such as Turkey and Romania gradually became important suppliers to the European market. In North America, NAFTA has made Mexico a privileged supplier of textiles to Canada and the US—the leading purchaser of clothing. Also, foreign investors have built up the clothing industry in Mexico.

Unlike the textile sector, the electronics sector is far more extensive and globally dispersed. One reason is that electronic parts and most final products are highly tradable, with a very high value to weight ratio, which makes it economical for the products to be manufactured far from the source of final demand. Another reason for the industry's product and distribution is highly "modular" (Sturgeon & Kawakami, 2011, p. 10). The electronics value chain is made up of a set of "value chain modules", each of which contains a set of closely related value-added production activities (Sturgeon, 2003, p. 12). These value chain modules include product design (e.g., computer-aided design), production planning and inventory, and logistic control (e.g., enterprise resource planning), as well as various aspects of the production process itself (e.g., assembly, test and inspection, materials handling). One of the most important implications of value chain modularity is that it makes it easier to accomplish work across a great distance. This creates opportunities for developing countries, both as production locations for multinational firms and as local firms seeking to participate in the industry as suppliers and contract manufacturers. Once a local supplier has gained a role in a GVC, rapid product innovation and short product life cycles keep creating opportunities for learning and industrial upgrading.

A handful of East Asian economies have taken advantage of the opportunities made available through value chain modularity to enhance their development experience (Whittaker et al., 2010). The electronics sector is the best example of the dramatic expansion of transnational production networks connected with East Asia. The economic rise of East Asia went hand-in-hand with the development of the electronics sector as an engine for East Asia's industrialization. The first phase of the global expansion of East Asian productional interests and capabilities in the electronics sector was driven by the emergence of Japanese electronics companies. Leading electronics companies in Japan, the US, and Europe modularized their production processes and offshored manufacturing and assembly tasks to South Korea, Taiwan, Hong Kong, and Singapore. In the second phase, a similar pattern evolved within the region, with South Korea and Taiwan increasingly offshoring their labor-intensive production activities to developing economies, principally Indonesia, Malaysia, Thailand, and the Philippines. In the most recent phase in the 2000s and 2010s, leading electronics companies further relocated their production to China to cut production costs. Figure 4.5 is the global economic structure in the electronics industry.

As Figure 4.5 demonstrates, the position of East Asia in the global economic structure underwent great changes. In 1995, Japan dominated the regional production networks and provided huge value-added to South Korea, Taiwan, China, Malaysia, Thailand, Singapore, and the Philippines. The structure in the 2005 map shows the deepening and widening of transnational production

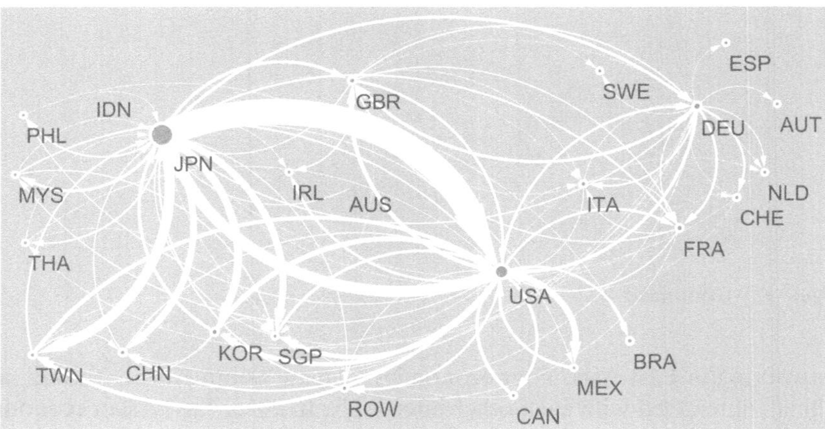

Figure 4.5 The Global Economic Structures of Electronics: 1995, 2005, and 2015.

Note: Author's compilation using Cytoscape and data from OECD-ICIO Tables.

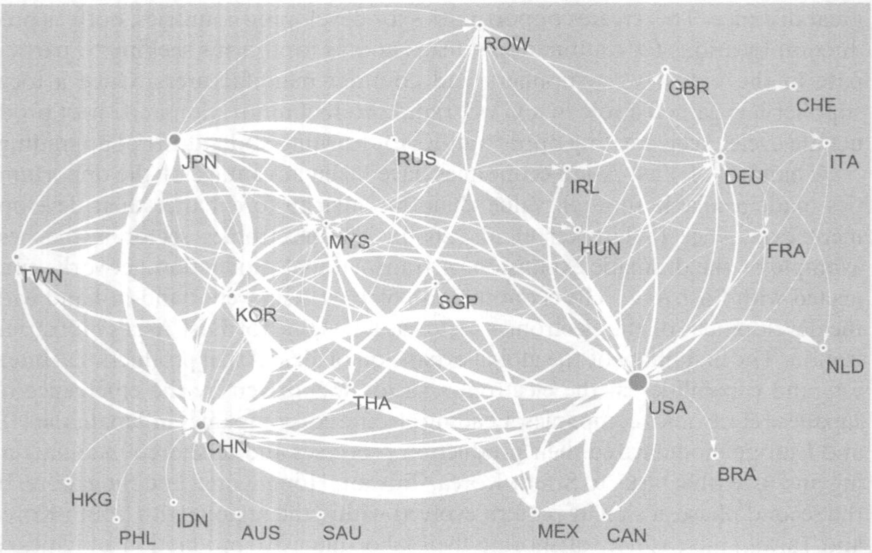

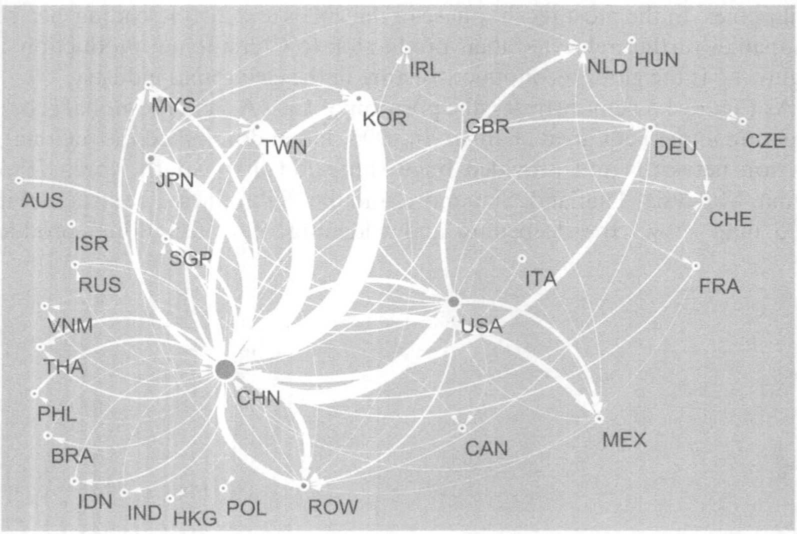

Figure 4.5 Continued

networking in East Asia. Four economies—Japan, South Korea, Taiwan, and China—interacted with each other intensively. In 2015, East Asian economies became significant global players. China dramatically increased its presence in the regional and GVCs of the sector, absorbing great value-added from South

Korea, Taiwan, and Japan within the region, as well as the US and Germany from outside the region.

The electronics sector in Europe and North America also underwent major restructuring from being highly localized to becoming highly globalized. In Europe, Germany, the hub economy, strengthened its involvement in East Asian production networks and provided an increasing amount of value-added into China. Eastern Europe was integrated with European production networks. Hungary, the Czech Republic, and Poland emerged as major low-cost supply bases in the region. In North America, the US was deeply integrated into the GVCs of the electronics sector, being more interconnected with East Asian partners than its regional counterparts. Meanwhile, Mexico became host to an electronics cluster that supplied the North American market via increased industry linkages with East Asia.

In contrast to the textile and electronics sectors that developed global-scale patterns of integration, the automobile sector surprisingly continued to strengthen regional production. The automobile sector is highly R&D intensive, with competition driven by innovation and quality. Investments needed for automobile production are high cost, large scale, and oriented toward longer cycles of production. Moreover, national governments create pressure on automakers to "build where they sell" and increase local content. This can explain that the automobile sector has high trade intensity, but assembly and production tend to be regionalized. It is built toward serving customers located near factories. Only a very small number of segments is fully global (Sturgeon & Van Biesebroeck, 2009).

Figure 4.6 is the global distribution of transnational production interests and capabilities in the automobile industry. We see three regional clusters of

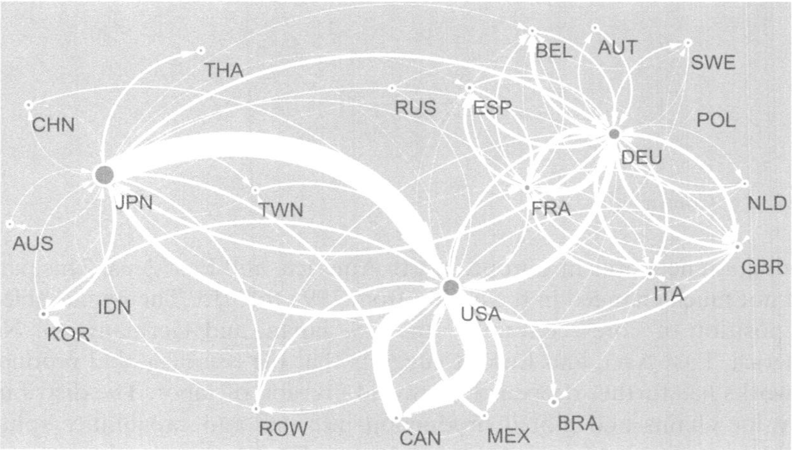

Figure 4.6 The Global Economic Structures of Automobiles: 1995, 2005, and 2015.

Note: Author's compilation using Cytoscape and data from OECD-ICIO Tables.

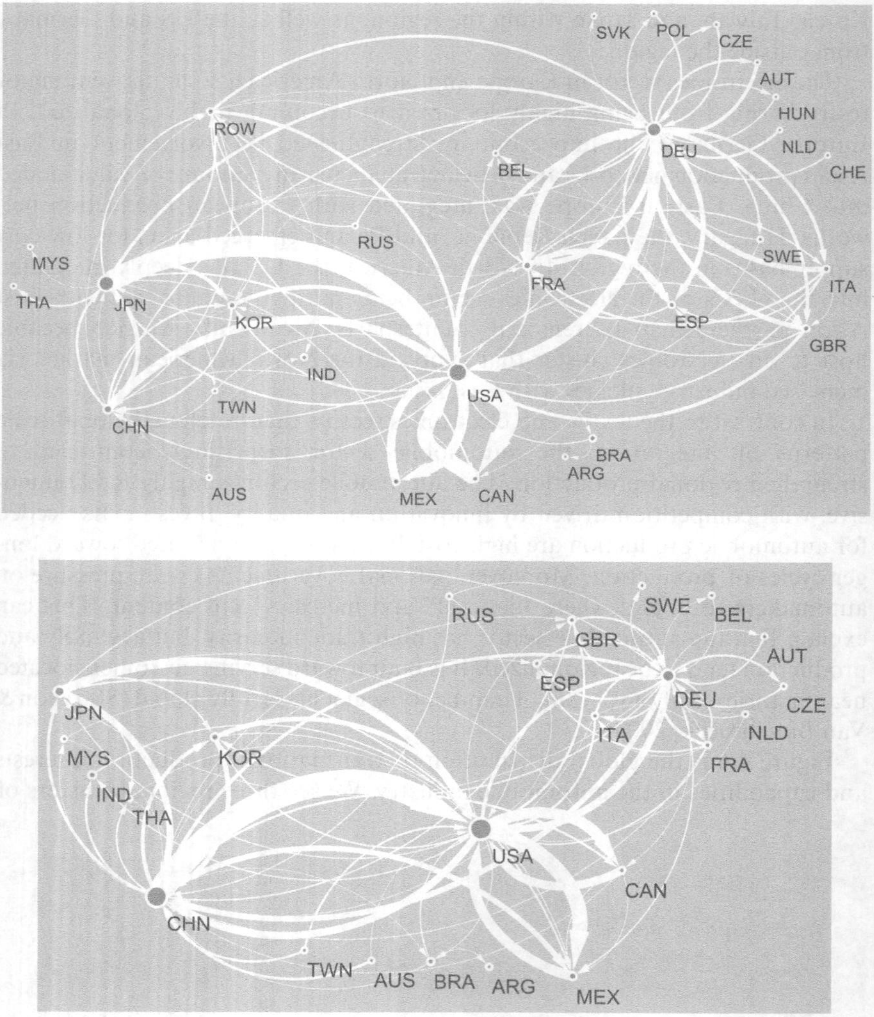

Figure 4.6 Continued

production networks in Europe, North America, and East Asia. This pattern had not much changed in the period from 1995 to 2015. The remarkable stable position of core economies—the US, Japan, and Germany—in North America, East Asia, and Europe suggests that the rise of global production networks has further deepened the world division of labor. The distribution of value chains and global production interests and capabilities split the world into core and periphery economies. Even when developing economies manage to get into the GVCs, they find themselves in low value-added positions.

In East Asia, Japan and South Korea were major production forces in the transformation of the auto industry from 1995 to 2015. In 1995, Japanese automaker investments were heavily concentrated in the US as the political pressure drove Japanese automakers to manufacture cars in the US, the largest target market for Japanese cars. Japan also exported auto parts and components to assembly economies, for example, Thailand, which then re-exported these intermediates products to be assembled into Japanese cars sold in the US market. Unlike Japan, China's automotive industry developed extensively through FDI in the form of joint ventures with international automobile manufacturers. While China was insignificant in 1995 in global car manufacturing, it became a production and export hub for auto parts and components serving the region and beyond, particularly the US. Other key players at the center of the regional networks were South Korea, Malaysia, and Taiwan.

Of the three regions, regional integration is the most advanced in North America. Under NAFTA's rules of origin, an automobile must contain at least 62.5% regional value content for it to be imported into a member country duty-free.[2] The regional content requirements of NAFTA introduced a substantial tariff cost on extra-regional automobile parts. As a result, automakers and suppliers were motivated to relocate value chains to North America. This in turn served to generate a surge of investment in the Southern US and Mexico.

Europe continued to be a primary production region accounting for 23% of the world's total automobile production in 2015. However, since the 2000s, the Eastern enlargement of the EU[3] has had a significant effect on the geographic distribution of automobiles across Europe, Turkey, and Morocco (Pavlínek, 2020). Several old assembly factories have been closed in Western Europe, while new ones have been opened in Eastern Europe.

To summarize, I have constructed the global economic structure on the global distribution of transnational production interests and capabilities. Findings on the structural character of the distribution suggest that there is a clear pattern of three concentrations in the distribution, in East Asia, North America, and Europe. The extent of concentration varies among the regions at different times and in different industries. What is unclear from the visual presentations is whether such a pattern of concentration suggests a difference in the level of regional integration of concentrated production interests and capabilities. I now turn to RCI analysis for further explanation.

4.2.2 Regional Concentration Index: Measuring the Levels of Regional Integration

In this section, I will build on the investigation in the previous section to focus on the intra-regional value chain trade in Europe, North America, and East Asia. I will use the same GVCs and RVCs data to construct an RCI. The RCI is a calibrated index and measures the extent to which a region is absorbing value-added from itself relative to how much the world is absorbing value-added from this region. This calibration addresses a key problem in the analysis of intra-regional trade share where regions with more members necessarily capture more of each other's trade and thus may overestimate the extent of integration.

To compute RCI, domestic flows of value-added are excluded, which is equivalent to setting the block diagonal elements of the VBY matrix to zero. The index is computed backward. It measures the extent to which a region is absorbing value-added from itself, relative to how much the world is absorbing the region's value-added. For a given region *q* and given sector *i*, the RCI is computed as:

$$RCI(b)_{(q,i)} = \frac{vby_{q,(q,i)} \,/\, vby_{*,(q,i)}}{vby_{*,(q,i)} \,/\, vby_{**}}$$

where an asterisk * denotes all traders.

Using the formula above, I construct annual RCI for the three regions for the period from 1995 to 2015 on all industries and the three individual industries. Figure 4.7 shows the regional concentration rates over the years in East Asia, Europe, and North America. An RCI close to 1 means value flows in the region to about the same extent as it does outside the region. The higher the index, the more a region disproportionately relies on producers within itself. Figure 4.7 first shows the levels of regional integration of the three regions in all industries and their changes over the years. The application of RCI establishes a clear ranking in regional integration among the three regions. East Asia had the lowest RCI (around 1), followed by Europe (around 3) and North America (between 1 and 1.5).

In the case of East Asia, the RCIs were declining between 1995 and 2012 when they went down to 0.81. It rose slightly to reach 1.15 in 2015. Europe had the highest level of regional integration, where the RCI was at 3.66 in 1998. Although there was a decline in the RCIs of Europe over time, it was always ahead of the other two regions. The RCI of North America stood between East Asia and Europe and was largely unchanged over time.

The patterns in the three industrial sectors in Figure 4.7 resonate with the findings in the mapping of the global economic structure in the previous section. As shown in sectoral RCIs in Figure 4.7, the levels of regional integration in textiles, electronics, and automobiles are not consistent with that in all industries. Although the RCI of Europe was the highest in all three sectors, those in East Asia and North America were different in different sectors. For instance, in textiles and electronics, East Asia had higher RCIs than North America.[4] The relatively higher RCIs in textiles and electronics for East Asia came probably from the early decades of Japan-led regional production networks where textiles and electronics were particularly important for export-oriented industrialization. However, in the 2000s and 2010s, textiles and electronics became increasingly globally interconnected. As is evident in the figure, the RCIs of textiles and electronics gradually dropped to less than 1 in

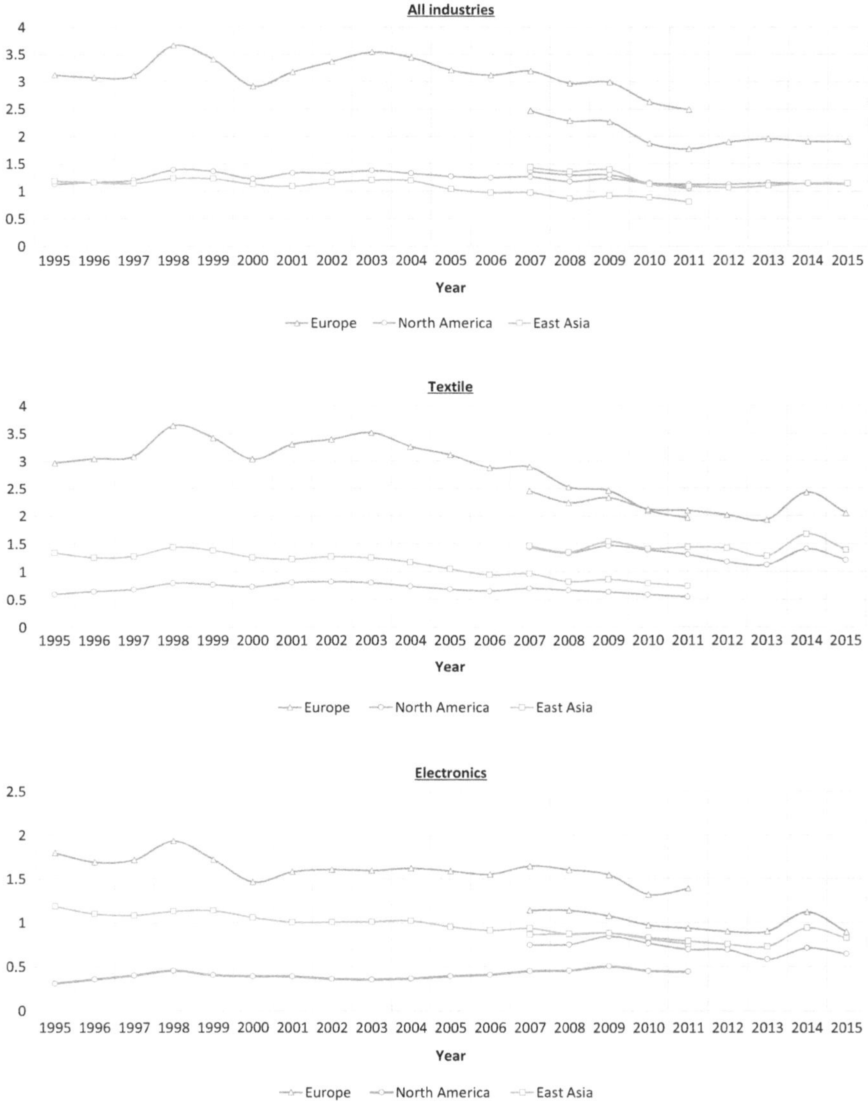

Figure 4.7 Yearly RCIs of East Asia, Europe, and North America.

Source: Author's compilation using the ADB-MRIO data (The RCI is calculated by the ADB-MRIO statistics team (more information can be found at their official website: https://mrio.adbx.online/wp-login.php). The data for years 1995–2011 are sourced from OECD (2018b) and years 2007–2015 from ADB (2021). There are some discrepancies between the two databases: OECD-ICIO and ADB-MRIO. However, as the research is more concerned with the relative level of the regional concentration rates of the three regions, these discrepancies do not affect our comparisons).

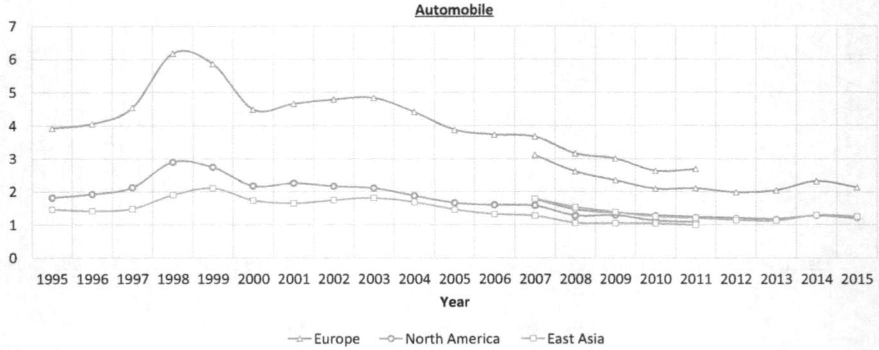

Figure 4.7 Continued

the 2010s. The automobile sector saw a different pattern and had the highest RCIs among the three sectors. The automobile sector was the most regionally concentrated. In regional comparison, Europe had the highest RCI, followed by North America and East Asia. Over time, the RCIs rose dramatically in the late 1990s then declined significantly in the 2000s and 2010s.

Taken together, the results from the analysis of the RCIs provide evidence that production networks within East Asia are less integrated than the two other regions. This does not mean the absence of truly RVCs in East Asia, but the empirical evidence here suggests that the majority of value chains in East Asia are primarily and increasingly globally interconnected.

4.3 Evidence for Hypothesis 1

This chapter has undertaken to test Hypothesis 1 against empirical evidence. I used the complex network method and OECD-ICIO table data to construct the global economic structure for observing the structural character of the distribution of transnational production interests and capabilities. I used the ADB-MRIO data to construct the RCI to determine the levels of regional integration in Europe, North America, and East Asia.

Analysis of the empirical materials largely confirms the theoretical expectations in Hypothesis 1 that the intra-regional interconnectivity of East Asia in all industrial sectors is lower than that of Europe and North America. Europe had the highest level of regional integration, with the highest RCIs in all industrial sectors (1.5–4), in textiles (2–4), electronics (1–2), and automobiles (2–6). North America had close regional connectivity in all industrial sectors and the automobile sector. In textiles and electronics though, it was overwhelmingly globally interconnected. The level of regional integration of North America varied at different industrial sectors: all industrial sectors (1–1.5), textiles (0.5–1.5), electronics (0–1), and automobiles (1–3). East Asia had the lowest levels of intra-regional connectivity in all industrial sectors with the lowest in

RCIs in all industrial sectors (0.5–1.5). There were also sectoral variations in East Asia: textiles (0.5–1.5), electronics (0.5–1.5), and automobiles (1–2). East Asia was the least regionally integrated and the most globally interconnected.

As explained in Hypothesis 1, different levels of regional integration in production networks are suspected to be an important factor for the different performances and outcomes in regionalism in Europe, North America, and East Asia, and the level in East Asia is suspected to be much lower. A lack of dominance of regionally integrated production interests and capabilities in East Asia accounts for the lack of development of institutional arrangements for a single regional economic community in East Asia. The empirical analysis of the global economic structure largely confirmed these theoretical expectations.

Notes

1 East Asian region here includes ten ASEAN nations and five Northeast Asian economies, Japan, South Korea, China, Hong Kong, and Taiwan. Europe comprises 28 members of the EU. North America includes the US, Canada, and Mexico.

2 Notably, a recent update of NAFTA, the US-Mexico-Canada Agreement (USMCA), came into force on 1 July 2020. The USMCA lifted the regional value content requirement of automobiles from 62.5% to 75%. The USMCA also contains new rules governing the use of steel and aluminum inputs in the automobile sector, a topic not addressed by NAFTA. It provides that at least 70% of the vehicle producer's purchases of steel and aluminum in the US, Mexico, and Canada must consist of originating goods.

3 Eight countries with economy in transition, the Czech Republic, Estonia, Hungary, Latvia, Lithuania, Poland, Slovakia, and Slovenia, and two market economies, Cyprus and Malta, joined the EU in 2004.

4 Although East Asia presented higher RCIs in textiles and electronics than North America, this did not cripple my judgment that East Asia had the lowest RCI at the all-industry level. East Asia's high RCIs in textiles and electronics were largely contributed by its internationally competitive industrial capabilities in these two sectors.

5 East Asian Economies in Transnational Production Networks

In Chapter 4, I investigated the three regional concentrations in the global economic structure and tested theoretical expectations of Hypothesis 1. In this chapter, I test Hypothesis 2. I investigate the global, regional, and national origins of value-added in the production networks in East Asia and determine the relations between the pattern of the divergence in the origins and divergent institutional choices of these nations for regional arrangements. In doing so, I construct the regional economic structure underlying the pattern of the distribution of value-added in production in the region. In addition to ASEAN+3 (Association of Southeast Asian Nations), there were various plans, initiatives, and projects for regional institutional arrangement, each with a different set of purposes, organizational mechanisms, membership scope, or focuses in regulation and governance: APEC, ASEAN, CP/TPP, RCEP, and many less prominent ones in between. If we recall, Hypothesis 2 theorizes that: *The weakness in East Asian regionalism was partly because of the divergent position of nations in the regional economic structure. The more divergent in their global/regional connectivity, the stronger their desire for different institutional arrangements in East Asian regionalism.*

While Hypothesis 1 considers each region as a productional unit, Hypothesis 2 treats each national economy as a separate productional unit, that is, Factory China, Factory Malaysia, and so on. Hypothesis 2 is built on the belief that regionalism is ultimately an interstate exercise of institution-building.

To test Hypothesis 2, this chapter proceeds in three parts. Section 5.1 disaggregates the final goods into domestic value-added (DVA) and foreign value-added (FVA) to identify value-added from within the nation and from outside the nation. Section 5.2 further decomposes FVA into regional value-added (RVA) and global value-added (GVA) to separate value-added regionally and globally. The DVA-RVA-GVA nexus is then transformed into a coordinate system for a description of the position of each East Asian economy in the regional economic structure. Section 5.3 discusses my overall findings.

DOI: 10.4324/9781032613321-5

5.1 Determining the Positions of East Asian Nations in the Distribution of DVA and FVA Production Interests and Capabilities

The international economic structure changes rapidly, and the same is true for the underlying structural interdependencies of the economies in the global system. Not all individual economies are equally affected by the structural forces. For example, a large and self-sufficient economy such as that of China and a small and open economy such as that of Singapore are influenced very differently by the structural forces. Great attention shall be paid to the unique and different positions of these nations to understand the effects of the structural forces on these nations' institutional preferences in East Asian regionalism. These positions, for this investigation, are essentially defined by the extent to which and the mode in which these nations participate in global value chains (GVCs) or where they are relocated in the transnational production networks.

Before 1985, successful industrialization by nations meant building domestic value chains. In recent decades, developing economies are presented with unprecedented opportunities to join GVCs without having to develop complete products or value chains themselves (Baldwin, 2011). The expansion of GVCs triggered a catching-up development strategy by developing economies that first foster linkage to transborder production networks (TPNs) and then use the learning opportunities to develop and consolidate domestic production relations and capabilities. In the short term, developing economies specialize in the production of simple goods and labor-intensive tasks. The long-term target is national industrial growth and moving up in the value chain to a higher value-added development stage. The literature suggests that upward mobility in GVCs does take place but does not work for all, and the gains are likely conditional on other factors (Ignatenko et al., 2019).

In East Asia, China and some ASEAN economies pursued this development strategy involving upward movement in GVCs. They sought to attract manufacturing Foreign Direct Investment (FDI) in the early stage of development and encourage multinationals to source more intermediates locally. A study by Asian Development Bank (ADB) summarizes the transition of East Asian developing economies as follows:

> The beginning of East Asia's remarkable transition in the 1970s and 1980s was initially powered by major Japanese multinational investments, investments which established subsidiaries across the region. But it was the unprecedented economic reforms unleashed by the People's Republic of China (PRC) in the late 1980s that provided the fodder for exponential expansion. 'Production networks' were born, coupled with a complex web of intermediate goods increasingly produced and traded among developing countries in Asia. The PRC led the charge as a final assembler

> of manufactured goods, with Southeast Asia benefiting considerably from the regional nature of many production processes. Along with this rapid growth came new jobs, higher incomes, and relative prosperity. Millions of people were lifted out of poverty. 'Factory Asia' catapulted Asia back onto the world map with its share of global output quickly rising. Several recent studies proclaim that the Asian Century is upon us, but only if the region can sustain its growth momentum and if structural economic transformation continues. Key to its success will be embracing policies that will ensure emerging Asia is not caught in the so-called middle-income trap.
>
> (2013, p. iv)

As a result of the export-led industrial production and embeddedness in the global production networks, the domestic productional forces of East Asian economies have been intertwined with foreign productional forces. Therefore, this section will conduct a split two-way analysis of productional contributions, domestic and foreign, to define the position of an economy in the international economic structure. Technically, I measure domestic and foreign productional contributions via the ratios of DVA and FVA. The DVA and FVA ratio stands for the share of domestic and foreign value-added components in the final goods and services. The DVA ratio and FVA ratio of a certain economy equates to 100%. Sections 5.2.1 and 5.2.2 will discuss DVA ratios and FVA ratios, respectively.

5.1.1 DVA Ratios

I look first at DVA ratios. I order East Asian economies based on their DVA ratios in 1995, 2005, and 2015 from the lowest to the highest and form a visual description of the structural relations among nations in East Asian regionalism (see Figure 5.1).

In 1995, Singapore ranked the lowest in DVA (61%), followed by a distant second, Malaysia (72%), and a third, Vietnam (78%). Not surprisingly, these three small and open economies sourced the most foreign inputs for domestic production. Conversely, the most self-reliant three were the three large economies in the region: Indonesia (88%), China (92%), and Japan (96%). These economies rely less on international production. The middle-ranking group includes Taiwan (80%), Thailand (80%), the Philippines (84%), South Korea (84%), and Hong Kong (86%).

In 2005, the bottom three economies and the top three economies remained the same. Singapore (64%), Malaysia (65%), and Vietnam (68%) took the bottom three places, while China (85%), Indonesia (85%), and Japan (93%) had the highest. However, in terms of change from 2000 to 2005, a substantial drop in DVA ratios of three developing economies is notable. The DVA ratio of Vietnam for the first time dropped to lower than 70%. Similarly, Thailand reached 70%, and China for the first time slipped below 90%. These three economies started to engage in TPNs and increasingly use foreign inputs to produce final products.

In 2015, the bottom three economies and the top three kept the same positions as they had been in 1995 and 2005. However, some minor changes are worth mentioning. Vietnam for the first time achieved the lowest DVA ratio

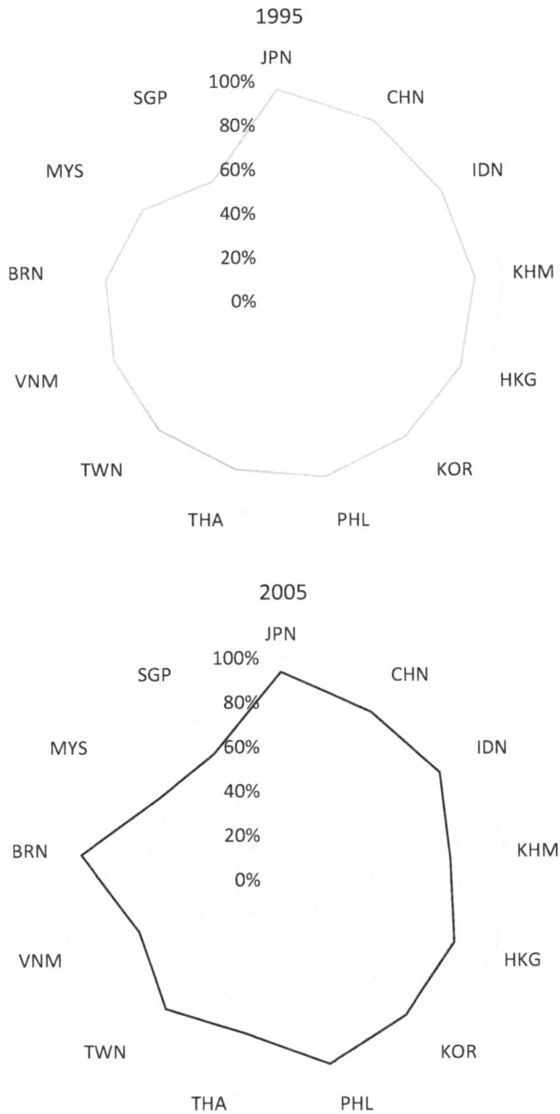

Figure 5.1 Structural Relations of East Asian Nations by DVA Ratio: 1995, 2005, and 2015.

Source: Author's compilation using OECD-ICIO data.

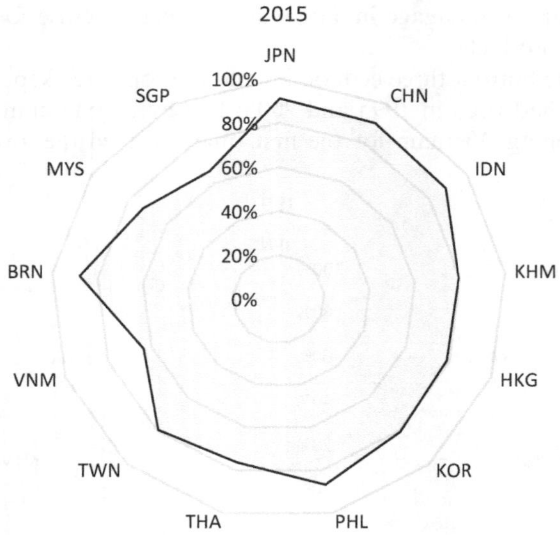

Figure 5.1 Continued

(63%), leaving Singapore (66%) and Malaysia (73%) behind. Among the top three, Japan maintained a consistent drop and further narrowed the gap between Japan and the other two: Japan (91%), China (90%), and Indonesia (89%).

In the above observations of the structural relations, we may note several characteristic features. First, larger economies tend to be more self-sufficient, a characteristic which is often attributed to the fact that they have larger domestic markets from which to draw their intermediate goods and services. Second, nearly all East Asian economies have seen an increase in their DVA ratios in the period. Third, their DVA ratios first fell and then rose.

5.1.2 FVA Ratios

The previous discussion on DVA ratios provides insight into the trend of self-reliance rates. In this section, I use the FVA ratios to determine the participation rates of nations in GVCs and the level of dependence on foreign productional forces. Not only do I calculate the FVA ratios of the sector in general, but I also pay attention to the three chosen sectors, that is, textiles, electronics, and automobiles. Therefore, each economy has four corresponding FVA ratios. Figure 5.2 compares the FVA contributions in all industries, textiles, electronics, and automobiles among East Asian economies.

The x-axis represents the 11 East Asian economies. From the left to the right, they are China, Japan, South Korea, Taiwan, Hong Kong, Indonesia, the Philippines, Thailand, Malaysia, Singapore, and Vietnam. The bars represent the absolute volume of an economy's final goods and services or known as

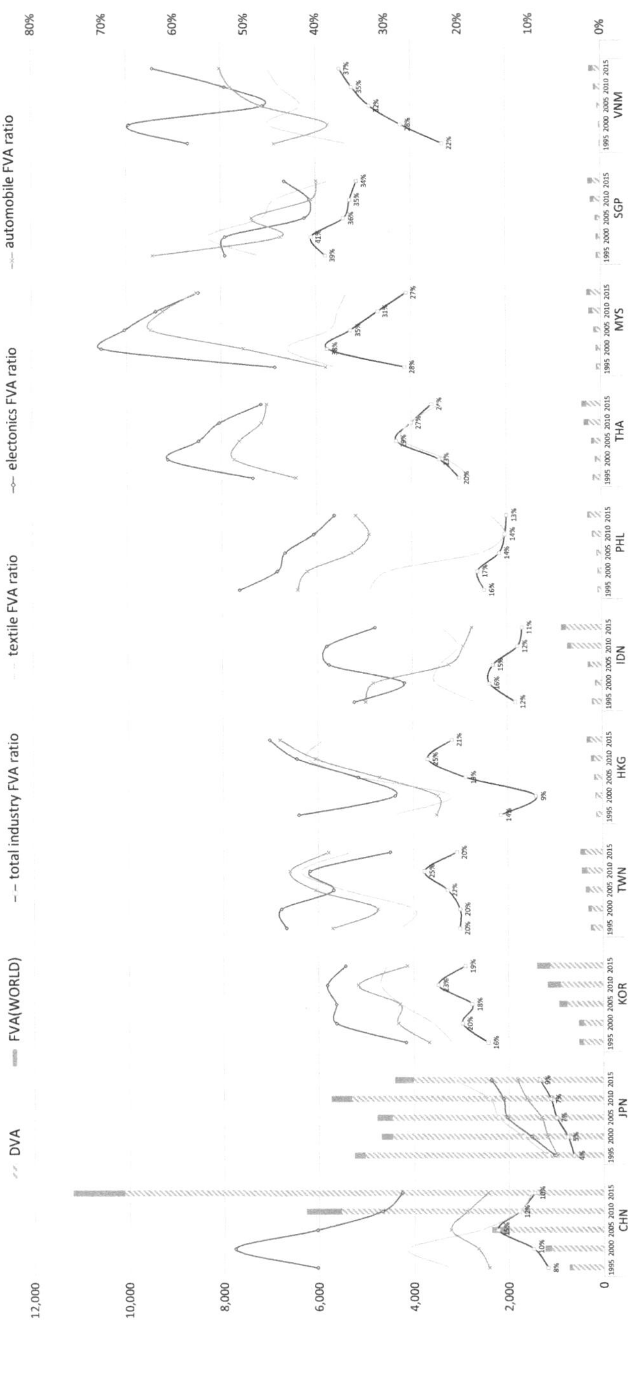

Figure 5.2 Structural Positions of East Asian Nations by FVA Ratios.

Source: Author's compilation.

gross domestic product (GDP). The bars are measured by the left y-axis (in billion dollars). According to the sources of value-added, each bar (the absolute volume) is divided into two parts: DVA and FVA. The lines represent the movement of FVA ratios for each economy/sector over the period, which is measured on the right y-axis (%). Each economy has four lines: all industries, textiles, electronics, and automobiles.

I first look at the bars and compare the productional capacities of the economies in the region. Over the past two decades, GVCs have helped developing economies grow faster. China overtook Japan as the region's largest economy and the world's second-largest economy. A number of medium- or small-sized economies also achieved extraordinary growth by reaping the benefits of being part of GVCs.

I then consider the lines and compare the rates of GVC participation for each economy/sector. In all industries (in red), Northeast Asian economies generally had lower FVA ratios than ASEAN member economies. In particular, large economies such as Japan and China had the lowest FVA ratios. From 1995 to 2015, the corresponding FVA ratios of Japan ranged from 4% to 9% and those of China from 8% to 15%. Meanwhile, medium-sized economies such as South Korea and Taiwan had average FVA ratios (15% to 25%). In contrast, the FVA ratios of the ASEAN economies (except Indonesia and the Philippines) were typically higher (20% to 40%).

Finally, I look at the three strategic sectors, textiles, electronics, and automobiles. All of the three sectors featured a high-level FVA ratio. Their FVA ratios typically exceeded the FVA ratios of all industries. This suggests the strong influence of international production networks in these three sectors. In some cases, the FVA ratios even exceed the DVA ratios. Such cases are as follows:

- Textiles: Singapore (2000)
- Electronics: China (2000), the Philippines (1995), Thailand (2000, 2005, 2010), Malaysia (2000, 2005, 2010, 2015), Singapore (1995, 2000), and Vietnam (1995, 2000, 2010, 2015)
- Automobiles: Thailand (2000), Malaysia (2000, 2005, 2010, 2015), Singapore (1995), and Vietnam (2010, 2015).

Among the three sectors, the FVA ratios of the electronics sector were much higher than those of the other sectors. This suggests a sophisticated division of labor and highly developed international production networks of electronics in East Asia. In the automobile industry, ASEAN+5 (the Philippines, Thailand, Malaysia, Singapore, and Vietnam) all had very high FVA ratios. This is an indication of a high level of integration of production networks in the automobile sector in ASEAN.

East Asian developing economies achieved fast industrialization and economic transformation by participating GVCs. This is shown in three stages as measured by DVA ratios. In the initial stage before participating GVCs, the economy has a high level of DVA ratios because of its self-sufficient and inward-looking economic structure. In the second stage, the economy calls for the capital, knowledge, and know-how of foreign producers. The economy links into GVCs by attracting export processing FDI and increasingly relying on foreign inputs to produce final products. The economy starts as a simple assembly site for foreign firms practicing a hierarchical international division of labor. As a result, this stage features an inevitable decline of DVA ratios. In the third stage, the established linkages with foreign firms play a catalytic role in industrial development. Network participation provides opportunities and incentives for the economy to develop its own technological and innovative capability. The economy grows beyond being a simple assembler and gradually replaces foreign inputs with domestic substitutes. As a result, the economy moves up in the value chain and its DVA ratio rises. Therefore, we see in the figure that DVA ratios first fall and then rise, and FVA ratios first rise and then fall.

The trend of movement in FVA ratios of the economies (except Japan and Vietnam with a consistent rise) was in inverted-U shape, reflecting the rise and then fall of foreign value-added ratios. This evidence was consistent with my expectation of the countries moving up in the GVC. Note that the years of the turning points vary by economy. The turning points relate to the stages of development, and the subsequent turning points of East Asian economies can be interpreted as supportive evidence for more advanced stages of economic development. The turning points can be seen as evidence of the structural change—moving up of nations in value chains from being final assemblers to developing their own production relations and capabilities. The divergence in the structural positions of these nations as indicated by these turning points is the original forces that drive the nation to develop their preferences and interests over different ideas and projects for regional institutional arrangements.

So far, I have conducted a split two-way analysis of the structural relations of East Asian nations in DVA and FVA. I find in this analysis that most of the East Asian economies adopted a development strategy and developed their international connections in stages through participation in GVCs. Because of the great importance of FVA, we further decompose FVA contributions and investigate their geographical origins.

5.2 Determining the Positions of East Asian Nations in the Structure of RVA and GVA Production Interests and Capabilities

In the distribution of FVA in East Asia discussed above, the global and regional sources of the FVA might also have an impact on the pattern of distribution and hence the positions of East Asian nations in the distribution. This section investigates this. To further explore the divergence and contention in the positions of East Asian economies, I further divide FVA into RVA and GVA. In a manner similar to the previous section, I discuss the structural relations and their shift over the period at the level of all industries and in the three individual industrial sectors.

5.2.1 Structure of RVA and GVA distribution in East Asian Economies

I first discuss the structural relations of RVA and GVA and the positions of nations at the level of all industries. Figure 5.3 shows different positions of East Asian economies and their structural relationship and their shift over the period from 1995 to 2015. A look at the shares of RVA and GVA reveals that production networks in East Asia were predominantly global.

To construct the structure in Figure 5.3 and plot the positions of East Asian economies, I use two methods: domestic-foreign split of value-added in final goods and regional-global split of value-added contributions in the FVA. Each quadrant on the matrix in Figure 5.3 represents a set of positions of national economies. Economies in Quadrants I and IV are open and outward-oriented economies with high FVA shares (>10%): those in Quadrant I are more regionally oriented while those in Quadrant IV are more globally interconnected. In contrast, economies in Quadrants II and III are self-sufficient economies with low FVA shares (<10%): the economies in Quadrant II are more regionally oriented while those in Quadrant III are more globally integrated.

A great majority of the East Asian economies are located in Quadrants I and IV. Vietnam (VNM in 1995, 2005, and 2015), Hong Kong (HKG in 1995), Indonesia (IDN in 2015), the Philippines (PHL in 2015), and Malaysia (MYS in 2015) are all economies located within Quadrant I. Vietnam was the most focused on participation in regional value chains (RVCs). Hong Kong was a regionally oriented economy in 1995 but subsequently moved to a globally interconnected economy. Indonesia, the Philippines, and Malaysia had a similar level of equal dependence on global and regional production partners.

Economies located in Quadrant IV are Singapore (SGP), South Korea (KOR), Taiwan (TWN), and Thailand (THA). Located on the far right, Singapore was the most globally integrated economy. South Korea, Taiwan, and Thailand also depended more on global partners than regional ones. All these economies were generally industrialized with their strong participation in GVCs.

No economies are positioned in Quadrant II, and only two countries, Japan (JPN) throughout the entire period and China (CHN in 1995, 2015), are located in Quadrant III. Both Japan and China had much greater economic interests and capabilities necessary to achieve a higher level of self-sufficiency. In terms of RVA/GVA ratios, Japan was the most globally interconnected economy in 1995. Over time, it strengthened its regional production partnerships, although integrative global forces still dominated. China started participation in RVCs in 1995. From 1995 to 2005, China became more internationally interconnected and its pace of global integration significantly exceeded its regional dependence. In 2015, China became a more self-sufficient economy but its FVA contributions were ever more globally connected.

The orientation in GVC participation of national economies in East Asia changed significantly over time. Table 5.1 summarizes the change. Overall, in terms of FVA share, nine out of the 11 economies (in the first and second

Figure 5.3 Changing Positions of East Asian Economies in the Regional Economic Structure, All Industries.

Table 5.1 Change in the Positions of East Asian Economies in the Regional Economic Structure by RVA/GVA Ratio and FVA Share

		FVA share		
		↗↗	↗↘	↘↘
RVA/ GVA ratio	↗↗	Japan, South Korea	Indonesia, Malaysia	
	↘↗	Vietnam, Hong Kong	Thailand	Singapore, the Philippines
	↘↘		China	
	→↘		Taiwan	

Notes: The first arrow represents the change in the first decade of 1995–2005 and the second decade of 2005–2015.

columns) experienced growth in FVA share from 1995 to 2005 (shown by the first ↗). The rise of FVA share in the first decade was associated with the export-oriented industrialization model. Under this model, most East Asian developing economies relied on foreign firms to jump-start their export in the early stage of industrial development. At this point, they focused on the assembly of imported materials.

In the second decade, they moved to a "more domestically integrated and higher value-added form of exporting" (Gereffi, 2018, p. 73). In this structural shift shown in Table 5.1, seven out of the 11 economies (in the second and third columns) show a decrease in FVA share from 2005 to 2015 (shown by the second ↘). This change, also known as industrial upgrading, contributed to the changes in FVA ratios and improved the positions of developing economies in the regional economic structures. Second, after the 2008 Global Financial Crisis, the economic "slowbalization"—understood as the slowdown of global integration—seriously disrupted GVCs (Titievskaia et al., 2020, p. 2). After years of global outsourcing and offshoring, the contraction of GVCs led to the decline of FVA share in East Asian economies in the 2010s.

In terms of the RVA/GVA ratio, six out of the 11 economies (in the second, third, and fourth rows) showed a decrease (↘) from 1995 to 2005. The dominant trend in the change of RVA/GVA ratios was influenced by the decline of Japan-centric regional production networks and a new wave of globalization. First, the 1990s saw Japan's "Lost Decade" that Japan was in a decade of sluggish economic growth and recession. As Japan lost its dominance in the region, the dependence of East Asian economies on Japan decreased. This contributed to the decrease of RVA share. Second, the decade of 1995–2005 was considered as a golden era of globalization or "hyperglobalization". For lower costs and efficiency, many multinational corporations (MNCs) from outside the region, mostly in the US but also Europe, outsourced their manufacturing activities to East Asia (Dent, 2016, p. 52). This participation of extra-regional forces linked Factory East Asia to globalized operations and thus increased the GVA share of East Asian economies. As a result of the structural change, the RVA/GVA ratios of most East Asian economies declined in the first decade.

In contrast, the second decade in 2005–2015 witnessed the rise of RVA/GVA ratios for most East Asian economies. There were at least two structural factors that reshaped the international connectivities of East Asia. First, China's astonishing rise shifted the region's development gravity in a more regionally oriented manner. As a result, China's neighboring economies became increasingly enmeshed in the regional production networks. Second, due to the slowbalization since the 2008 crisis, supply chains were sourced from closer to home, which led to deeper links within national borders and regional blocs. Therefore, the RVA/GVA ratios of most East Asian economies rose in the second decade.

After examining the overall trend, I now explore the divergent dynamics of each national economy. Japan and South Korea were the only two economies that showed a consistent rise in both FVA share (↗↗) and RVA/GVA ratios (↗↗). This means that the domestic production activities of Japan and South Korea became increasingly integrated with the international economy, especially with the regional economy. In this structural shift, I see different pathways of development in the two economies. As we learned from Figure 5.3, Japan was unique as being the least open but the most globally interconnected economy in the region. Japan was once the leading goose in the flying geese pattern of regional growth in the 1960s–1980s. This was "a model of sequential catch-up through teacher-learner relations among the nations along the stages of industrial upgrading" (Ozawa, 2001, p. 2). But it began to open its economy through structural reforms from the 1990s. It intensified its economic linkages with China, and, as a result, Japan's integration occurred in a more regionally oriented manner. Despite the significant change, Japan was still the least open economy and the third globally oriented economy after China and Singapore in 2015.

The change in South Korea was mainly because it increasingly participated in globalization through the "state-firm-global production networks relations" (Yeung, 2016). South Korea grew with the domination of chaebols (i.e., large business conglomerates controlled by their founding families) such as Samsung, LG, Hyundai, and SK in major industrial sectors including electronics and automobiles. These chaebol giant corporations took direct initiatives to participate in global production networks and became a dominant force transforming South Korea into a mature and globalized economy.

The steady increase in FVA share (↗↗) in Vietnam and Hong Kong was also remarkable, but they represent a different set of dynamics in the development of their RVA/GVA ratios (↘↗). They first declined and then rose. Even though this was very similar in the two, each had a very different story. Vietnam went through a transition from a centrally planned economy into an open economy in this same period. Its government took significant steps toward integrating with the global economy. For example, Vietnam joined the ASEAN free trade agreement (FTA) in 1995, signed an FTA with the US in 2000, joined World Trade Organization (WTO) in 2007, and engaged in mega-FTAs such as CP/TPP in the 2010s. These institutional efforts paid off. Since the 2010s, labor-intensive manufacturing activities were increasingly relocated to Vietnam in response to an increase in China's manufacturing costs, and Vietnam became a regional production hub outside China.

The dramatic drop in Hong Kong's RVA/GVA ratio between 1995 and 2005 can be partially explained by the structural shift in its economy from manufacturing production toward services. Since the 1990s, with the "hollowing out" of the manufacturing sectors, Hong Kong transformed from an industrialized city to a center of manufacturing-related services. Specifically, transport and financial services were the two major pillars in Hong Kong's service industry (Chiang, 2016, p. 40). In transport services, Hong Kong played an intermediary role (such as re-export and offshore trade) between the mainland and other countries. In financial services, global financial institutions set up offices or branches in Hong Kong to serve the demand of foreign manufacturers on the mainland.

The increase in the regional content in Hong Kong's GVC participation, as reflected in the upward movement of its RVA/GVA ratio between 2005 and 2015, was mainly due to its intensified economic integration through trade, financial links, and tourism with the mainland. Hong Kong has played a unique role as a bridge connecting China's economy with the rest of the world. China and Hong Kong signed "The Mainland and Hong Kong Closer Economic Partnership Arrangement" or "Closer Economic Partnership Arrangement" (CEPA) on 29 June 2003. This further accelerated Hong Kong's shift toward closer integration with the mainland.

As shown by the second column in Table 5.1, the FVA share in Thailand, Malaysia, Indonesia, China, and Taiwan all showed a dynamic pattern of rise and fall (↗↘). However, there is a significant disparity in the pattern of movement of their RVA/GVA ratios. The RVA/GVA ratio of Thailand first fell and then surged (↘↗). Thailand was an example of an East Asian economy transforming from a global manufacturer to a regional production hub.

Both Malaysia and Indonesia show a continuous rise in both decades (↗↗) in RVA/GVA ratios. This reflects their increasing dependence on RVCs. Malaysia chose export-oriented industrialization (EOI) strategy from the 1980s. It was deeply involved in GVCs in 1995, ranking second among East Asian economies only after Singapore. Malaysia diversified its economic focus from natural resources-oriented (tin and rubber) to manufacturing-oriented (especially electronics). This strengthened its intra-regional sourcing. Indonesia was very different in this respect. According to Djidin (1997), before the 1980s, Indonesia was opposed to EOI policies, the Indonesian economy was targeted at the domestic market and supported by import substitution industrialization (ISI). In the 1980s and 1990s, the collapse of oil prices brought strong pressure on the government to promote non-oil exports. Indonesia's economic policy went through a change from relying on ISI strategy to mixed measures of ISI and EOI. The inclusion of EOI measures facilitated the participation of Indonesia in regional production networks. This in turn contributed to the continuous increase in its RVA/GVA share from 1995 to 2015.

China's steady fall in RVA/GVA ratio (↘↘) is largely related to its rapid integration of domestic manufacturing into global production networks. According to Ahmad (2021), China went through various stages of the development of its GVC participation and became the center of the world's GVC. First, China pushed domestic firms into international production networks by reducing tariffs, deregulating FDI policies, and strengthening supporting infrastructure. Second, Chinese firms developed partnerships with global leading companies, particularly in the development of manufacturing low value-added products. Third, China gradually shifted production from processing trade toward more advanced and technology-intensive sectors with heavy investment in R&D and prioritizing technology transfer from global companies to domestic companies. Because of these efforts, China became big enough to act as a global connectivity platform and a nexus of most production networks for the rest of the region.

Taiwan (→↘) evolved to become the world's premier high-tech hardware manufacturing hub from the 1990s. According to Yeung (2016), Taiwan's most prized technology companies, Foxconn and TSMC, are original equipment manufacturers (OEM) and original design manufacturers (ODM) for global consumer electronic brands. Taiwanese firms initially served as low-cost subcontractors to their OEM customers located in North America, Western Europe, and Japan. The ODM arrangement is a more sophisticated form of GVC development. Through this form, Taiwanese firms became much more involved in product and process design in accordance with a general design layout supplied by their global partners. The partnership with global lead firms was the engine of economic growth for Taiwan as well as a key contributor to the decline of its RVA/GVA ratio.

Singapore and the Philippines, situated in the last column of Table 5.1, share a similar pattern in the shift of FVA shares (↘↘) and RVA/GVA ratios (↘↗). While the switch of RVA/GVA ratios was in line with the overall trend across the region, the continuous drop of their FVA shares stands out as the rest of East Asian economies experienced an upsurge in general. The reasons behind the drop in their FVA shares were quite different for the two. In the case of Singapore, it developed an international-oriented economy and has been fully engaged in global production networks since the 1980s. Even with a minor drop in FVA share in the period, Singapore was still a top open economy in the region. The Philippines was weak in GVC participation.[1] It was less competitive than its neighbors to attract MNCs in terms of logistics performance, infrastructure, and quality of institutions.

Overall, East Asia was a highly diverse region in the structural relations of East Asian nations in GVC participation and experienced significant economic structural changes from 1995 to 2015. I have identified at least three distinct groups of economies based on their positions in the regional economic structure: regional manufacturing hubs (such as Vietnam), open and global players (such as Singapore, South Korea, Taiwan, and Thailand), highly self-sufficient but globally interconnected production powers (Japan and China).

5.2.2 Textiles, Electronics, and Automobiles

While the analysis of the regional economic structure of all industries provides insight into the positions of nations in East Asian regionalism, a close-up look at the structural forces in the textile, electronics, and automobile sectors can provide further on the pattern at the industrial level. Almost all East Asian governments actively and carefully selected sectors that better utilized their comparative advantages and assisted EOI. This pattern of state behavior was influenced partly by the flying geese logic of their regional growth strategy. Early industrialized countries like Japan became global economic leaders, in part, by mastering the export of textiles, electronics, and automobiles. It is this industrialization model that many other countries seek to emulate. In this section, I will focus on the three selected industrial sectors and determine the extent of divergence among East Asian economies in the evolving distribution of production interests and capabilities for the same period.

5.2.2.1 Textiles

Labor-intensive manufacturing sectors such as textiles played a significant role in the overall industrialization of East Asian economies. Driven by the flying geese logic of regional industrial growth, East Asian economies formed a dynamic division of labor in textile manufacturing. According to Smith (1996, p. 218), export-oriented textile manufacturing in East Asia took off in Japan in the late 1950s and the early 1960s and was a key low-wage labor-intensive industry that underlaid the "economic miracle" in Hong Kong, South Korea, and Taiwan in the 1970s and 1980s. However, these newly industrialized economies (NIEs) faced great competition from China and ASEAN-developing economies in the late 1980s and 1990s. Textile producers in NIEs sought to outsource production to China and ASEAN-4 where labor was cheaper and more compliant with trading rules.[2] In the 2000s and 2010s, Vietnam was poised to become a player in textile production. Figure 5.4 shows the evolving structure of the distribution of GVCs in East Asia and the changing positions of East Asian economies in the textile sector.

Compared to the pattern at the all-industry level, the pattern in the textile sector shows a stronger regional orientation. East Asian economies use more inputs from within the region than from outside the region. In 1995, value-added in textiles was globally concentrated in three regional factories: Europe, North America, and East Asia. However, in 2015, production networks in textiles were dominated by Factory East Asia.

If we look at individual East Asian economies in terms of their level of industrialization, both Japan and South Korea evolved from a more globally oriented position in 1995 to a more regionally focused position in 2015. Japan moved from Quadrant III and South Korea from Quadrant IV to Quadrant I. Japan and South Korea, as early industrializers in East Asia, were closely

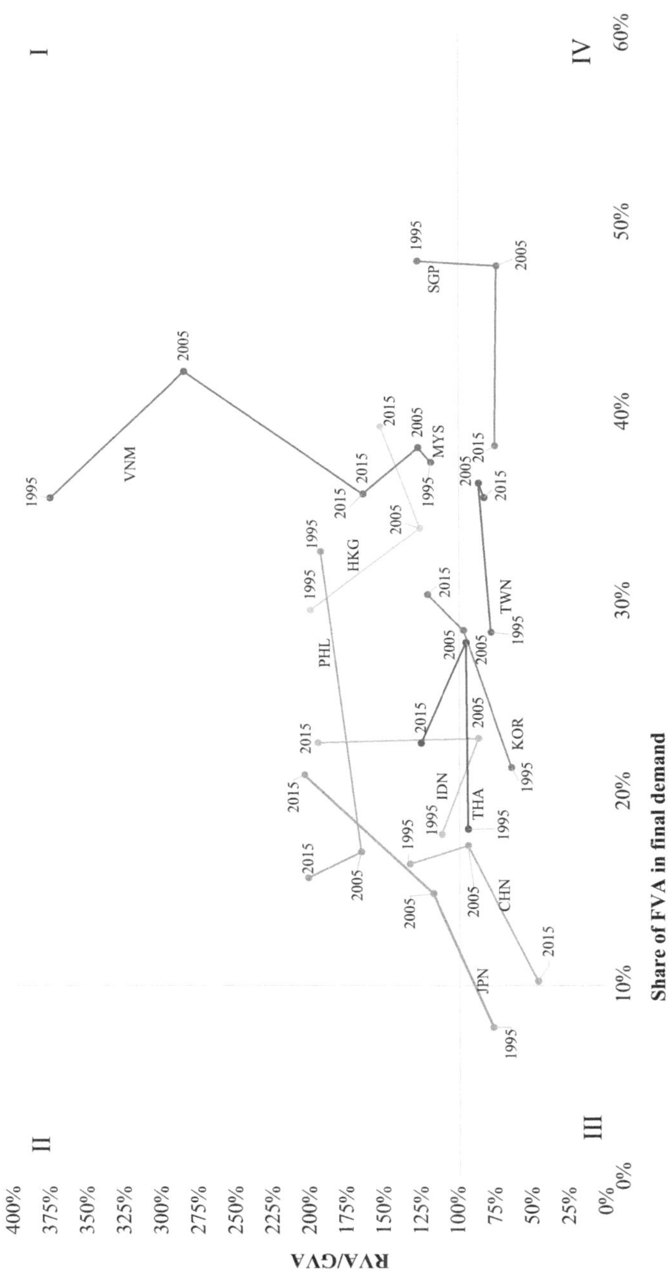

Figure 5.4 Changing Positions of East Asian Economies in the Regional Economic Structure, Textiles.

integrated into the global production networks. But, during the two decades under consideration, both Japan and South Korea increasingly sourced textile production from East Asian neighbors.

The three newly industrialized economies—Hong Kong, Taiwan, and, to a less extent, Singapore—also developed internationally competitive manufacturing interests and capabilities in the textile sector in the 1970s. Following the steps of Japan and South Korea, they phased out labor-intensive operations to lower-cost economies in Southeast Asia and China in the 1980s and early 1990s. This trend was in accord with the stage theory of comparative advantage. While Hong Kong and Taiwan moved labor-intensive operations of textiles offshore, they still kept high value-added tasks such as designing and retailing at home. This explains the increase in their FVA share from 1995 to 2015.

From the 1980s, the textile sector became a major export-oriented industry in Indonesia, Thailand, and Malaysia and had a significant share in their industrial output. In the first decade, the rise of FVA was quite sharp in Indonesia and Thailand and to a less extent in Malaysia. In the second decade, their FVA share declined partly due to their stronger domestic production capacities. In terms of RVA/GVA share, the dramatic increase of all three economies from 2005 to 2015 is noticeable.

Two newly emerging textile exporters, China and Vietnam, share similarities in the change of FVA share (↗↘) and RVA/GVA ratios (↘↘) despite the differences in their positions. China evolved from a regional production hub (Quadrant I) to a global hub (Quadrant IV) and became the center of the textile industry. Vietnam, located in Quadrant I in the entire period, emerged as a new regional assembly site. Like China, Vietnam became increasingly integrated with the GVCs. Domestically, with the increase in productivity and quality, both countries focused on moving up in the value chain.

In sum, although the textile sector proved to be more regionally integrated than that in all industries, there were significant variations among East Asian economies in individual strategic industrial sectors.

5.2.2.2 Electronics

The electronics sector provides a different illustration of regional economic structural dynamics. In *Race to the Swift*, Woo describes the electronics industry as:

> really a deus ex machina for the upstarts of the late twentieth century—like Taiwan and Korea—because it so neatly fills the lacuna between the light and heavy phases of industrialization. It is a bridge between the two phases, and offers the best advantages while avoiding the worst pitfalls of a lead-off industry such as textiles.
>
> (1991, p. 144)

Indeed, electronics has been a strategic sector in East Asian industrial transformation.

According to Dedrick and Kraemer (1998, p. 49), the spread of electronics production to East Asia in the period from 1960 to 1980 was a very important factor in East Asia becoming a major production hub. Many global lead firms such as IBM were globalizing their production to develop a better and cheaper supplier base. In the paradigm shift of electronics, East Asian economies caught the opportunities and participated in the global production networks. Developed economies such as Japan, South Korea, and Taiwan specialized in high value-added activities such as design and manufacturing of key components, while the main contribution from latecomers (ASEAN-developing economies and China) was in low-cost final assembly work. Figure 5.5 illustrates the changing positions of East Asian economies in the distribution of GVCs in the region in electronics in the period from 1995 to 2015.

Compared to the pattern in all industries and similar to the textile sector, the electronics sector also saw greater regional concentration. Most of the economies were located in Quadrant I, open and globally connected. This was facilitated by two structural conditions. First, the change in the way of industrial organization in electronics in favor of global sourcing created an unprecedented window of opportunity for East Asian firms to "plug" into emerging global production networks (Yeung, 2016, p. 84). Second, electronics is a "heterogeneous" industry with different types of production activities ranging from highly sophisticated design to simple component assembly (Chowdhury, 1988, p. 246). East Asian economies were in various stages of their industrialization and development posture and possessed diverse manufacturing capabilities. This wide range of industrial capabilities among East Asian economies provided a favorable condition for taking over the entire value chain of an electronic product. East Asia became a primary site for global production in the electronics sector.

Several structural factors contributed to the growth of the exceptional global connectivities of Japan (1995, 2005), South Korea and Indonesia (1995), and Hong Kong and Singapore (2005, 2015). Japan's electronics sector developed in parallel with the global industry and sourced globally in the 1990s and early 2000s. Despite significant state interventions in the 1970s and 1980s, South Korea was still heavily dependent on the US and Japan for its components in 1995. Indonesia was chosen by global companies to locate production from 1985 onward[3] and thus also absorbed global components to assemble final products in 1995. Both Hong Kong and Singapore were chosen by MNCs as the regional headquarters.[4]

Variations among East Asian economies from the overall pattern separate the countries into seven groups. The first group—South Korea, Indonesia, Thailand, and Malaysia—showed a rise and then a fall of FVA share in the two decades (↗↘) but a continuous rise of RVA/GVA ratio (↗↗). South Korea successfully transformed from a modest economy into a high-tech export power with a very strong domestic electronics industry. Indonesia, Thailand, and Malaysia were key locations for manufacturing electronic products for

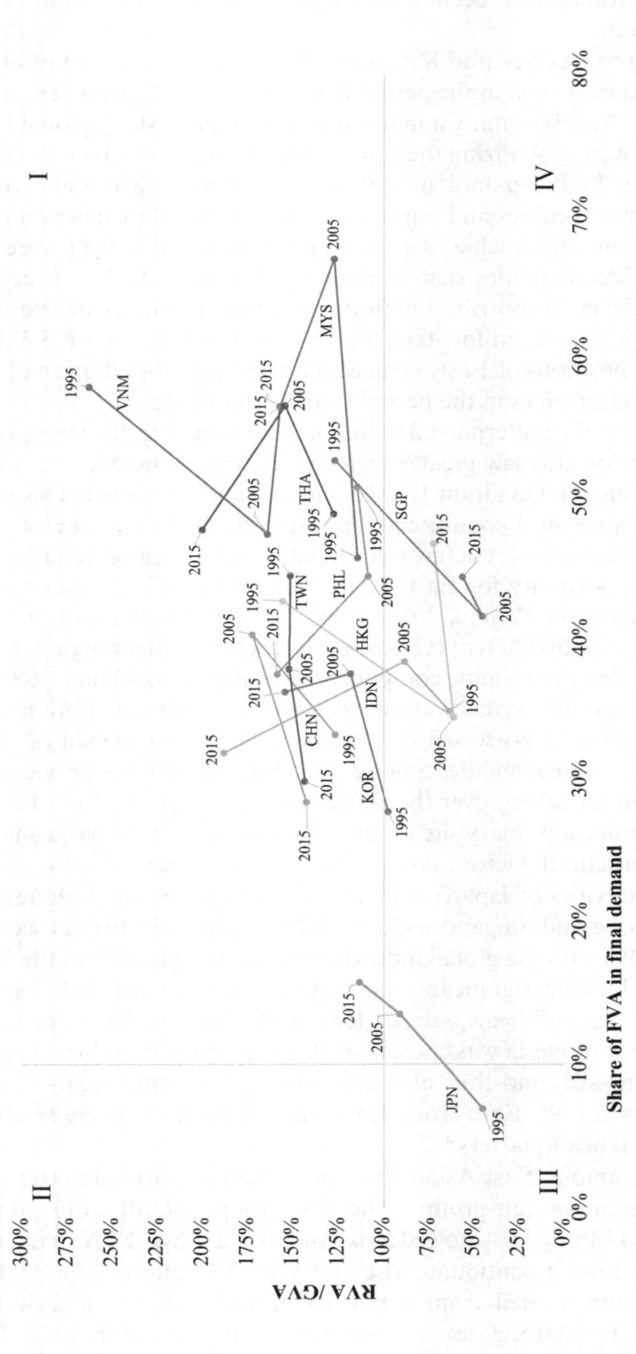

Figure 5.5 Changing Positions of East Asian Economies in the Regional Economic Structures, Electronics.

foreign firms. Particularly, these three countries attracted Japanese and South Korean investors to establish large industrial areas, which were mostly assembly operations. All four economies developed local supplier industries and upgraded their electronics industries rapidly, indicated by the falling trend of FVA share[5] from 2005 to 2015.

The second group—Hong Kong and Singapore—shows an opposite trend in FVA share (↘↗) and a switch in RVA/GVA ratio (↘↗). Neither of them had an indigenously owned and fully integrated value chain, but both secured a unique place in the global electronics industry. Singapore developed as a production platform for the hard disk drive and a business hub for coordinating supply networks in East Asia. Hong Kong, on the other hand, served as the link between the global production system and China (Dedrick & Kraemer, 1998, pp. 70–72; Yeung, 2016, pp. 92–93). The hub function contributed to their outstanding global connectivities and their increasing integration into GVCs in the second decade.

Each of the remaining five economies stood out as a different type, and the unique trend of Japan shows ↗↗ in FVA share and ↗↗ in RVA/GVA ratio, Taiwan ↘↘, →↘, the Philippines ↘↘, ↘↗, China ↗↘, ↗↘, and Vietnam ↘↗, ↘↘. The Japanese electronics sector was well-established and held a global reputation for its technological prowess in the 1990s. However, the global presence of Japanese firms was greatly diminished with the rising competition from the US firms and the rise of South Korean rivals (Sturgeon, 2007). An increase in activity by foreign companies in the Japanese market also signaled a significant increase in FVA share. As a result, Japan had a continuous increase in both FVA share and RVA/GVA ratio.

Taiwan became the leading supplier of components to the world. During the period from 1995 to 2015, Taiwan outsourced lower value-added manufacturing activities offshore. It focused on OEM systems to the global leading firms, "strategic coupling" between its own manufacturing capability and the US leading firms (Yeung, 2016). As a result, Taiwan's FVA share fell dramatically (↘↘), and its RVA/GVA ratio declined slightly (→↘).

Electronics also played an important role in the Philippine economy from the 1970s. The Philippines started with semiconductor assembly activities. Most inputs were imported, and even components purchased within the Philippines primarily came from foreign-owned firms, while domestic firms only provided assembling. In 1995, the Philippines thus demonstrated a high FVA share. However, over the entire period, the Philippines had a continuous decline in FVA share (↘↘). The fall in FVA share was largely because of the decline in imports of electronic components. First, the Philippines increased domestic purchases of electronic components. Second and most importantly, one of the largest global electronics companies (Intel) left the Philippines between 2007 and 2014. This significantly reduced the participation of the Philippines in GVCs.[6] In terms of the RVA/GVA ratio, Japanese investment and to a lesser extent Korean investment dominated in the 1990s and into the 2000s. In the 2010s, these trends became more globally oriented.

The economic influence of China rose dramatically in the late 1990s and early 2000s. China entered GVCs as a low-end supplier. Export orientation was a salient feature of China's electronics industry. However, from 2005 to 2015, China shifted its development strategy toward self-dependent innovation and moved up in the value chains.[7] The growth in technologies, manufacturing capabilities, and infrastructure made China a global player in the electronics industry. China's FVA share moved in the trend (↗↘). In terms of RVA/GVA share, China's electronics sector demonstrated the same trend (↗↘). In the first decade, China's electronics industry was dominated by Taiwanese firms with processing and manufacturing links. In the second decade, the global electronics industry accelerated its outsourcing to China. The position of China's electronics changed from a regional hub to an important global processing and manufacturing base.

As China moved up in the value chain, Vietnam took its place and emerged as an important electronics assembler and exporter. This shows in its FVA share trend (↘↗). In terms of RVA/GVA ratios, before 1995, Vietnam attracted substantial investments mainly from regional multinational giants such as Samsung and Mitsubishi. In the period after 1995, Vietnam became increasingly attractive to Western leading firms (such as Jabil, Compa, and Nokia/Microsoft). The RVA/GVA ratio of Vietnam fell significantly (↘↘) in this period.

Overall, electronics is one of the world's most globalized industries, with electronics MNCs having established offshore production plants and activities in East Asia. What emerged in the two decades was a transnational production system stretching throughout East Asia. The electronics sectors in Japan, the NIEs, the ASEAN countries, and China grew and expanded under differing conditions at different periods. Each East Asian economy kept seeking a greater value-added place in the international division of labor in the industry. As a result, the positions of East Asian economies in the regional economic structure were different and dynamic.

5.2.2.3 *Automobiles*

Compared with light industries (textiles and electronics), the automobile sector is more difficult to develop because its international competitiveness is influenced by factors of scale, technology, brand name, recognition, and reputation. In particular, the scale of the economy is much more important. The automobile industry can be more successful and internationally competitive in larger economies. Figure 5.6 shows the changing positions of East Asian economies in the regional distribution of production networks in the automobile sector from 1995 to 2015.

The overall structure of transnational value-added in the automobile sector is different from that of all industries, textiles, or electronics. Accordingly, East Asian economies fell into two groups. Economies in the first group (located in Quadrants III and IV) share a high level of global interconnectedness.

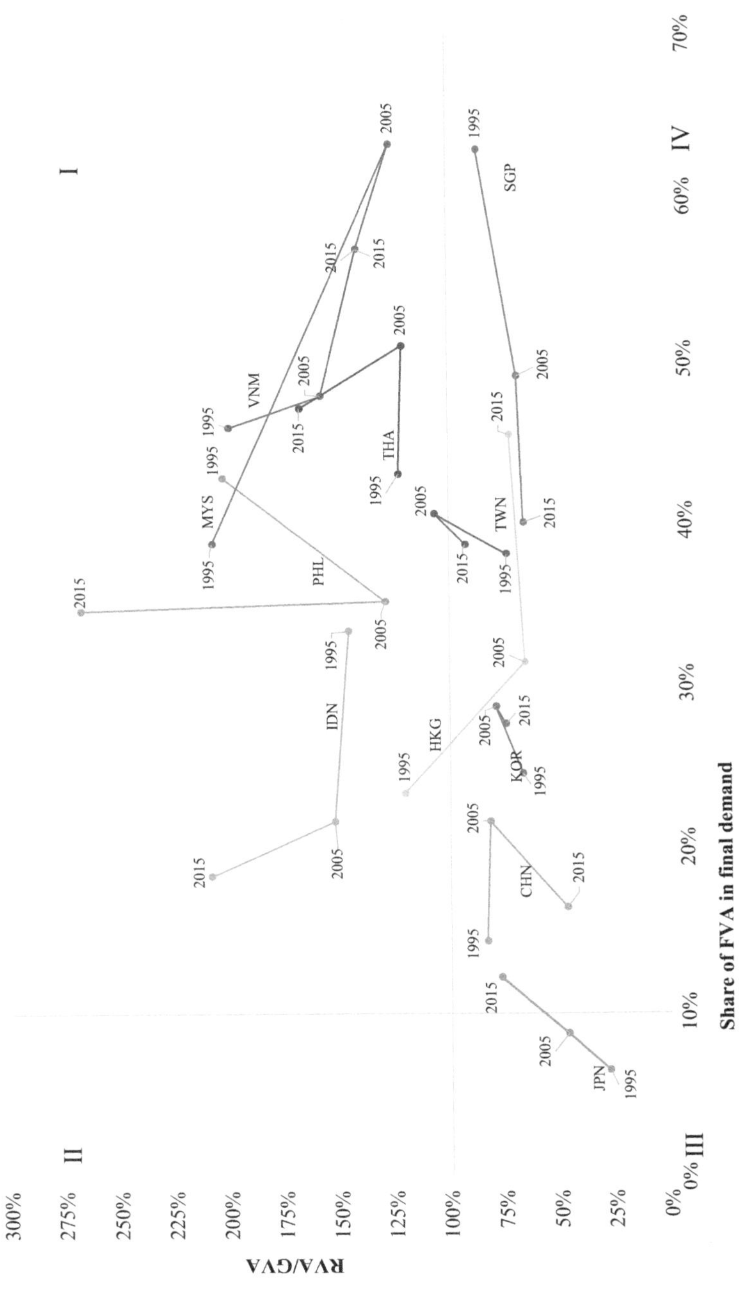

Figure 5.6 Changing Positions of East Asian Economies in the Regional Economic Structure, Automobiles.

They are Japan, China, South Korea, Hong Kong, Taiwan, and Singapore. Because of their small size, Hong Kong, Taiwan, and Singapore did not have an indigenously owned and fully integrated value chain. In the following discussions, I consider the three countries of large automobile production: Japan, China, and South Korea. The second group features greater regional orientation and are five Southeast Asian developing economies (located in Quadrants I and II): Indonesia, the Philippines, Thailand, Vietnam, and Malaysia. All these economies have automobiles as a strategic sector to help the industrialization of their national economy.[8]

Japan, China, and South Korea were the most globally oriented players in the region. Bilateral disputes in automobile trade between the US on the one hand and Japan and South Korea on the other in the 1980s and 1990s led to the establishment of large assembling facilities of Japanese and South Korean automakers in North America (Kasahara, 2019, p. 85). China's production and consumption potentials attracted global automobile companies to establish operations in the Chinese market mostly through joint ventures with Chinese counterpart companies.

In contrast, Southeast Asian economies were more regionally oriented. Two reasons contributed to this intra-regional sourcing. First, Japanese firms, and particularly Toyota, played a central role, as they have in the automobile industries of Thailand, Malaysia, Indonesia, and Vietnam (Doner, 1991; Doner & Wad, 2014). Second, with the formal implementation of the ASEAN FTA, intra-ASEAN automotive trade increased fast. Consequently, regional integration in the automotive industry rose in Southeast Asia.

In terms of change in the position in the regional structure over the period, each East Asian economy shows a unique trend in the movement of FVA share and RVA/GVA ratio: Japan (↗↗, ↗↗) China (↗↘, →↘), South Korea (↗↘, ↗↘), Indonesia (↘↘, ↗↗), Thailand (↗↘, →↗), Malaysia (↗↘, ↘↗), and Vietnam (↗↗, ↘↘). While Japan internationalized its automobiles by sourcing more components in the region, China also internationalized its automobiles in the region in the first decade, but shifted its strategy in the second decade. The change in South Korea's position was insignificant. Indonesia showed de-internationalization and also strengthened regional ties. From 1995 to 2015, Thailand[9] increased international sourcing significantly. From 2005 to 2015, Thailand saw modest growth in domestic inputs. The Malaysian automobile industry is Southeast Asia's leader in indigenous car manufacturing. Malaysia shifted its foreign sourcing from a global focus to a regional focus. The government of Vietnam treated the automobile industry as a "spearhead industry" in its attempt to upgrade industrial production and capability (Hansen, 2016, p. 551). Vietnam's automobiles saw the influence of international, especially global production forces.

5.3 Evidence for Testing Hypothesis 2

One methodological innovation in the empirical investigation and analysis in this chapter is to establish the positions of East Asian economies in the structure of the distribution of value chains in the region and the divergence and dynamic change of these positions. I used DVA/FVA ratios and RVA/GVA ratios of the national economies to determine these positions and their shift over time. The economy-sector analysis of the GVCs data offers insights into the influence of transnational production interests and capabilities of national, regional, and global origins on complexity, contentiousness, and divergence in the nations' interests and options for regional institutions in East Asia.

More specifically, our investigation and analysis established the following. First, in FVA ratios, most East Asian economies manifested an inverted-U shape from 1995 to 2015, that is, FVA ratios first rose and then fell. But the turning points varied. When entering GVCs, these economies initially attempted to specialize in final assembly and then, at later stages of development, moved to higher value-added activities within the chains over time.

Moreover, there were complexities and dynamics in the global and regional connectedness of the regional economies in East Asia. I have identified at least three distinct groups of economies that had three different types of positions in the regional economic structure. They are regional manufacturing hubs, Vietnam, open and global players, Singapore, South Korea, Taiwan, and Thailand, highly self-sufficient but globally interconnected production powers, Japan and China. East Asian economies also varied significantly from one another in the pattern of change in their position over this period.

The sectoral patterns were further more different: the textile sector saw a more globally dispersed structure with more FVA sources; the electronics sector was mainly concentrated in ASEAN+3 and therefore was more regionally oriented; and the automobile sector had a stronger orientation of domestic sourcing. Particularly, ASEAN members are found to have sourced more within the sub-region.

Determining the extent of participation of East Asian economies in the distribution of transborder value-added in East Asia established the complex and dynamic divergence in the positions of nations in East Asian regionalism and largely confirmed the theoretical expectations in Hypothesis 2. This complex and dynamic divergence not only made it hard for nations to agree on the scope and purpose of a regional economic community, but also motivated themselves to propose, engage, and bargain hard for multiple different projects for regional institutions, because of the divergent and often conflicting positions of the nations in the regional economic structure and the intergovernmental nature of these projects that require consensus and commitment of these very nations.

Notes

1 For more information about the participation of the Philippines in various value chains, please refer to a series of research reports by the Global Value Chains Center of Duke University, which are available in https://gvcc.duke.edu/cggcproject/philippines/.

2 From 1974 until the end of the Uruguay Round (1995), the textile trade was governed by the Multifiber Arrangement (MFA), which imposed quotas on the amount of clothing and textile exports from Japan, South Korea, and later other textile giants to developed countries.

3 According to Gale Raj-Reichert (2019), from 1985 onward, the government of Indonesia replaced its import substitution industrialization model with an export-oriented development model. Global electronics firms from Europe, the US, Japan, South Korea, and Singapore were attracted to relocate manufacturing operations to Indonesia. However, from the late 1990s, a new wave of FDI in the labor-intensive manufacturing operations was led by a new group of Japanese firms, which led to the increasing regionalization of the Indonesian electronics in 2005.

4 Successful globalization requires coordination of geographically dispersed activities, which has contributed to the growth of regional headquarters activities.

5 However, Indonesia showed a smaller drop in FVA share from 2005 to 2015 because it lagged behind its neighboring countries with a weaker domestic component supplier industry (Rasiah et al., 2014).

6 One report stated that in 2008, Intel's exports from the Philippines totaled US$5 billion (approximately one-third of semiconductor exports).

7 For instance, in the integrated circuit industry, since the start of the 21st century, China has made considerable progress in the independent design and development of integrated circuit chips, mastery of core technology, and possession of independent intellectual property rights (Yue & Evenett, 2010, p. 26).

8 As a study by IDE-JETRO (1995) puts it, the automobile sector occupies a significant proportion in the whole economy due to its extensive upstream and downstream linkages to a broad range of sectors.

9 Thailand, known as the "Detroit of Asia", has long been recognized as the primary manufacturer of automobiles among ASEAN countries and has gained traction in the automobile export industry (Medina, 2019).

6 Sectoral Economic Structures and Choices over CP/TPP and RCEP

In Chapters 4 and 5, I built the models of global and regional structures and developed evidence to verify Hypotheses 1 and 2 centered on the two key features of the problem in East Asian regionalism: no single region-wide institutional architecture for an East Asian economic community and multiple and competing initiatives and projects for organizing transnational production in the region. In this chapter, I explore the third feature in the problem: the bifurcation in the development of regional institutions. CP/TPP and RCEP, supported by two different groups of economies, are the latest in the alphabet soup of trade agreements involving East Asia. CP/TPP and RCEP offer two different sets of institutional arrangements for the transnational organization of production in the Asia-Pacific region. While the US-led TPP and Japan-led CP/TPP go deep into behind-the-border measures, the ASEAN-led RCEP focuses on traditional trade tariffs. These are the two mega-regional institutional arrangements that were finally agreed upon by the member states. What I intend to determine in this chapter is, as theorized in Hypothesis 3, whether a services-focused economy is more interested in CP/TPP, while a more agriculture/manufacturing-oriented economy is more likely to support RCEP. The assumption is that the CP/TPP and RCEP write two different sets of rules for transnational economic activities in the region, with the former focusing on services-dominated interests and capabilities, while the latter on agriculture/manufacturing-dominated interests and capabilities.

This exercise requires me to establish the critical differences between CP/TPP and RCEP; construct the sectoral economic structures of CP/TPP and RCEP to determine their sectoral focuses and priorities, and those of the individual East Asian economies to determine their positions in the regional economic structure; and establish the link between the sectoral economic structures and the institutional choices of the East Asian states over CP/TPP and/or RCEP.

The chapter has three sections. Section 6.1 investigates the sectoral focuses of the CP/TPP and RCEP in making trade rules, and, I hope, establishes that CP/TPP and RCEP write the different rules for transborder trade, investment, and manufacturing organization in the region. Section 6.2 uses the skyline chart method to visualize the sectoral economic structures of CP/TPP and

DOI: 10.4324/9781032613321-6

RCEP as two regional groups and uses their self-sufficiency rates (SSRs) and agriculture-manufacturing-services ratios (AMSR) for a more precise comparison of their sectoral focuses. I then use the same skyline chart method to visualize the sectoral economic structures of each East Asian economy and determine their positions in the regional sectoral structures. Section 6.3 examines the evolution of the institutional preferences of states in East Asian regionalism into their final and different decisions to join or not join CP/TPP and/or RCEP, and the role of the sectoral focus and priorities of the regional economic structures of CP/TPP and RCEP. Finally, Section 6.4 summarizes the findings as evidence against Hypothesis 3.

6.1 Sectoral Focuses and Priorities of the Trade Rules under CP/TPP and RCEP

Before I compare the rules of CP/TPP and RCEP, I discuss the differences between TPP and CP/TPP first. Most provisions of the CP/TPP are similar or identical to the original TPP. However, 22 provisions of the TPP that were once favored by the US, but generally opposed by other signatories, were suspended in the CP/TPP (US-ASEAN Business Council, n.d.). One of the main differences in the CP/TPP is the removal of certain provisions regarding intellectual property (IP). TPP adopts the highest standards in IP protection at a level similar to the protections found in domestic laws of the US. These IP protection rules are designed by the US to promote its competitiveness in the IP-dependent industries, from software and information technology, music, books, and movies to pharmaceuticals, food products, and consumer and industrial goods. These agenda-setting acts of the US are central to understanding the TPP. Though the US favored longer copyright terms, automatic patent extensions, and separate protections for new technologies, these provisions were unpopular among other signatories and ultimately removed from the CP/TPP. The CP/TPP also features modifications to the original TPP in the investment chapter, certain implementation timelines, and labor and environmental rules. These suspended provisions, however, can also be reinstated, leaving the door open for the US to join the agreement.

CP/TPP and RCEP are supported by two different groups of economies and have different blueprints for governing future trade and investment in the Asia-Pacific region. CP/TPP is led by developed economies such as Japan, Singapore, Australia, and New Zealand. RCEP is advocated by ASEAN-developing economies and China. Both agreements use the regional platform as a basis for negotiating future WTO rules (Horn et al., 2010). Table 6.1 summarizes the major differences. As shown, CP/TPP and RCEP address a wide range of issues from traditional market access issues (such as trade in goods) to the behind-the-border measures (such as investment and IPR) albeit with varying degrees of ambition and substance. I review the provisions of these two mega-regional FTAs and compare the differences in their rules.

The major issues listed in the first seven rows of Table 6.1—tariff elimination; national treatment and market access; ROOs; customs administration

Table 6.1 Provisions of the CP/TPP and RCEP Agreements

Major issues	*CP/TPP content*	*RCEP differences*
Estimated tariff elimination	95%	80%–90%
National treatment and market access	Application of national and MFN treatment, transparent tariffs	
ROOs	Yarn-forward requirements for textile products	No yarn-forward requirements for textile products
Customs administration and trade facilitation	Enhanced customs cooperation, trade facilitation, express shipment, administration of customs penalties	
Trade remedies	Rules for safeguards, temporary protection, antidumping, and countervailing duties	
Sanitary and phytosanitary measures	Rules for sanitary and phytosanitary measures, equivalence recognition, science and risk analysis, audits, certification, and transparency	
Technical barriers to trade	Enhanced cooperation on standards for technical regulations, conformity assessment	
Investment	National treatment, MFN treatment, compensation for expropriation, rules for financial transfers, bar performance requirements, investor-state dispute settlement (ISDS) with improved safeguards for public welfare regulations; phase-out of equity limits in some countries	Instead of negative lists, also permits positive lists for exceptions; ISDS provisions will not be activated unless members decide to do so three years after the agreement is signed
Trade in services	Disciplines on market restrictions, local presence requirements, regulations, criteria for service providers; special provisions for financial services for offering new products and restricting regulations, for educational services in enhancing offerings, and for telecommunications services on interconnection, roaming	Instead of negative lists also permits positive lists for exceptions
Temporary entry for businesspersons	Disciplines on regulating the temporary entry of businesspersons	
Electronic commerce	Prohibition of customs duties on electronic transmissions, discriminatory treatment of digital products; legal framework for e-commerce; limited restrictions on cross-border transmission of data and location of computing facilities	No coverage of cross-border data flows and data localization requirements; no moratorium on customs duties on electronic transmissions

(*Continued*)

Table 6.1 (Continued)

Major issues	*CP/TPP content*	*RCEP differences*
Government procurement	National treatment and nondiscrimination, governance of procurement, expanded range of organizations covered	A new area of cooperation that is not in any existing ASEAN agreements
Competition and regulatory policy	Assurance of fairness in competition law, private right of action; enhanced regulatory coherence, transparency, anticorruption measures	
IP	Commitments to ratify international agreements on IP; suspension of US-promoted provisions for expanded IP protections under TPP	Add new digital copyright rules such as genetic resources, traditional knowledge, and folklore
SOEs	Limits on noncommercial assistance to SOEs	Not covered
Labor	Commitments to implement laws and regulations supporting ILO Declaration on Labor Rights; institutions for review and a Labor Council for monitoring	Not covered
Environment	Recognition of multilateral environmental agreements; provisions on ship pollution, biodiversity, invasive species, marine fisheries, conservation	Not covered

Source: Petri and Plummer (2020, pp. 7–9), MFAT of New Zealand (2021), and Whiting (2021).

and trade facilitation; trade remedies; sanitary and phytosanitary measures; technical trade barriers—address barriers to trade in goods. There are two significant differences between CP/TPP and RCEP regarding rules for trade in goods. On tariff elimination, CP/TPP reduces tariffs to zero on an estimated 95% of tariff lines. By contrast, the tariff concessions in RCEP exclude several products considered sensitive, particularly in the agricultural sectors, and cover 80%–90% of the products, and even for these goods tariffs will not be fully eliminated in the transition period. Nevertheless, RCEP is regarded as "a value chain accelerator" because a single "Made in RCEP" origin certificate allows products to move across borders more efficiently and lower compliance costs for business (Wilson, 2020).

With regard to the rules of origins (ROOs), the rules are incredibly complex for textile products. CP/TPP has yarn-forward ROOs, which require that only fabric produced from yarn would quantify for the trade agreement's duty-free status. RCEP is not yarn-forward.

More significantly, CP/TPP attempts to establish rules domestically and verseas consistent to grant greater access to investment and services in CP/TPP markets and secure a level playing field for investors and service providers. For example, the investment and services chapters adopt an approach of "negative list", which requires that countries allow full access to their markets, except in sectors listed. RCEP members use a mix of positive and negative lists for managing inflow services and investment. While countries with dual membership in RCEP and CP/TPP choose to use negative lists, the RCEP-only members opt to schedule services using a positive list approach. Only those services and investment sectors listed in the schedules of commitments are opened for RCEP participation.

Moreover, CP/TPP is an ambitious agreement in addressing new issues such as e-commerce, government procurement, competition, IPR, SOEs, labor, and environment. By contrast, RCEP-only includes chapters on e-commerce,[1] government procurement, competition, and IPR, and the commitments are less extensive or in-depth than those in the CP/TPP.

Specifically, under the framework of CP/TPP, the e-commerce chapter covers a range of issues including customs duties, data localization, electronic authentication, and electronics signature, and so on. It is worth noting that data localization rules, requiring foreign companies to store data within a member's borders, are prohibited under CP/TPP (except for security and confidentiality of communication). This provision expresses the interests of digital service providers (predominantly based in developed economies), which no longer have to establish costly servers in CP/TPP markets (APEC, 2017). Under the framework of RCEP, the provisions on e-commerce do not provide a moratorium on customs duties on electronic transmissions nor cover cross-border data flows and data localization requirements.

Regarding government procurement, CP/TPP's commitments addressing barriers in government procurement (such as national treatment and nondiscrimination) allow companies of CP/TPP countries to have more opportunities to bid for government projects that were previously unavailable to foreign bidders. By contrast, RCEP's government procurement chapter[2] sends signals of support for deeper regional economic cooperation but lacks substantive content due to the cautious positions of developing economies.

The competition chapter of CP/TPP helps ensure fairness in competition by enhancing regulatory coherence, transparency, anticorruption measures. RCEP also includes a competition chapter, which contains obligations requiring RCEP parties to maintain competition laws and regulations to a limited extent.

Although CP/TPP suspends the US-promoted provisions for expanded IP protections under TPP, the IP chapter of CP/TPP still reflects a shared commitment to streamline IP transactions. The IP chapter benefits the developed member countries most who have the most IP resources and endeavor (such as trademark, copyrights, pharmaceutical patents, industrial designs, and business secrets). RCEP members represent a diverse mix of developed, developing, and least-developed economies with significant variations in IP resources. RCEP's IP chapter goes beyond the protection of industrial and commercial resources (included in the CP/TPP) and adds new digital copyright rules such as genetic resources, traditional knowledge, and folklore. These new digital copyright rules resolve the key concerns of developing and least-developed economies that have an abundance of genetic resources and traditional knowledge but lack industrial and commercial resources.

Another major difference between CP/TPP and RCEP is that the CP/TPP contains major commitments on SOEs, labor, and environment, which are not addressed in RCEP. The SOEs chapter of CP/TPP sets limits on noncommercial assistance to SOEs. The labor chapter undertakes commitments to implement laws and regulations supporting International Labor Organization Declaration on Labor Rights and establishes institutions for review and a Labor Council for monitoring. The environment chapter recognizes multilateral environmental agreements and includes provisions on ship pollution, biodiversity, invasive species, marine fisheries, and conservation. By contrast, RCEP does not involve such rules. As Whiting (2021) explains, some developing economies see their comparative advantage in the government-sponsored technological catch-up strategy (in the form of SOEs), different labor standards, and different environmental provisions.

To summarize, the ambitions and high standards in the TPP and CP/TPP agreement largely reflect the interests of developed countries in trade negotiations. The modest and tariff-focused commitments in the RCEP agreement are a response from developing economies. RCEP provides a single rulebook covering 15 economies (after the withdrawal of India). Significantly, it offers cumulative and favorable ROOs for manufacturers participating in regional value chains.

6.2 Sectoral Economic Structures of CP/TPP, RCEP, and East Asian Economies

This section virtually describes and compares the sectoral focuses of CP/TPP and RCEP and those of the East Asian economies. Existing discussions about TPP overwhelmingly focused on its strategic significance as part of the larger US engagement with East Asia. However, the withdrawal of the US did not lead to the derailment of TPP, as many expected. Instead, Japan took the lead updating TPP into CP/TPP with very minor modifications. RCEP, on the other hand, was framed as a strategic response by China to US engagement. But the enthusiasm of the business community toward the conclusion of RCEP also indicated that the deal is of economic significance. This section analyzes the sectoral economic structures of CP/TPP and RCEP to determine their different sectoral focuses and those of the individual East Asian economies to determine their different positions in the regional economic structures.

Specifically, I use skyline chart methods to virtually describe the sectoral economic structures and compare their unique structural characters. There are two primary indicators to the structures presented in the skyline charts: SSRs and the AMSR. The flatness of the self-sufficiency line (the red line, as indicated in Figure 6.1) measures the self-sufficiency level of an economy. According to Leontief (1963), a mature and self-sufficient economy tends to have a flat self-sufficiency line above the 100% horizon. The shares of agriculture, manufacturing, and services represent the industrial structure of an economy, indicating the level of economic development. The Law of Petty Clark states that with the increase in national income per capita, the main focus of the economy shifts from agriculture to manufacturing, and then from manufacturing to services (Clark, 1951).

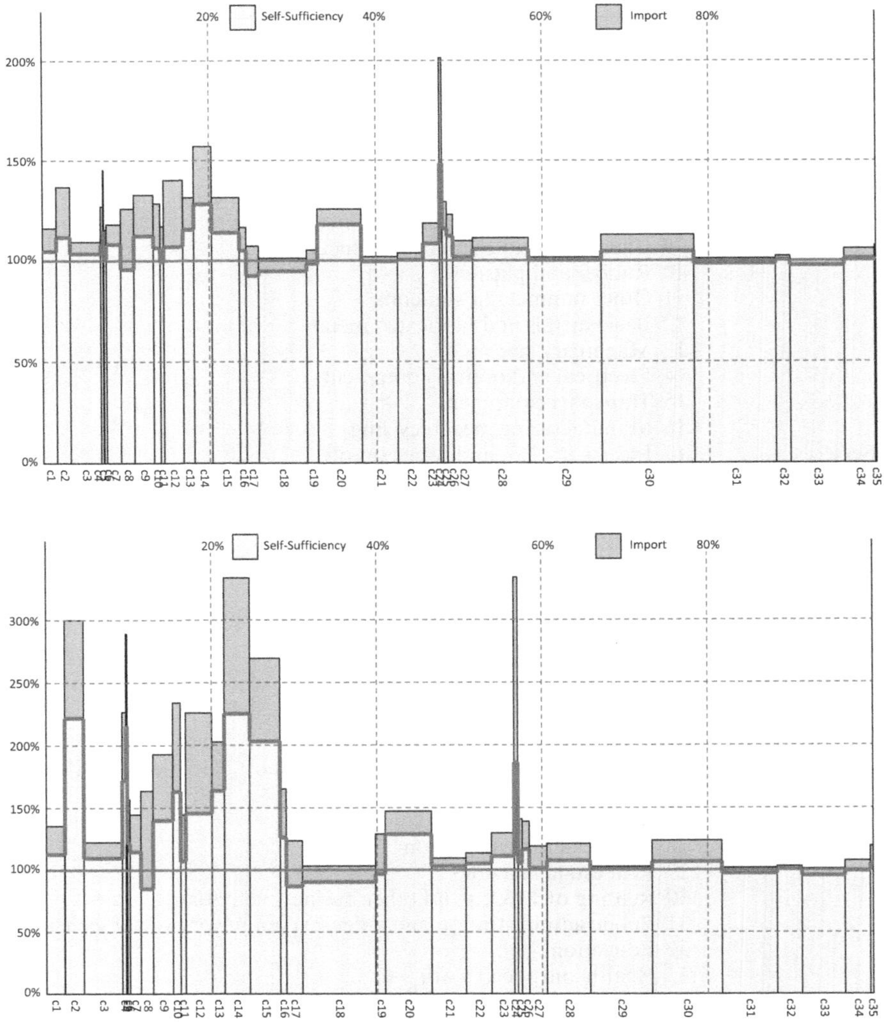

Figure 6.1 Skyline Charts of TPP and CP/TPP, 2015.

6.2.1 Sectoral Economic Structures of CP/TPP and RCEP

I use the ADB-MRIO tables data to produce the skyline charts of CP/TPP and RCEP. Table 6.2 below organizes 35 industries in the ADB-MRIO tables into three sectors: agriculture (industry 1–2), manufacturing (industry 5–18), and services (19–35).

Figure 6.1 shows the skyline charts of TPP and CP/TPP. There are two major findings. First, the self-sufficiency line in the skyline chart of TPP is

Table 6.2 ADB's Categorization of Industries into Agriculture, Manufacturing, and Services

Agriculture and mining	1	Agriculture, hunting, forestry, and fishing
	2	Mining and quarrying
Manufacturing	3	Food, beverages, and tobacco
	4	Textiles and textile products
	5	Leather, leather products, and footwear
	6	Wood and products of wood and cork
	7	Pulp, paper, paper products, printing, and publishing
	8	Coke, refined petroleum, and nuclear fuel
	9	Chemicals and chemical products
	10	Rubber and plastics
	11	Other nonmetallic minerals
	12	Basic metals and fabricated metal
	13	Machinery, nec
	14	Electrical and optical equipment
	15	Transport equipment
	16	Manufacturing, nec; recycling
Services	17	Electricity, gas, and water supply
	18	Construction
	19	Sale, maintenance, and repair of motor vehicles and motorcycles; retail sale of fuel
	20	Wholesale trade and commission trade, except motor vehicles and motorcycles
	21	Retail trade, except motor vehicles and motorcycles; repair of household goods
	22	Hotels and restaurants
	23	Inland transport
	24	Water transport
	25	Air transport
	26	Other supporting and auxiliary transport activities; activities of travel agencies
	27	Post and telecommunications
	28	Financial intermediation
	29	Real estate activities
	30	Renting of M&Eq and other business activities
	31	Public administration and defense; compulsory social security
	32	Education
	33	Health and social work
	34	Other community, social, and personal services
	35	Private households with employed persons

Source: ADB-MRIO Tables.

flatter than CP/TPP, representing different levels of self-sufficiency under the two regional frameworks. Second, both TPP and CP/TPP have a services-oriented sectoral economic structure.

First, in terms of self-sufficiency, the skyline of TPP is much flatter than that of CP/TPP, showing very little over- or underproduction of the regional economy. The TPP chart features few humps (125%–150%) over C14 (electrical and optical equipment), C20 (wholesale trade and commission trade), and C25 (air transport). By contrast, the CP/TPP chart is particularly noticeable for the highly overshooting production surpluses with humps over a variety of sectors. It shows remarkably large humps (≥200%) in C2 (mining and quarrying), C5 (leather, leather products, and footwear), C14 (electrical and optical equipment), and C15 (transport equipment). Besides, it reveals humps (≥150%) in C4 (textiles and textile products), C10 (rubber and plastics), C13 (machinery), and C24 (water transport). Both TPP and CP/TPP skyline charts stay high above the self-sufficient benchmark for the whole range of industries. This suggests that these two regional groups possess great productional capabilities, which not only satisfy their regional demand but also export products and services around the world. Second, in terms of industrial structure, TPP has a complete industrial profile where the services make up around 75% of the total output. The CP/TPP chart exhibits a similar pattern to that of TPP in that the output share of the service sector is remarkably large.

Comparing the charts of CP/TPP and TPP with RCEP (Figure 6.2), the difference is apparent both in SSR and AMSR.

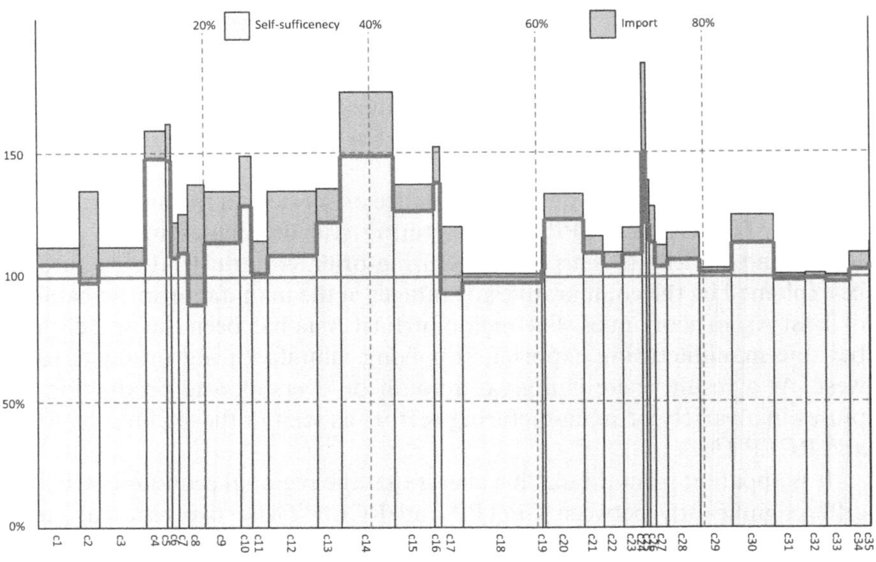

Figure 6.2 Skyline Charts of RCEP and RCEP 15, 2015.

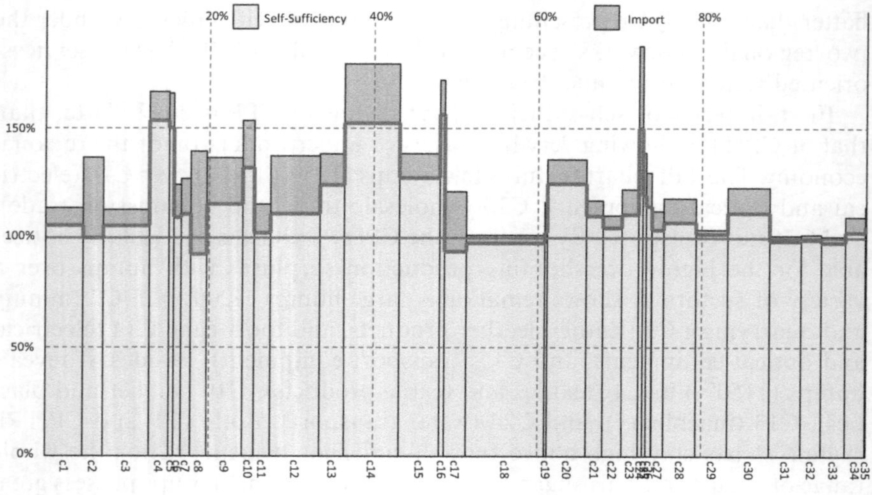

Figure 6.2 Continued

First, the skyline charts of both RCEP and RCEP 15 without India are not flat, with prominent skyscrapers in the manufacturing sectors such as C4 (textiles and textile products), C5 (leather, leather products, and footwear), C10 (rubber and plastics), C14 (electrical and optical equipment), C15 (transport equipment), and C16 (manufacturing; recycling). This overproduction in manufacturing reveals the role of Factory Asia in the world economy: a network of low-cost production bases that produce parts and components for consumer goods export. Since the late 1980s, abundant and cheap labor combined with export-driven, investment-friendly government policies has attracted multinational companies in advanced economies to set up manufacturing and export platforms in the region. East Asia has come to be viewed as Factory Asia.

Second, in contrast to the predominance of services in the industrial structures of TPP and CP/TPP, manufacturing still dominates in the cases of RCEP and RCEP 15. This manufacturing-oriented industrial structure can be explained by the comparative advantages in the manufacturing capabilities of East Asian economies. The region of East Asia has been the world's number one manufacturing exporter, supplying manufacturing products to the west. As a result, there is a great amount of overshooting production surpluses in a variety of manufacturing sectors as seen in the skylines of RCEP and RCEP 15.

It is apparent from the skyline charts that the regional economic structures differ significantly between CP/TPP and RCEP. These two regional groups including East Asian economies in different development stages and as a result, the coherence of the regional economic structures varies. The ranking of self-sufficiency levels is as follows: TPP, CP/TPP, RCEP, RCEP 15. In terms of AMSRs, the regional economy of CP/TPP is services-oriented, while the industrial structure of RCEP has the predominance of manufacturing.

The differences in sectoral economic structures largely determine what kind of rules are adopted by these regional groups. For example, CP/TPP focuses more on services targeted rules, particularly in research and development or business services. CP/TPP rules set high standards in trade in services, investment, and behind-the-border issues to enhance comparative advantages of services-dominated economies. In contrast, RCEP represents the core interests of developing economies and incentivizes manufacturing sectors to locate as much of their supply chains as possible within the regional bloc with the rules designed in its framework.

6.2.2 The Positions of East Asian Economies in the Sectoral Economic Structures

Now that I have established the sectoral economic structures of the CP/TPP and RCEP, I proceed in this section to establish the positions of East Asian economies in these structures. I do so by building the sectoral economic structures of individual East Asian economies, analyze their sectoral focuses, and connect them to those of the regional economic structures. It is worth noting that I use the OECD National Input-Output Tables, rather than the ADB-MRIO tables for data availability reasons. The categorization of industries under OECD is different from ADB. Table 6.3 shows the OECD way of industry categorization: agriculture and mining (C1-4), manufacturing (C5-20), and services (C21-36).

Using the OECD National Input-Output Tables data, I construct the sectoral economic structure of each East Asian economy in a skyline chart: China, Japan, South Korea, Singapore, Malaysia, Thailand, Indonesia, Philippines, and Vietnam. I discuss these structures in two groups for a clear discussion of how the sectoral focuses emerged to be the primary connecting basis for their nations to group into CP/TPP and RCEP from their perceived attempts for sub-regional grouping in Northeast Asia and Southeast Asia.

I first compare the sectoral economic structures of the three economies in Northeast Asia, China, Japan, and South Korea (see Figures 6.3, 6.4, and 6.5).

The sectoral economic structures of China and Japan were unparalleled in East Asia with complete industrial profiles in manufacturing and services. Their skyline charts share some similarities as well as apparent differences. Both China and Japan had underproduction in agriculture, huge overproduction capacity (much more than self-sufficiency) in manufacturing, and very little over- or underproduction in services. However, China was more dependent on manufacturing, and the share of services was much less than that of Japan. Moreover, the primary manufacturing sectors were different: China's

Table 6.3 OECD's Categorization of Industries into Agriculture, Manufacturing, and Services

Agriculture and mining	1	Agriculture, forestry, and fishing
	2	Mining and extraction of energy-producing products
	3	Mining and quarrying of non-energy-producing products
	4	Mining support service activities
Manufacturing	5	Food products, beverages, and tobacco
	6	Textiles, wearing apparel, leather, and related products
	7	Wood and products of wood and cork
	8	Paper products and printing
	9	Coke and refined petroleum products
	10	Chemicals and pharmaceutical products
	11	Rubber and plastic products
	12	Other nonmetallic mineral products
	13	Basic metals
	14	Fabricated metal products
	15	Computer, electronic, and optical products
	16	Electrical equipment
	17	Machinery and equipment, n.e.c.
	18	Motor vehicles, trailers, and semi-trailers
	19	Other transport equipment
	20	Other manufacturing; repair and installation of machinery and equipment
Services	21	Electricity, gas, water supply, sewerage, waste, and remediation services
	22	Construction
	23	Wholesale and retail trade; repair of motor vehicles
	24	Transportation and storage
	25	Accommodation and food services
	26	Publishing, audiovisual, and broadcasting activities
	27	Telecommunications
	28	IT and other information services
	29	Financial and insurance activities
	30	Real estate activities
	31	Other business sector services
	32	Public admin. and defense; compulsory social security
	33	Education
	34	Human health and social work
	35	Arts, entertainment, recreation, and other service activities
	36	Private households with employed persons

Source: OECD Inter-Country Input-Output (ICIO) Tables.

chart has two great "humps" in textile (C6) and electronics (C15), while Japan's chart has a prominent tower in automobiles (C18). There were great complementarities in the international division of labor between the biggest two economies in the region.

Substantially different from those of China and Japan, the sectoral economic structure of South Korea saw a much higher level of export orientation with its SSR in some manufacturing sectors over 250%. Much smaller in economic size,

South Korea appeared to be an open trading nation in the region. Regarding the AMSR, South Korea stood between China and Japan. South Korea had a very small portion of agriculture and a large part of manufacturing industries (chemicals, electronics, and automobiles) and services (wholesale and retail trade, transportation, and financial and insurance activities).

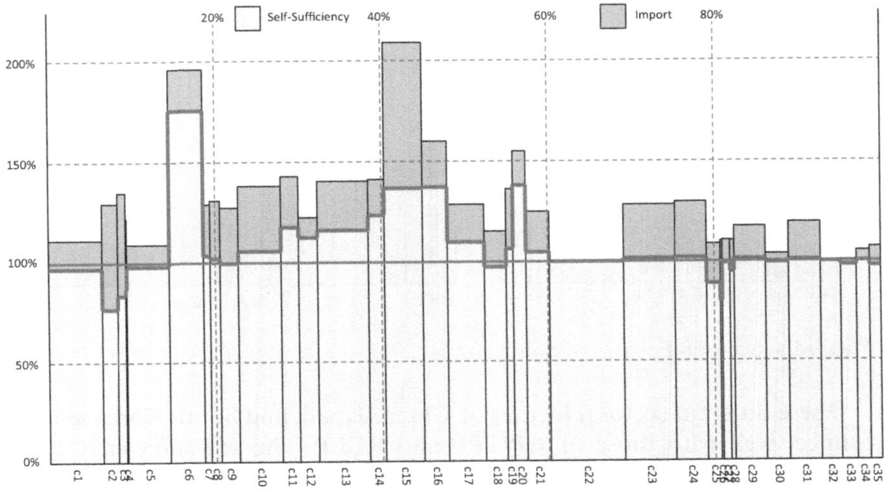

Figure 6.3 Sectoral Focuses of China, 2015.

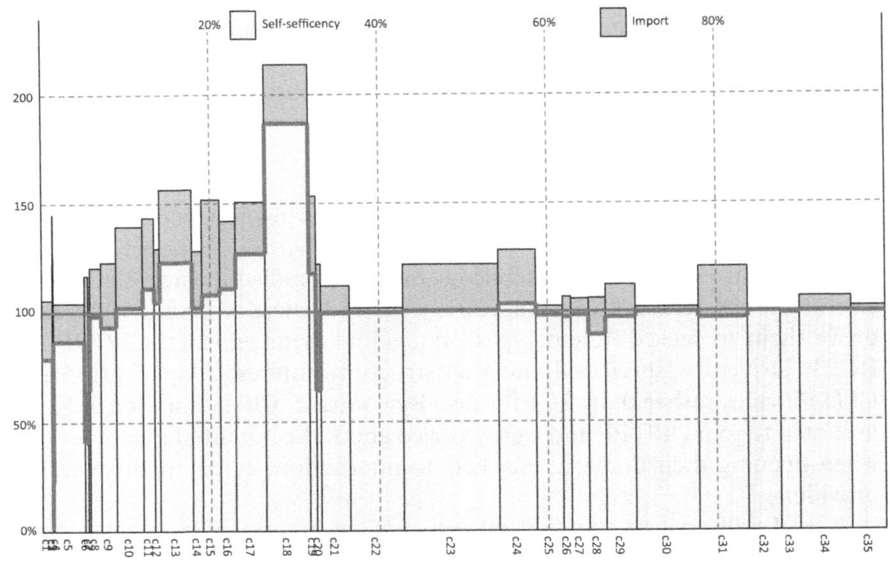

Figure 6.4 Sectoral Focuses of Japan, 2015.

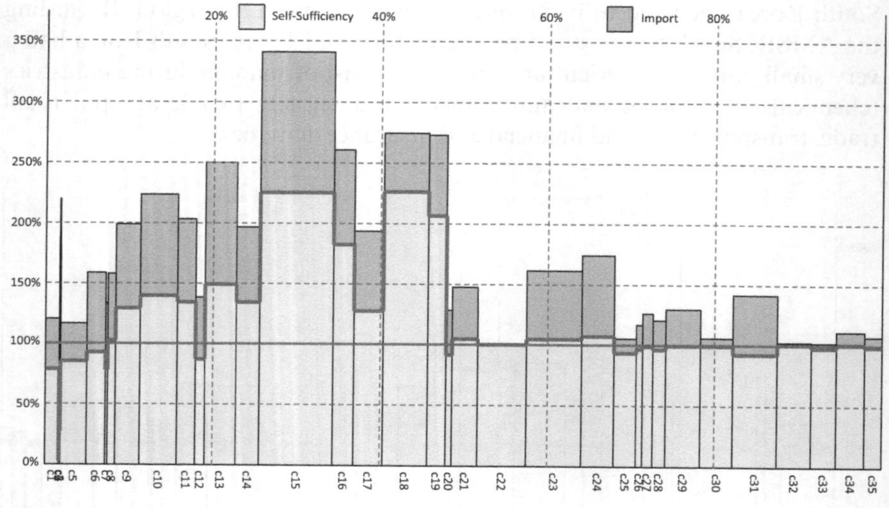

Figure 6.5 Sectoral Focuses of South Korea, 2015.

These different sectoral focuses of China, Japan, and South Korea seem to connect well with those of CP/TPP and RCEP. The self-sufficiency levels influenced their attitude toward international trade agreements. South Korea, as a small trading nation, invested more time and energy in international trade negotiations than Japan and China and became an FTA hub in Northeast Asia. The sectoral focuses in AMSR match to a great extent with those of the CP/TPP and RCEP. Japan wanted beneficial arrangements more from the investment and the services sector than from trade in goods and hoped to build a high-standard FTA beyond substantial tariff reduction, including liberalization of services, IP rights, environment, and labor policy. However, China's sectoral economic structure was mainly manufacturing-oriented and thus preferred a tariff-focused FTA. The conflict between China's unwillingness to entirely open its services market and Japan's high expectations for a CJK FTA, together with South Korea's concern over competition from Japanese manufacturing companies stalled the negotiation process of the trilateral FTA (Zhang, 2019). Instead, these structural differences drove them to seek different types of regional arrangements: CP/TPP and RCEP. Driven by services-dominated structural interests, Japan prioritized CP/TPP rules rather than RCEP rules. By contrast, China and South Korea hesitated to join CP/TPP and were worried about the potential loss in services when opening their domestic markets to internationally competitive service providers.

Now I will analyze the sectoral economic structures of Southeast Asian economies in an order of the levels of economic development. Among the Southeast Asian nations, only Singapore (Figure 6.6) reached an advanced level

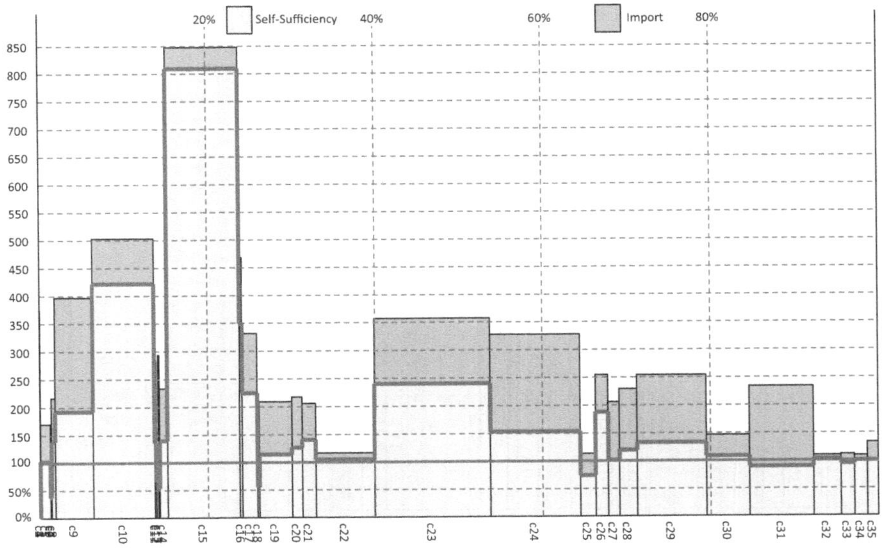

Figure 6.6 Sectoral Focuses of Singapore, 2015.

of industrialization. Malaysia (Figure 6.7), Thailand (Figure 6.8), Indonesia (Figure 6.9), and the Philippines (Figure 6.10) had significant economic development with export-oriented industrialization. Vietnam did not integrate with the global economy until its economic and political reforms launched in 1986, and it became a rapid-growing economy in the latest wave of industrial development more recently (Figure 6.11).

The skyline charts of Southeast Asian economies show a great variety of sectoral economic structures. Singapore was outstanding for its squeezed agriculture sector (C1-4) and manufacturing (C5-20) on the left half of the chart but the predominance of the services sector (C21-35). Singapore had a large composition ratio of C23 (wholesale and retail trade; repair of motor vehicles), C24 (transportation and storage), and C29 (financial and insurance activities). These show Singapore's sectoral focuses and priorities in logistics and financial services.

Malaysia, Thailand, Indonesia, the Philippines, and Vietnam are referred to as Tiger Cub Economies because they are the newly industrialized economies, following a similar export-driven model of economic development. I discuss and compare the sectoral focuses of these five economies in Figure 6.7, Figure 6.8, Figure 6.9, Figure 6.10, and Figure 6.11.

The skyline charts of these five economies share two significant similarities. First, all these five economies had marked ups and downs. All five economies had remarkable overproduction (200%–600%) in several manufacturing sectors (indicated by skyscrapers) and significant underproduction in other sectors

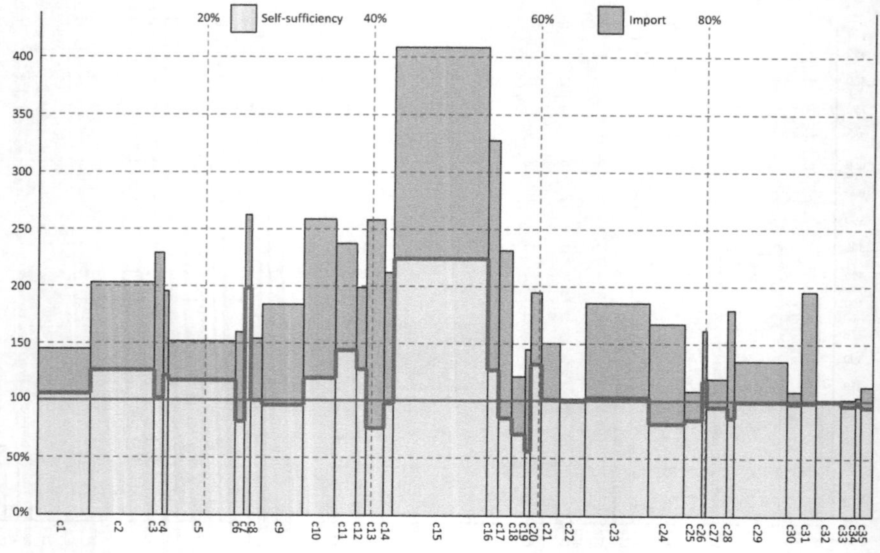

Figure 6.7 Sectoral Focuses of Malaysia, 2015.

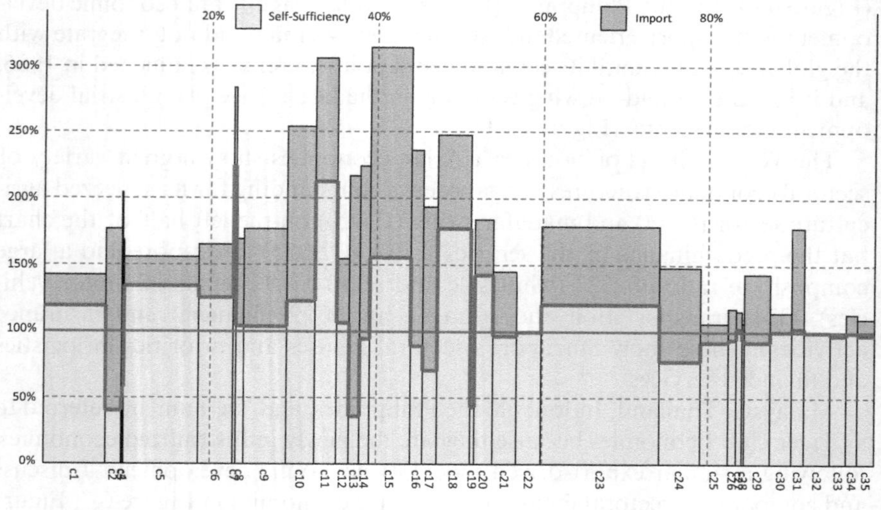

Figure 6.8 Sectoral Focuses of Thailand, 2015.

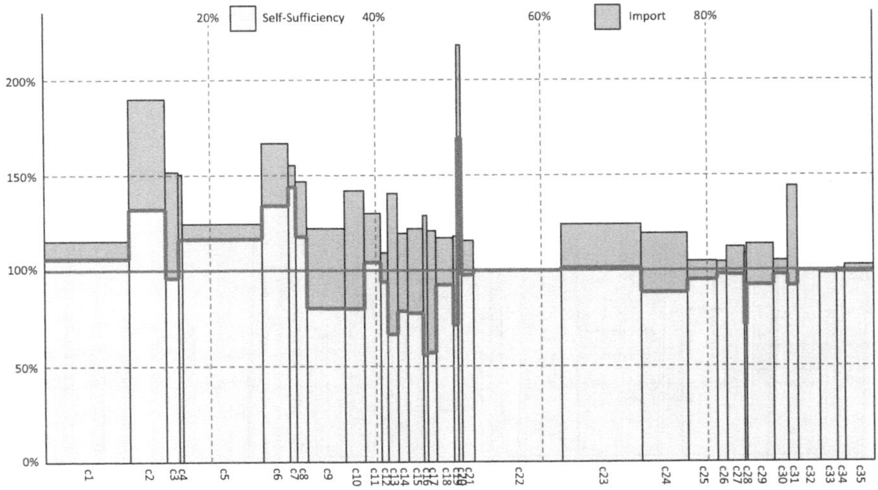

Figure 6.9 Sectoral Focuses of Indonesia, 2015.

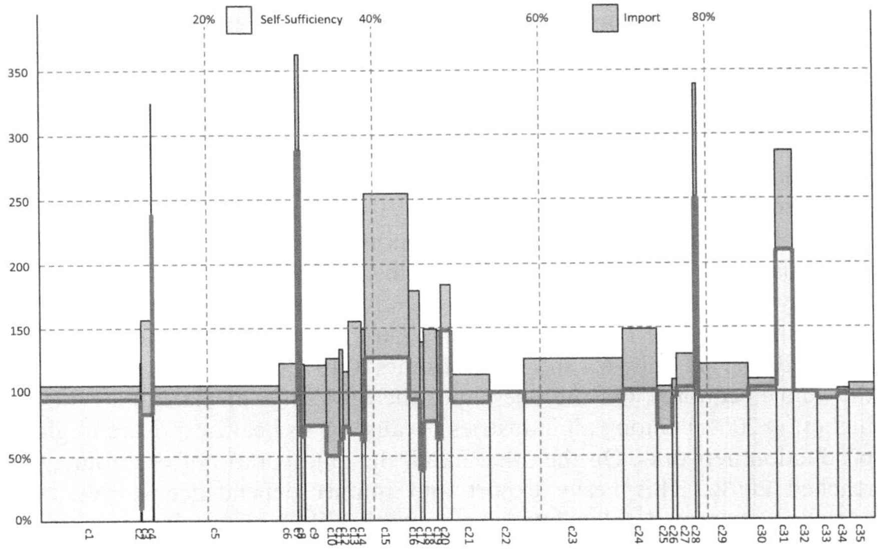

Figure 6.10 Sectoral Focuses of the Philippines, 2015.

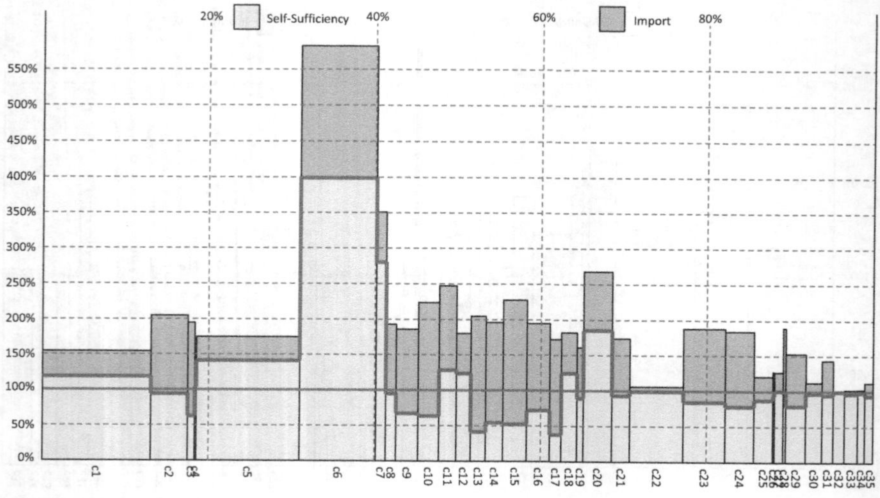

Figure 6.11 Sectoral Focuses of Vietnam, 2015.

(indicated by slumps). These skyscrapers and slumps are closely related to their export-driven development model. These small economies specialized in and built internationally competitive production capacities in key manufacturing sectors but became heavily dependent on international supplies in other sectors. Second, the sectoral structures of all these five economies were dominated by manufacturing, rather than agriculture or services. Regional production networks in manufacturing sectors provided an environment conducive to rapid industrial growth and transformation of the predominantly agricultural economies into modern industrial economies.

Despite these two similarities, each economy was unique in sectoral focuses. Malaysia had a diversified sectoral economic structure. Malaysia evolved successfully from one that was initially agriculture and resources-based (oil, gas, and palm oil) in the 1990s to one with robust manufacturing and service sectors in 2015. As Figure 6.7 shows, electronics (C15) occupied a large portion of the whole economy. On the one hand, the SSR ratio of electronics was the highest (>200%) among all industries because of its heavy exposure to global production networks. On the other hand, the import ratio of electronics also reached 200%. This heavy export and import dependence suggests that Malaysia performed well in integrating into the GVCs of the electronics industry but was mainly in low-value-added production (Raj-Reichert, 2020). In other words, Malaysia failed to develop a broad and multitier base of support industries, which gave rise to "an inverted production pyramid—a huge and rapidly growing final product sector that rests on a weak and much smaller domestic base of support industries" (Ernst, 2002, p. 40).

In contrast to the predominance of one single manufacturing sector in Malaysia, Thailand saw marked overproduction in a variety of industries: C10 (chemicals), C11 (rubber and plastic products), C15 (electronics), and C18 (motor vehicles, trailers, and semi-trailers). Moreover, benefited from its successful tourism, Thailand also developed a huge service economy. As shown in Figure 6.8, C23 (wholesale and retail trade) occupied a great portion of the whole economy of Thailand.

Indonesia was the largest but only less globalized and less competitive economy of ASEAN. On the one hand, Indonesia has been blessed with great and commercializable natural resources. Its economic structure is heavily dependent on the exports of oil and gas. According to Vanzetti, McGuire, and Prabowo (2005), trade reform in Indonesia tended to be closely tied to the price of oil. During the period of high oil prices, protection increased. At times of low oil prices, major trade liberalization reforms were implemented when the government realized the urgency to diversify its export base.[3] On the other hand, Indonesia lost its competitive edge in the manufacturing sectors, unlike its East Asian neighbors. As Figure 6.9 shows, Indonesia's production capacity in most of the manufacturing industries was not self-sufficient. This is in marked contrast to the situation in its East Asian neighbors. Low levels of labor productivity undermined Indonesia's cost advantage, and countries such as Malaysia and Thailand outperformed despite their higher wages.

Compared with its neighbors, the performance of the Philippines in manufacturing capacity was weak. As illustrated in Figure 6.10, it recorded only mild overproduction (around 250%) in its most productive C15 (electronics). This was in stark contrast to the overwhelming manufacturing capacities of Malaysia, Thailand, Indonesia, and Vietnam. Besides, the Philippines developed a large portion of services (such as IT, financial services, and other business sector services) without having the structural transformation of the economy from agriculture to manufacturing.

The sectoral focuses of Vietnam had an unparalleled high level of specialization in textiles. Its SSR was over 550%. Vietnam's textile industry developed strongly and played an essential role in the growth of the national economy.

The diversity in the sectoral focuses and priorities of Southeast Asian economies was not only the obstacle to the building of an ASEAN economic community but also put each of them in a different position in the regional economic structures of the CP/TPP and RCEP.

6.3 Shaping of the Institutional Choices of East Asian States over CP/TPP and/or RCEP

In the previous section, I have established the difference in the sectoral focuses of the regional economic structures of CP/TPP and RCEP and the diversity in the positions of East Asian national economies in these regional economic structures. In this section, I discuss in detail how these sectoral forces shape the choices of these states to join CP/TPP and/or RCEP as regional institutional arrangements for transborder trade, investment, and production organization.

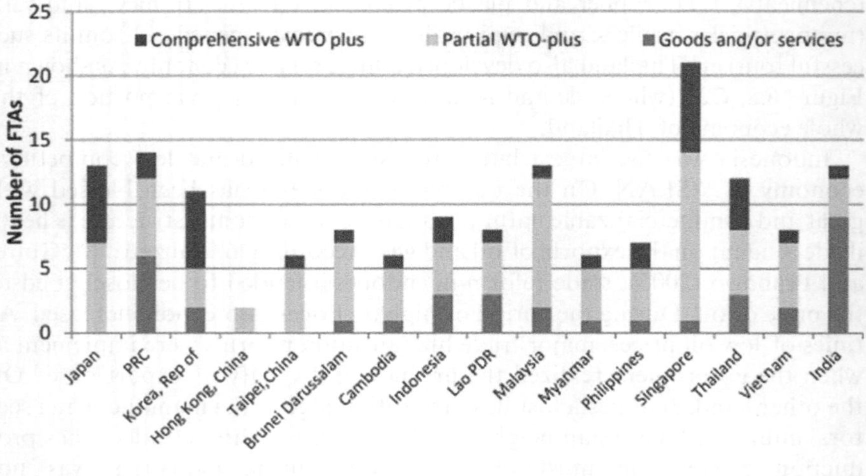

Figure 6.12 The Depth of Free Trade Agreements in East Asia.

Graph credit: Kawai and Wignaraja (2014, p. 18).

Specifically, I discuss how the different sectoral focuses of the regional economic structures influenced the preference of the East Asian states over different types of regional institutional arrangements, in terms of the scope of the sectors covered in the trade rules negotiation and agreement. In doing so, I identify the effects of the structural forces on the East Asian states in their final decision to join or not join the two regional institutional arrangements of CP/TPP and RCEP.

Existing studies suggest that there are significant variations in the extent of East Asian countries' involvement in regional institutional arrangements. Some opt for narrow agreements that deal with goods and/or services. Others prefer somewhat broader agreements covering goods, services, and partial WTO-plus commitments. And still, others pursue comprehensive agreements covering goods, services, and comprehensive WTO-plus commitments. Figure 6.12 shows such diversity. Three advanced economies—Japan, Singapore, and South Korea—strongly favor a WTO-plus approach to FTAs and are increasingly emphasizing comprehensive agreements (indicated in deep blue). In contrast, China and ASEAN developing economies focus on traditional goods and/or services (in light blue) and partial WTO-plus provisions (in light orange).

With this concept of the different types of regional institutional arrangement, I discuss the shaping of the institutional preference of states in East Asian regionalism over different types of trade agreements, and in particular over the CP/TPP and RCEP. Table 6.4 shows the evolution of the institutional preferences of each East Asian economy from the 1980s to 2010s.

Table 6.4 Shaping of Divergent Institutional Preferences of States in East Asian Regionalism

	1989–1997	*1997–2000s*	*2010s*
China	• Questing to enter the GATT/WTO • Open regionalism • Cautious cooperation toward APEC	• ASEAN+3 > ASEAN+6	• Firm supporter of RCEP • Evolution from suspicion to support toward CP/TPP • China-centered hub-and-spoke bilateralism: BRI
Japan	• Firm supporter of GATT/WTO • Initiator of APEC	• ASEAN+6 > ASEAN+3	• Firm supporter of TPP • Initiator of CP/TPP • Initiator and supporter of RCEP
South Korea	• Global multilateralism	• Bilateral globalism	• Role of middle power • Firm supporter of RCEP • Hesitate to join CP/TPP • Bilateral FTA hub: US, China, EU
Singapore	• Firm supporter of GATT/WTO • Firm supporter of APEC	• ASEAN+6 > ASEAN+3 • Bilateralism	• CP/TPP and RCEP • Bilateral FTA hub: Japan, US, China, EU
Malaysia	• Initiator of EAEG • Suspicion toward APEC	• ASEAN+3 > ASEAN+6	• CP/TPP and RCEP
Thailand	• Propose ASEAN FTA • Firm supporter of APEC	• A multilevel FTA strategy	• RCEP
Indonesia	• Evolution from suspicion to support toward APEC • Leader in ASEAN	• ASEAN+6 > ASEAN+3	• RCEP
The Philippines	• Supporter of ASEAN and APEC	• ASEAN+3 > ASEAN+6	• RCEP
Vietnam	• Latecomer in regionalism and a proactive player	• ASEAN+3 and ASEAN+6	• CP/TPP and RCEP • FTA hub

6.3.1 China

I start with the evolving preferences of China over different types of regional institutional arrangements. For much of the post-war period, China remained a large, underdeveloped, and relatively autarkic economy (Lardy, 1994). China treated all discussions of regional economic cooperation with deep suspicion. Its approach to economic regionalism was shaped by worries of the hegemonic intentions of the US and Japan (Moore & Yang, 1999). China purposefully refrained from joining any regional framework.

By the 1990s, China's attitude toward regionalism gradually evolved from suspicion to cautious engagement. Largely driven by the fear of exclusion, China joined the APEC in 1991. China opposed the idea of establishing an FTA in the Asia-Pacific and wanted to make sure that APEC represented a model of open regionalism (Moore & Yang, 1999). Chinese leaders emphasized that regional economic cooperation should be in line with the GATT principles. With this set of values as its guide, Beijing used its participation in APEC to promote an open and nonexclusive trading system. It was willing to "take its chances with a relative institutional vacuum in East Asia rather than risk the consequences of more formalized regional institutions with real policy coordination and rule-making teeth" (Moore & Yang, 1999, p. 409).

In response to the 1997 Asian financial crisis (AFC), China became a key promoter for an exclusive regional trading group. The crisis moved China to make serious commitments to regional cooperation in East Asia. China's contribution to the crisis control was its pledge not to devalue its currency (Terada, 2012). China regarded ASEAN+3 as a natural grouping for East Asia's trade and investment (Kawai & Wignaraja, 2007). To minimize resistance toward ASEAN+3, China adopted a multitrack strategy on the regional community-building process, including ASEAN+1 and China-Japan-South Korea (CJK) trilateral FTA. First, China proceeded to sign an FTA with ASEAN in 2002. In the negotiations, China was willing to "give more, and take less" (Chin & Stubbs, 2011, p. 289). Following China's move, Japan and South Korea also launched negotiations with ASEAN.

Second, China took a leading role in negotiating for a CJK FTA in the early years. The very early idea of creating a CJK FTA was made by then Chinese Premier Zhu Rongji in 2002. But the conflict between China and Japan over the scope and coverage of CJK FTA stalled the negotiation process. While Japan hoped to build a high-standard FTA covering services, IP rights, environment, and labor policy, China expected merely a moderate level of tariff reduction and limited abolishment of non-trade barriers (Zhang, 2019). As a result, the project did not move further.

By the 2010s, China took a more proactive attitude toward trans-regional and bilateral arrangements, reflecting its changing growth agenda, interests, and priorities. China took a leading role in promoting RCEP and regarded RCEP as part of a broader program of trade deals. China also moved forward in the bilateral front, pushing for a long series of bilateral FTAs and eventually the Belt and Road Initiative. On one hand, China became more and more active in forging FTAs with partners in East Asia and other regions of the world. As of December 2020, China had signed 16 bilateral FTA agreements (see Appendix 2). Among these bilateral FTAs, most of them address traditional tariff issues and contain few advanced provisions. According to Salidjanova (2015), China's agreements fall short of high standards in areas such as investment, government procurement, IPR, labor, and the environment. On the other hand, the BRI is a platform for expanding global trade and investment, which connects China to the world. The BRI consists of the

"Belt"—Silk Road Economic Belt—and the "Road"—21st Century Maritime Silk Road.[4] Under the BRI scheme, the Chinese government usually negotiates an intergovernmental partnership with the project country that provides political and institutional support and insurance for Chinese enterprises to participate in the transborder industrial projects. In doing so, the Chinese government combines mechanisms and arrangements of both Official Development Assistance (ODA) and FDI for development financing (Huang, 2020. The sectoral focuses of the BRI are overwhelmingly in manufacturing, infrastructure, and transportation, reflecting the sectoral focuses of the Chinese economies at this stage of economic development.

In this process of China's emergence as a principal supporter of the RCEP and its leading founding member, not with CP/TPP, we see the effects of the different sectoral focuses of the regional economic structures on China's choice of RCEP over CP/TPP. This is because of China's primary interests in ruling traditional sectors and concern over the influence of the services and high-tech dominance of the US and Japanese economic forces.

6.3.2 Japan

Japan's institutional selection also unfolded in three distinct phases. The first phase from 1945 to 1997 featured Japan's firm support for global multilateralism but ambivalence toward regionalism. Maintaining strong support for a nondiscriminatory and rule-based multilateral trading system was a pillar of Japan's external economic policy. In the aftermath of World War II, Japan benefited from the GATT and WTO-led waves of global trade liberalization. Japan showed no interest or even criticized regional and bilateral free trade deals. For instance, the Ministry of International Trade and Industry (MITI) of Japan published a White Paper in 1998 and put its priority in negotiations of trade arrangements on "the steady implementation of WTO rules, and constant surveillance of and countermeasures for protectionist behaviors of foreign countries" (1998). Then-Minister of Foreign Affairs (MOFA) of Japan, Yohei Kono, explained why Japan favored global multilateralism: "Japan is working hard for the strengthening the WTO. This is quite a natural consequence of Japan's dependence on multilateral trade; Japan's trade structure does not show particular dependence on particular regions" (2001).

Consequently, in trade policy practice, Japan was ambivalent toward regionalism. Japan perceived regional trade agreements as negative because they might weaken efforts in the global trading system. Instead of inward-looking regionalism, Japan worked together with others, especially Australia, for more than three decades to realize a goal of the pan-Pacific regional framework, from the establishment of the Pacific Basin Economic Council in 1967 to the launch of the APEC project in 1989 (Ravenhill, 2001). In all of these initiatives, Japan's approach to the Asia-Pacific region involved a delicate balance in two sets of objectives. First, Japan relied on access to the US market and US involvement with the broader region of Asia-Pacific. Second, Japan wanted to bring ASEAN into the working of closer Japan-US economic relations.

In the second phase (1997–2010), in contrast to China's support on the ASEAN+3 framework, Japan approached ASEAN+6 as an appropriate group for trade and investment cooperation (Kawai & Wignaraja, 2007). In 2007, Japan officially proposed ASEAN+6 as a regional institutional framework for organizing transborder production and distribution in the region. This vision of ASEAN+6 includes not only East Asian countries (ASEAN+3), but also India, Australia, and New Zealand.

In the 2010s, Japan's FTA engagement entered the third phase with its focus shifting from East Asia to the Asia-Pacific. Japan was involved with both CP/TPP and RCEP, but emerged as a principal supporter and a leading organizer of CP/TPP. In addition to that, Japan also engaged with the US, EU, and other countries to build a global FTA network. According to MOFA (2015), Japan aimed to increase the FTA coverage[5] in its trade relations to 70% by 2018 from about 19% in 2012. As of December 2020, Japan signed up the two regional FTAs, CP/TPP and RCEP, and 17 bilateral FTAs (see Appendix 2). In order of the effective dates, Japan's bilateral FTA partners include Singapore, Mexico, Malaysia, Chile, Thailand, Brunei, Indonesia, ASEAN, Philippines, Switzerland, Vietnam, India, Peru, Australia, Mongolia, the EU, and the UK.

Japan engaged with both CP/TPP and RCEP, but had a clear priority in CP/TPP. The Abe administration (2012–2020) undoubtedly placed TPP at the top of the diplomatic agenda. Abe took TPP as a centerpiece of his economic growth strategy as he believed TPP would create trade and investment opportunities overseas and advancing domestic reforms in services and agricultural liberalization. As the US withdrew from TPP in 2017, Japan proceeded to take over the leadership role in moving the TPP forward to become CP/TPP. In reaching the CP/TPP agreement, Japan was instrumental in leading the way (Terada, 2018). Moreover, in setting the agenda for RCEP, Japan insisted to include nontariff issues in negotiations. Japan wanted strong rules in the areas of investment, IP, and dispute settlement. Due to Japan's insistence, new working groups on competition, IP, economic and technical cooperation, and dispute settlement were established in RCEP negotiations (Hamanaka, 2014). In both cases, CP/TPP and RCEP, Japan's engagement was influenced by its position in the regional economies structures as defined by sectoral focus and priorities. More generally, the shifts in Japan's attitude/approach toward regional institutional arrangements over the years were shaped by changes in the sectoral focuses and priorities of its economy and in its sectoral relations with other trading partners.

6.3.3 South Korea

Like Japan, South Korea was also a firm supporter of the global trading system and an insignificant player in regional institution-building before the 1997 AFC (Krieckhaus, 2018). Benefiting from the global trade network and the

GATT trading system, South Korea transformed itself from one of the poorest countries in the world to a successfully industrializing economy. The South Korean economy was heavily dependent on global trade and believed in the primacy of the global trading system.

However, South Korea developed a great passion for regionalism after 1997 by actively involving in a variety of regional initiatives including ASEAN+3, ASEAN+1, and China-Japan-South Korea trilateralism. In the ASEAN+3 track, the South Korean government proposed an East Asian Vision Group (EAVG) in 1998 and an Economic Cooperation Research Group in 2001 (Cheong, 2008; Kwon, 2004). In the ASEAN+1 track, South Korea also signed an FTA with ASEAN in 2006. In the trilateral track, South Korea aimed to become "a Northeast Asia business hub" and actively participated in the negotiation of a CJK trilateral FTA (M. Zhang, 2016). For instance, the South Korean government prioritized the bilateral FTA negotiations with Japan and China[6] and intended to use the bilateral FTA to help with the process of economic integration in Northeast Asia.

More recently in the 2010s, South Korea's enthusiasm toward East Asian regionalism diminished sharply, showing less interest for East Asian economic integration with its neighboring countries. Instead, it shifted focus toward building a global FTA hub network (Park, 2015). The then-trade minister Taeho Bark emphasized the importance for the economy:

> As a global FTA hub nation, Korea will emerge as the gateway for a multitude of American, European, and Chinese investors seeking access to these enormous and dynamic markets. The entry into force of these three FTAs is of great significance to South Korea not only in expanding trade, investment and boosting the economy but also rapidly increasing South Korea's FTA trade coverage.
>
> (Bark, 2012)

As of December 2020 (see Appendix 2), South Korea signed up 17 bilateral FTAs. South Korea had a broad FTA territory and became a "linchpin" of economic integration in East Asia through aggressive pursuit of FTAs (Lee, 2015).

The global scale of South Korea's economy blurred its interests in a regional trade arrangement. Its ambiguous position of the regional economic structures with priorities in both manufacturing and services sectors makes both CP/TPP and RCEP attractive and acceptable to South Korea. South Korea has actively engaged with RCEP and still wait for the opportunity to join CP/TPP.

6.3.4 *Singapore*

Singapore's government tended to distance itself from the concept of an exclusive East Asian bloc and, like South Korea, stressed the need for a global trading system. In the first phase (1989–1997), Singapore strongly advocated trade liberalization under the APEC framework rather than an ASEAN-centered approach. For instance, it successfully bid to host the APEC Secretariat by offering to meet the body's local costs for its first two years (1989–1991) (Ravenhill, 2001, pp. 105–106). It showed little interest or faith in ASEAN's own efforts for regional economic integration. As Thompson (2006, p. 183) commented on the unique role of Singapore in the context of ASEAN, "Singapore ... is in Southeast Asia but not, someone might say, of Southeast Asia".

After the 1997 AFC, Singapore opposed the exclusive East Asian regional bloc, ASEAN+3, and supported Japan's proposal of ASEAN+6 (Hund, 2003). Singapore promoted the formation of the ASEAN-Australia-New Zealand FTA and insisted that neither Australia nor New Zealand should be excluded from East Asian regionalism. In 2002, Singapore's then-Prime Minister Goh Chok Tong stated that he did not believe in the idea of molding East Asia into another regional bloc similar to NAFTA and the EU. He was quoted as saying "What we fear most is that the world will be split into three economic blocs", and "to prevent this happening, both Singapore and Japan should establish FTAs with countries outside East Asia" (Kwan, 2002).

In 2003, Singapore released a new national development strategy to raise its profile as a leading global city. The core of this vision was a strategy to strengthen relations with developed economies such as the US, Japan, and the EU. Pursuing the strategy, Singapore signed various bilateral FTAs and had the broadest geographical coverage in its agreements. Singapore implemented or concluded agreements with the largest economies in East Asia (China, Japan, and South Korea) as well as outside East Asia (including the US and EU, and India). It is particularly noteworthy that the Singapore-US FTA was the first US FTA with an Asian nation which took into effect in 2004.

In the 2010s, Singapore joined both CP/TPP and RCEP. Singapore thus saw these two agreements as mutually reinforcing pathways toward an eventual Free Trade Area of the Asia-Pacific (FTAAP) (Ministry of Trade and Industry, 2014). Singapore leaders repeatedly spoke up for CP/TPP, even as they were also among the first to ratify RCEP. Like South Korea, the global scale of its economies and trade relations, and the sectorial focuses of its economy led Singapore to be interested in global trade arrangements, and enthusiastic for both CP/TPP and RCEP.

6.3.5 Malaysia

Malaysia has always been "a fervent promoter" of East Asian regionalism (Hund, 2003, p. 386). In the first phase (1989–1997), the Malaysian government was the most resolute opponent against trade and investment liberalization under APEC (Ravenhill, 2001, pp. 108–112), regarding liberal multilateralism as an instrument of Western economic domination. In response to the challenge of the West, then Prime Minister of Malaysia, Mahathir, stressed that Asian countries must develop an Asian identity and an alternative strategy for development (Yu, 2003, p. 278). In a 1991 speech to the UN, Mahathir said: "In East Asia, we are told we may not call ourselves East Asians as Europeans call themselves Europeans and Americans call themselves Americans" (Awanohara, 1991, p. 13).

To counter the perceived threat posed by APEC and to strengthen the economic sovereignty of East Asian countries, the Malaysian government proposed the idea of an East Asian Economic Group (EAEG),[7] the embryo of ASEAN+3. Unlike that of APEC, the idea of EAEG was to build a strictly regional organization for an East Asian economic community. It was designed to reinvigorate regional economies through trade liberalization and strengthen ties among member states. However, most East Asian countries were concerned that an exclusive bloc in the region might result in more protective regionalism in Europe and North America. Tighter blocs in these regions meant higher barriers into these markets, which would be bad for East Asian economies after all. The EAEG proposal did not become a reality but paved the way for its successor: ASEAN+3.

In the 2000s, the Malaysian government stepped up its rhetoric and called for "formalized" East Asian regional integration under the ASEAN+3 framework (Leong, 2000). On the one hand, the Malaysian government initiated a public debate about the viability of an East Asian monetary union and welcomed the ASEAN+3 currency swap arrangements. On the other hand, Malaysia criticized the bilateral FTAs by ASEAN members (particularly, Singapore). Malaysia believed that a focus on bilateral FTAs might harm the solidarity among ASEAN and East Asian nations, and allow economies outside the region to dominate the regional market. As we already know, Malaysia's regionalist efforts did not pay off, and its enthusiasm toward ASEAN+3 cooled.

In the 2010s, trans-regionalism and bilateralism became a domino effect that East Asian countries competed in trade and investment liberalization to attract the participation of external economies in transborder production networks. In this context, Malaysia transformed its regional focus to a multi-layer strategy (Nambiar, 2015). First, following the steps of its neighbors, Malaysia implemented seven bilateral FTAs as of December 2020 (see Appendix 2). Second, at the regional level, through ASEAN, Malaysia signed regional FTAs with China, Japan, Korea, India, Australia, and New Zealand. Third and most importantly, Malaysia joined both CP/TPP and RCEP. It is worth mentioning that two factors motivated Malaysia to join the CP/TPP negotiations. The first reason was the participation of the US in the TPP, which significantly enhanced the economic weight of the free trade area (Wu, 2019). The second motivation was to "lock-in or lend greater external visibility to current domestic reforms" (Ayub & Jalil, 2018, pp. 104–105). Similarly, the signing of RCEP was anticipated to benefit local industries as the mega FTA would lower barriers to entry for Malaysian goods and services in East Asia. With market barriers lowered and ROOs streamlined, Malaysia expected that its investments from more developed countries in the RCEP region and beyond would increase (Azhar, 2020; Ernst & Young Tax Consultants, 2021).

Malaysia's early focus on an East Asian regional economic community has a lot to do with its position in the regional economic structure as a developing economy in sectoral focuses and priorities. This position has not led Malaysia to choose RCEP over TPP/CP/TPP. This can be explained by the influence of additional forces such as the accommodating trade policy and complimentary domestic regulatory framework it has adopted in the fierce competitive liberalization with its neighbors to attract and retain FDI.

6.3.6 Thailand

Thailand has been a champion of outward-looking regionalism since the 1990s. Thailand proposed the formation of the ASEAN FTA indicating its intent and determination to eliminate the country's protective trade regime. Like other ASEAN countries, Thailand viewed AFTA as an investment-driven integration that would serve as a "training ground" for global competition (Chirathivat and Mallikamas, 2004, p. 39). Thailand also played an active role in supporting APEC.

After the 1997 financial crisis, Thailand started to pursue a multilevel FTA strategy aggressively. On the one hand, Thailand and generally the East Asian region felt the need to promote a regional economic community. On the other hand, Thailand was the second ASEAN economy after Singapore to actively pursue bilateral FTAs driven by their dissatisfaction with the ASEAN and APEC processes.[8]

More recently in the 2010s, Thailand played an active role within ASEAN in promoting closer regional integration by supporting RCEP. By contrast, due to its lack of the necessary preparedness and consensus for the high-quality trade and investment rules, Thailand showed caution toward CP/TPP. According to the Bangkok Post (2020), Thailand still needed to enact a new legislature to catch up with global trading rules such as CP/TPP.

Thailand was a flexible player in regionalist projects and adjusted its strategy swiftly, from initiator of an ASEAN-centered approach to a firm supporter of RCEP-only, to accord with its economic interests. Unlike in Malaysia, sectoral focuses of the regional economic structures did influence Thailand to choose RCEP over CP/TPP.

6.3.7 Indonesia

Indonesia has always been ambivalent toward trade liberalization, and its road to trade liberalization has been "long and winding" (Vanzetti et al., 2005, p. 4). In the first phase, when APEC was established in 1989 and the ASEAN FTA was established in 1992, Indonesia initially shared Malaysia's lack of enthusiasm. Indonesia was very cautious and unwilling to join APEC and ASEAN due to the general suspicion that trade liberalization would be less beneficial to Indonesia (Intal & Chen, 2017, p. 73). In the initial negotiations of ASEAN, Indonesia asked for a 15-year transition period when joining ASEAN. Similarly, later in 1994, it converted to promote trade liberalization through APEC.[9]

In the 2000s, although Indonesia backed Japan's initiative of ASEAN+6 rather than ASEAN+3, its trade liberalization move was still very limited. On the one hand, the Indonesian government did not make any substantial promises under the framework of ASEAN+3. Instead, it supported an open and nonexclusive East Asian regionalism and welcomed the participation of Australia and New Zealand. On the other hand, Indonesia had reservations when signing FTAs with the "+6" countries (namely, China, South Korea, Japan, Australia, New Zealand, India). Particularly, the ASEAN-China FTA was challenging for Indonesia due to its concern about the influx of inexpensive goods from China into its market (Artner, 2017; Tan, 2015).

In the 2010s, there was also hesitation in Indonesia about joining RCEP and CP/TPP. Particularly, Indonesia regarded CP/TPP rules as too ambitious and onerous to comply with. Sahu (2016) interpreted this hesitation as fears that further liberalization would worsen the balance of trade. Eventually, Indonesia joined RCEP but not CP/TPP. This can be partly explained by the matching of sectoral focuses of RCEP and Indonesia.

6.3.8 The Philippines

Since the late 1980s, the Philippines government shifted from a protectionist to a more open trade policy. Philippines was a member of the APEC in 1989 as well as the ASEAN FTA in 1992. The 1997 AFC further underscored the benefits of establishing formal economic links to the more developed economies of Japan and South Korea and the dynamic market of China "as a means of averting any possible future crisis" (Stubbs, 2002, p. 449). In the 2000s, the Philippines supported ASEAN+3 and the idea of an East Asian economic community.

In the 2010s, the Philippines was less active than its neighbors in promoting bilateral FTAs. It engaged in FTA negotiations mainly as part of ASEAN (e.g., ASEAN-China, ASEAN-Japan). Bilaterally, the Philippines signed up only two FTAs, one with Japan and one with EFTA (composed of Iceland, Liechtenstein, Norway, and Switzerland). Moreover, the Philippines put its full weight behind RCEP but criticized CP/TPP by highlighting the restrictive nature of its provision. The Philippines is a good example of how a country's position in the regional economic structures shaped its choice of RCEP over CP/TPP. It was in the lowest level of economic development in the region for decades and has not much seen the development of the manufacturing sector of its own. As a result, for the Philippines, manufacturing-oriented RCEP was more relevant than the service-focused CP/TPP framework.

6.3.9 Vietnam

Vietnam started to participate in global value chains after its launch of the "Doi Moi" (reform) policy in the late 1980s, and it was a latecomer in regional economic integration. It did not become a member of ASEAN until 1995,

APEC until 1998, or WTO until 2007. In the 2000s, Vietnam was an active member of both ASEAN+3 and ASEAN+6. It regarded ASEAN+3 as "a major mechanism for China to increase its influence in the regional architecture without US participation" (Quyet, 2013, p. 99–100). It saw the framework of ASEAN+6 as a Japan-led counterweight to ASEAN+3 with the inclusion of Australia, New Zealand, and India. It sought to steer a middle path in economic affairs between China and Japan.

In the 2010s, Vietnam transformed its trade policies to position itself as an FTA hub and create a web of economic interdependence. It was the only ASEAN country, apart from Singapore, that signed up an FTA with the EU in 2019 and was pursuing a bilateral FTA with the US. It intended to attract exporting companies from the EU and the US to produce in Vietnam and export to partners outside ASEAN.

Toward the contentious CP/TPP and RCEP, Vietnam consciously adopted a dual-track approach by signing both. The high-standard agreement with the CP/TPP partners forced Vietnam to conduct substantial institutional reforms toward enhanced market efficiency in areas such as investment, competition, IPR, and SOEs (Deprez, 2018). RCEP would help particularly in combining several ASEAN+1 FTAs into one set of trade rules, reducing tariffs (manufacturing costs), and thus linking regional supply chains. Through these two preferential trade agreements, Vietnam wanted to engage itself with the East Asian production networks and global value and supply chains. Like Malaysia, though, the sectoral focuses of the regional economic structures influenced Vietnam's institutional choice to a great extent. Other factors such as geopolitics and the international economic strategy of the state pushed Vietnam not only into RCEP but also CP/TPP which the sectoral focuses alone can't fully explain.

From the discussions above, I analyzed the shaping of institutional preferences of East Asian states over different types of regional arrangements and the extent to which the sectoral focuses and priorities of the regional economic structures influenced their choices over CP/TPP and RCEP.

6.4 Evidence on Hypothesis 3

In the sections above, I have constructed sectoral economic structures of CP/TPP, RCEP, and each East Asian economy. I established the positions of the East Asian national economies in the two regional economic structures. Now I test Hypothesis 3 and summarize the findings on the effects of sectoral economic structures on the institutional choices of East Asian states to join CP/TPP and/or RCEP. Table 6.5 lists the key points of the findings.

The center column in Table 6.5 focuses on countries with dual membership in CP/TPP and RCEP. The cases of Japan and Singapore on the bottom row are expected in Hypothesis 3, while Malaysia and Vietnam on the top row are not. For Japan and Singapore, services dominated their sectoral economic structures. The services prioritized rules of CP/TPP fitted their structural

Table 6.5 Determining the Relationship between the Institutional Choices and Sectoral Economic Structures

	CP/TPP and RCEP	*RCEP-only*
Institutional choices	Japan, Singapore, Malaysia, Vietnam	ASEAN, China, South Korea
Expectations by sectoral focus and priority	Japan, Singapore	ASEAN, China, South Korea

interests and opened avenues for service exporters. For Malaysia and Vietnam, although RCEP's tariffs-focused rules served their current structural interests best, they also participated in CP/TPP because of the influence of two other factors. The first was the particular international economic strategy the states adopted at the time. Both Malaysia and Vietnam used their participation in CP/TPP to signal the principle of trade and investment liberalization in their trade policy. The second factor was geopolitical considerations. Malaysia and Vietnam attempted to maintain an equal distance between the great powers. Their participation in the CP/TPP was an expression of a "hedging" strategy to diversify their economic concentration, avoid becoming overdependent on China, and balance diplomatic relations with China and the US (Wu, 2019).

On the right column of RCEP-only, institutional choices and structural expectations match perfectly for China, South Korea, and most ASEAN countries. These tariffs-prioritizing economies embraced RCEP-only and took a cautious approach toward CP/TPP. The overwhelming choice of these economies over RCEP showed the strong influence of manufacturing-oriented sectoral economic structures. The sectoral focuses and priorities of South Korea could have pushed it to take both the CP/TPP and RCEP as Singapore had done. However, South Korea's international economic strategy of global economic liberalization, heavy reliance on manufacturing with China, and unsettled geopolitical relations with Japan seemed to make it cautious about taking up with CP/TPP at the time.

Overall, while there were other factors such as geopolitics at play, investigation in this chapter significantly supports Hypothesis 3 that sectoral focuses and priorities of the economic structures influenced the institutional choices of East Asian states over CP/TPP and RCEP. A services-focused economy is more interested in CP/TPP, while a more agriculture/manufacturing-oriented economy is more likely to support RCEP.

Notes

1 According to MFAT of New Zealand (2021), RCEP's electronic commerce chapter allows businesses and consumers to transact online with confidence, protects the privacy and rights of consumers, and establishes a framework for discussing fast-changing and emerging issues.

2 Government procurement is a new area that is not covered in any existing ASEAN FTAs.

3 For instance, due to weak oil prices in the 1980s, Indonesia had a hard time in slow economic growth. The Indonesian government accorded high priority to developing non-oil and gas exports and developed a more outward-looking trade regime.

4 The Belt is proposed to connect the Western part of China to Western Europe via Central Asia, Iran, Turkey, Russia, the Caucasus, and the Balkans. Besides, linking Eurasia by land; and the Road is designed to connect China with South Asia, Southeast Asia, the Middle East, Africa, and Europe through a strip of seaports through the South China Sea, the Indian Ocean, and the Mediterranean Sea.

5 FTA coverage rate refers to the ratio of the value in trade with countries that already signed FTAs with a country to its total trade value.

6 As early as in 1998, the Japanese Ambassador to South Korea, Okura Kazuo, proposed a bilateral FTA between the two parties. In the same year when then-South Korean President Kim Dae Jung visited Japan, he responded to the proposal and called for Japan's cooperation in building economic partnership for the 21st century. In 2000, the Institute of Developing Economies, Japan External Trade Organization (IDE-JETRO) and the Korea Institute for International Economic Policy (KIEP) jointly proposed a bilateral FTA.

7 The initiative of the East Asia Economic Group (EAEG) was proposed for the first time in December 1990 at the meeting with Li Peng, then Chinese Premier. Later in July and October 1997 during the ASEAN ministerial meetings, the initiative was officially put on table. The title was changed to East Asia Economic Caucus in the process.

8 As of December 2020, there were 19 FTA deals in Thailand, 15 of which were initiated in the early 2000s (see Appendix 2).

9 For more about the turnaround of Indonesia's views on APEC, see Ravenhill (2001, pp. 106–108).

7 Findings and Implications

The previous three chapters have tested my three hypotheses and examined the evidence on the effects of structural dynamics on the institutional preferences of the states in East Asian regionalism. Chapter 4 constructed the global economic structure and examined the levels of intra-regional connectivity of industrial production in Europe, North America, and East Asia in the global economic structure. Chapter 5 constructed the structures of regional production networks and the positions of East Asian states in the structures. It elucidates how these led to multiple and contending initiatives and projects for East Asian regionalism. Chapter 6 constructed the sectoral economic structures of CP/TPP and RCEP and the divergent positions of East Asian states in the structures that led to the different choices of these states to join or not join CP/TPP and RCEP in the end.

In this chapter, I bring these findings together and discuss to what extent the structural theory on the weakness of East Asian regionalism we set out for this project matches with the empirical evidence. I begin with a brief revisit of my proposed structural theory and the three hypotheses. I then discuss to what extent the findings confirmed the three hypotheses and what that means for our structural explanation of the problem in East Asian regionalism. Finally, I will restate the theory and summarize all these discussions into an overall thesis for this book.

7.1 Revisiting the Theory and Hypotheses

With the emergence of global value chains and global production networks, the growing importance of production structures has led people to focus on what is called the governance of transborder production. This book also has focused on how the structural dynamics in production and distribution and the power relations manifested in the international division of labor have shaped the institutional preferences of states in East Asian regionalism.

This study is an investigation of the structural causes of the weakness of East Asian regionalism from the late 1980s to the 2010s. The underlying logic of the structural theory I laid out in Chapter 2 is the following: first, the international economic structure is the distribution of economic interests and

DOI: 10.4324/9781032613321-7

capabilities of states within the world economic system. Particular positions of states in the structure affect their national interests and hence their preferences for and choices over different types of institutional arrangements for production and distribution in the region. Second, a regional economic structure influences nations to opt for and compete over multiple sets of particular institutional arrangements. Third, different and contending institutional preferences of East Asian states, in particular, determined by their different positions in the structure, make their agreement on a single regional institution of economic integration difficult, if not impossible. I set up three hypotheses in Chapter 3 to test the theory. More specifically, these three hypotheses were designed to test causal mechanisms in the theory that link structural dynamics at different levels—global, regional, and sectoral—to the institutional preferences of the states.

Contrary to the popular belief of liberal institutionalism, Hypothesis 1 suggested that the global economic structure determined the shaping of an East Asian economic community for East Asian regionalism. According to liberal institutionalism, the top-down institutional designs have contributed greatly to the success of regionalism in Europe and North America. My structural theory suggests a bottom-up causal relationship between material forces and institutional arrangements and assumes that a certain level of regional economic integration is a necessary condition for regional institution-building. Hypothesis 1 operationalized this causal relationship and used regional concentration indexes of these three regional units to determine their levels of regional economic integration. Hypothesis 1 indicated that a more regionally concentrated economic structure makes it easier to cultivate an exclusive and highly institutionalized regional arrangement. Accordingly, in comparison with Europe and North America, East Asia is the least regionally oriented and the most globally interconnected, which is the structural reason why a single, unitary institutional arrangement was not able to develop in East Asia.

Hypothesis 2 assumes the same structure-institution logic working at the regional level and takes each East Asian national economy as a production unit. These units are positioned differently in the structure of transnational production networks measured by the influence of the value-added from national, regional, and global origins. Because of their different positions in the international economic structure, East Asian states have different and conflicting interests in institutional arrangements for the regional economic organization. Hypothesis 2 suggests, therefore, that the more globally interconnected the country, the greater its incentive for building global platforms. The more regionally concentrated countries are, the more interested they are in regional projects. These conflicting structural dynamics led to multiple and contending initiatives and projects in East Asian regionalism.

Hypothesis 3 focuses on sectoral economic structures and institutional relationships in East Asian regionalism. Hypothesis 3 suspects that East Asian states of similar sectoral focuses and priorities in their national economic structures formed different groups with different positions in the sectoral economic structures of CP/TPP and RCEP. Hypothesis 3, therefore, assumed that developed, services-dominated economies are likely to support CP/TPP which has sectoral focuses and priorities in services. In contrast, manufacturing concentrated economies are likely to join RCEP, which focuses on traditional tariffs of trade in goods. This led to the rise of the two competing institutional arrangements in East Asia and tense relations among the states over these two initiatives.

Each hypothesis is designed to show one aspect of the causal link between international economic structures and the states' institutional preferences in East Asian regionalism. To test these hypotheses, I designed methods and data for constructing the international economic structures in Chapter 3. I developed three sets of indicators for each hypothesis: the levels of regional concentration (Hypothesis 1), global-regional connectivity (Hypothesis 2), and sectoral focuses and priorities (Hypothesis 3). I explained the use of the value-added production method and GVC data for the test and analysis. Compared with the conventional method of national accounts using GDP, I used the value-added production as a more accurate way to the empirical description of the structures because it records which economy value-added comes from and which economy it goes to. This relational method allowed us to determine the international distribution of production interests and capabilities of East Asia.

7.2 Key Findings from Empirical Investigation and Analysis

Empirical construction of the global, regional, and sectoral economic structures and analysis of the positions of the states in these structures match well in general with what is suspected in the three hypotheses. Evidence on the three hypotheses is largely positive, but ambiguous in some minor areas, particularly in Hypothesis 3. I discuss below to what extent these findings support the structural theory and, based on this, attempt to summarize the theoretical and empirical discussion into an overall explanation for the problem in East Asian regionalism.

7.2.1 Finding I: East Asia Does Not Have the Material Basis for a Stand-Alone Production Community

Constructing the global economic structure and comparing the levels of regional concentration in Chapter 4, I tested whether there were three regional concentrations in the global distribution of value chains and whether East Asia's RCI was much lower than Europe or North America. I used the complex network method to map global economic structure for observing regional concentrations of production forces in the world. Three regional clusters of production activities are evident from this exercise: Germany-centered Europe, US-led North America, and East Asia (Japan-led in 1995 and China-centered in 2015). In contrast to the regionally oriented and more balanced production networks in Europe, East Asia has strong global and hierarchical production linkages (mainly) with North America. East Asia shifted from Japan-led regional production networks in 1985 to the US-Japan economic alliance in 1995, followed by the China-Japan-US tripolar network in 2005, and more recently, the China-centered regional production networks in 2015. These hierarchical and global production networks in East Asia involved unequal exchange and competing industrial powers and had profound implications for East Asia's inability to develop a stand-alone economic community.

Second, further analysis of the levels of regional concentration in Europe, North America, and East Asia confirmed that the RCI of East Asia was much lower than that of Europe or North America. East Asia relied on producers within itself as much as it did on those from outside the region. The findings on regional concentration levels confirmed that production networks in East Asia were not as regionally concentrated as that of Europe and North America and lacked a regionally oriented production basis to support the organizing of East Asia as a coherent economic community.

As a region, East Asia has been traditionally influenced by forces of regional and global production networking. The Japan-led regional industrial activities during the 1960s–1980s provided a good basis to push for regional economic integration. However, as a result of the increasing international fragmentation of production, the focus of East Asian production networks shifted from East Asia to the wider world in the past 30 years. In particular, with the rise of China as a World Factory, transborder production networks in the region gradually shifted from being Japan-dominated to China-dominated. The increasingly penetrating global production forces weakened the drive for regional economic integration and community building in East Asia. The idea of East Asian regionalism as a project for economic integration (more than economic cooperation) and regional economic community was unpopular and politically contentious.

We also investigated this relationship and analyzed the RCIs at sectoral levels intending to see if there were sectoral complications. As textiles, electronics, and automobiles were the most significant sectors in its industrialization, East Asia was in different positions in the global structures of these three sectors. Our structural analysis found that from 1995 to 2015, the textile sector shifted from Europe and East Asian developed economies to East Asian developing economies. The electronics sector was increasingly centered on East Asia, but its global connections were significant. In contrast to textiles and electronics, the automobile sector continued regional production in Europe, North America, and East Asia. These findings reflect different patterns of the distribution of production networks in key industrial sectors. The textile sector is highly labor-intensive, sensitive to price fluctuations, relatively easy for developing economies to set up, and thus had the most dynamic global structure of production networks. Electronics is highly R&D intensive and highly tradable, and its production networking has been traditionally influenced by global and regional forces. Automobile production tends to be regionalized because of economic and political considerations.

Considered together, Chapter 4 showed that the production networks in East Asia were not as regionally concentrated as those of Europe and North America and lacked a regionally oriented production basis to support the organizing of East Asia as a single production unit.

7.2.2 *Finding II: Nations' Complex Global-Regional Connectivity Led to Multiple and Competing Initiatives and Projects in East Asian Regionalism*

Examining the varying and rapidly changing positions of each East Asian national economy in the regional economic structure, I tested Hypothesis 2 to determine the complexity of their positions as influenced by different sets of forces in transborder value-added of global and regional origins. With the rise of regional value chains (RVCs) and GVCs, East Asian economies typically intensified their involvement with the international production networks. The exact effects of the international production forces, however, were felt differently among East Asian economies in different periods. To highlight this complexity, I used the RVA/GVA ratios of these national economies, that is, the extent to which a national economy is more integrated into RVCs or GVCs. Because of these different positions, we can further argue that nations favor either exclusive, regional institutional arrangements or open, global institutional arrangements. This was theorized in Hypothesis 2 as leading to the contentious rise of too many regional projects with different membership scopes and a mix of close/open arrangements in East Asian regionalism.

Investigation and analysis of the RVA/GVA ratios showed that from 1995 to 2015, most East Asian economies were more globally interconnected than regionally oriented in the structure. Singapore was the most globally connected economy: 84% (1995), 43% (2005), and 54% (2015). The two industrial powers—Japan and China—also depended much more on global partners than on regional counterparts. The regional-global ratios of Japan were: 37% (1995), 41% (2005), and 59% (2015), and the ratios of China were: 97% (1995), 77% (2005), and 47% (2015). In another group, although their levels of dependence on global sources were not as heavy as in the previous cases - South Korea, Taiwan, and Thailand - were also more reliant on value-added of global origins than that of regional origins in their production networks. However, Vietnam (182% in 1995, 142% in 2005, 173% in 2015), Hong Kong (134% in 1995), the Philippines (102% in 1995, 116% in 2015), Indonesia (111% in 2015), and Malaysia (106% in 2015) had the most regional value-added in their production networks in the region.

These varying positions of East Asian economies in the regional economic structures of production networks match very well with their different institutional preferences and explain their inability to agree on a single regional institutional architecture. The majority of the East Asian economies were more globally interconnected and welcomed extra-regional players in the regional institution building process. For instance, Singapore was a staunch advocate of the global trade system, as its Minister for Foreign Affairs argued for "no alternative to multilateralism" in tackling global issues (UN, 2017). Similarly, another global hub economy, South Korea, also made participation in global economic governance a cornerstone of its foreign policy (Pacheco Pardo, et al., 2019). More importantly, core economies in the region—Japan and China—were also keen supporters for a global institutional setting to protect their globally dispersed economic interests and relations. Japan had been one of the global industrial powers and built a worldwide division of labor and production networks since the 1970s. In the 2010s, China emerged as a key player in the process of East Asian integration and created both "centripetal" and "centrifugal" forces that operated at the same time (Amako, et al., 2013). The centripetal forces relate to the fact that China started up its industrialization via participation in RVCs. The centrifugal aspect refers to China using this regional interconnectedness as a platform to engage with GVCs. In other words, while both Japan and China helped in many ways to make East Asia a more cohesive region, they also pushed for a consolidation of trans-regional cooperation with the rest of the world, especially the US. Overall, these globally dispersed economic connections diverted the attention of East Asian economies away from building a single regional architecture.

In contrast, Malaysia had a greater regional concentration of production networks. Malaysia was a strong supporter of the idea of a single and regional organization for East Asia at some stages. For example, then-Malaysian Prime Minister Mahathir bin Mohamad proposed an East Asia Economic Group (EAEG) in 1989, intended to arrange trade relations among East Asian countries only. Malaysia also pushed through the ASEAN+3 cooperation at the height of the 1997 Asian financial crisis. In addition, Malaysia initiated and institutionalized a special working group for the idea of a Singapore-Kunming Rail Link (SKRL) to promote and coordinate the construction of a rail network across East Asia. However, these proposals have not eventuated.

Vietnam was found to have the most regionally oriented production networks. However, it was less enthusiastic about the idea of an exclusive East Asian regionalism, and its trade policy became more globally oriented in the 2010s. Compared with Malaysia, Vietnam had a different position in the regional economic structure. Value-added in its production networks had a mix of regional and global sources. For instance, the value-added components from China to Vietnam, which dominated Vietnam's RVA, not only came from Chinese enterprises but also foreign MNCs in China, such as Japan, South Korea, the EU, and the US.[1] Therefore, in the process of opening the country to capitalism and FDI, Vietnam joined several regional, trans-regional, and global platforms such as ASEAN (1995),[2] APEC (1998), WTO (2007), and more recently, CP/TPP and RCEP. The rationale for these efforts was to enhance the country's attractiveness as a global FDI destination and manufacturing hub.

In summary, the varying levels of global and regional connectivity made it hard for East Asian nations to form a collective institutional vision for a regional economic community. Different positions of the national economies in the regional economic structure significantly influenced these states to favor different types of regional arrangements with different scopes of membership and close or open mechanisms.

7.2.3 *Finding III: Different Sectoral Focuses and Priorities of the Sectoral Economic Structure Led to Difficult and Different Choices of the Nations over CP/TPP and/or RCEP*

In testing Hypothesis 3, I constructed the sectoral economic structures of CP/TPP, RCEP, and individual East Asian national economies by using skyline charts: the self-sufficiency rates (SSR) and agriculture-manufacturing-services ratios (AMSR). I determined whether there was a distinct pattern of sectoral focuses and priorities in the CP/TPP structure and the RCEP structure and the extent to which the patterns match with those of the East Asian economies who joined CP/TPP and/or RCEP. I explored the role of sectoral dynamics of the structure that led these nations to their institutional decisions.

I first used skyline charts—the SSRs and AMSRs—to show that CP/TPP and RCEP had different sectoral focuses or priorities in setting up trade rules. It was observed that the SSR and the AMSR of CP/TPP and RCEP varied significantly. The SSR of TPP was the highest because it included the largest and most mature economy in the world, the US. In the case of CP/TPP (excluding the US), the rate was significantly lower. The rate of RCEP stood between that of TPP and CP/TPP, which means that RCEP (mostly East Asian economies) as a group was less self-sufficient than TPP but more regionally integrated than CP/TPP. For the same reason, the AMSRs also differed substantially. TPP had the highest services ratios, followed by CP/TPP and then RCEP. While TPP and CP/TPP prioritized services and investment-related topics, RCEP mainly focused on manufacturing-related tariff issues.

We then used the same SSRs and AMSRs to determine the extent of the match between the sectoral focuses and priorities of individual East Asian economies and their final decisions to join CP/TPP and/or RCEP. On the one hand, the SSRs of East Asian economies had bumps (overproduction and competitive edges) and dips (underproduction and external dependence) in particular sectors. East Asian economies had similar bumps in customer products manufacturing, especially in the textile and electronics sectors. But dips occurred in different sectors across different economies. For instance, for China, Japan, and South Korea, the dips were mainly in agriculture and mining. But for most Southeast Asian economies, their dips were mainly in heavy manufacturing industries such as chemicals and refining, rubber, and plastic products.

On the other hand, the AMSRs also varied significantly across East Asian economies. The service sectors were the main drivers of growth and employment in Singapore and Japan, for example, financial services in Singapore and transport services in Japan. In contrast, the rest of the developing economies had agriculture and manufacturing-oriented sectoral profiles.

Developed economies (such as Japan and Singapore) preferred CP/TPP over RCEP. The majority of developing economies joined RCEP-only. Their institutional choices to join CP/TPP and/or RCEP can be largely explained by their differences in sectoral focuses and priorities. The SSRs demonstrated the overlapping overproduction in certain sectors (e.g., textiles and electronics), which meant that East Asian economies had similar comparative advantages and thus were competing. Moreover, the divergence in the AMSRs among East Asian economies led to their different trade negotiation priorities. For instance, Japan and Singapore had a services-dominated economy. To increase market access for their services providers, these two economies emerged as leading supporters for CP/TPP. Developing countries were more concerned with traditional market access because of their dominant agriculture and manufacturing ratios. RCEP particularly catered to these concerns. These two sets of sectoral interests and priorities became the key supporting forces for the two contending initiatives for regional institutional arrangement and for the East Asian states to favor one over the other or join both.

However, Malaysia and Vietnam joined both CP/TPP and RCEP. While their participation in RCEP was predicted in Hypothesis 3 because of their particular sectoral focuses and priorities. Their inclusion in CP/TPP was not expected in Hypothesis 3. This suggested that there were other forces such as geopolitics at play in the shaping of their institutional decisions to join CP/TPP.

Overall, Hypothesis 3 survived the test. My investigations have successfully established the relationship between the sectoral focuses and priorities and the institutional preferences of East Asian states for regionalism in general and their decisions to join CP/TPP and/or RCEP in particular.

7.3 A Structural Theory of East Asian Regionalism

With these findings as evidence, how does our structural theory stand now in explaining the weakness in East Asian regionalism? Table 7.1 summarizes the evidence on the three sets of logical relations proposed in the structural theory.

The first problem of East Asian regionalism is the lack of sincere efforts for a single, region-wide institutional architecture for regional economic organization. Evidence confirmed that the level of regional concentration in East Asia was not as high as that of Europe and North America. Thus, the East Asian economy lacked the material basis to organize itself as a productionally integrated economic community. The second problem is the "noodle bowl" of multilateral initiatives and projects in East Asian regionalism. The evidence established that each national economy is influenced uniquely by a different mixture of productional forces of global and regional origins. This complex global and regional connectivity lessened the desire and weakened the ability of East Asian national economies to form a collective institutional vision for a regional economic community. This lack of interest and inability further drove them to propose and pursue many different projects for regional institutional arrangement. The third problem is the emergence of two separate but

Table 7.1 Evidence for the Structural Theory

International economic structure	*Economic community*	*Theory* *Structural forces*	*Outcomes in East Asian regionalism*	*Evidence*
Global	East Asia, Europe, and North America	Low level of regional concentration of global production networks in East Asia	No efforts for a single region-wide institutional arrangement in East Asia	Confirmed
Regional	East Asian national economies	Complex global-regional connectivity in the nations' production networks	Noodle bowl of multilateral initiatives and projects	Confirmed
Sectoral	CP/TPP, RCEP, and East Asian national economies	Contention of sectoral focuses and priorities in CP/TPP and RCEP production networks	Emergence of two contending projects with different scopes of membership and mechanisms of open and close regionalism	Confirmed, except for Malaysia and Vietnam

overlapping, contending, and competing regional arrangements in East Asia. Evidence supported that contention between the two sets of sectoral focuses and priorities in the CP/TPP structure and RCEP structure drove groups of East Asian economies of similar sectoral focuses and priorities to join CP/TPP and/or RCEP. The global, regional, and sectoral structural forces did not support a single, region-wide institutional framework in East Asia, and thus contributed to weak regionalism.

Together, my evidence from the empirical investigation and analysis established convincingly the positive logical relationship between the three sets of structural forces and the three sets of outcomes in the 40-year development of East Asian regionalism. Based on the supportive evidence and the confirmation of the structural theory, we can make a general theoretical argument: different positions of states in the international economic structure significantly influence and indeed complicate their interests in and capabilities for different types of institutional arrangement for regional economic organization.

Such a theoretical claim is significant because of the theoretical context in which this structural theory was proposed in the first place. Liberal institutionalism hoped to convince us that weak regionalism in East Asia was due to the lack of institutional building in East Asia. My structure-institutional investigation and analysis, however, show that the weakness is not caused by weak institutions. Rather, it is because East Asian economies do not need robust institutions. While market forces called our attention to the power of material forces in driving institutional activities and decisions of these states, my structure-institutional investigation and analysis demonstrate that it was the networking effects of the material forces and the relative positions of states in these networks that shaped specifically their interests and capabilities in pursuing a particular set of institutional arrangement for regional economic organization. This book has undertaken structural investigation and analysis to advance an explanation of the problem in East Asian regionalism. This book draws attention to the critical importance of the driving power of the structural forces over others: 1) the institutional preferences and choices of nations in East Asian regionalism, and 2) the shaping of the institutional architecture for the organization of transnational production in East Asia.

Notes

1 There is a limitation in my input-output data, which cannot differentiate the value-added contributions of a country into contributions of local firms or foreign MNCs. This limitation partly exaggerates the regional concentration of Vietnam's economic structure.
2 Vietnam did not join ASEAN until 1995.

8 Conclusion

This final chapter summarizes the whole project and discusses methods, data organization and analysis, and findings. I will explain how this project was executed and how my project contributes to the wider scholarship on the topic. This book makes original contributions to scholarship on the problem of East Asian regionalism, advances the structural and institutional analysis of the international political economy, and contributes to our understanding of how the world economic system works.

8.1 Summary of the Book

I wrote this book to investigate the structural causes of the problem in East Asian regionalism in the past 40 years. In contrast to more successful projects in Europe and North America, institutional building in East Asian regionalism has been weak. There have been contending initiatives for an economic community in the region, from APEC to ASEAN+3, from EAS to CP/TPP and RCEP, and many less prominent initiatives in between. However, all of these proposals and projects have not led to the formation of a single, region-wide architecture for a regional economic community, but rather, in the end, two separate, overlapping, and conflicting regional arrangements for the region.

My initial puzzle arose from my dissatisfaction with the explanations of liberal institutionalism and market force theory for this circumstance. Liberal institutional theory suggests that East Asian states had little experience in international institution building and lacked a shared regional identity to support a regional economic community. Liberal institutional theory accords excessive attention to international institutions and their role in generating interstate cooperation. The theory fails to see the real material interests and dynamics at work behind the problem of East Asian regionalism. Market force theory, on the other hand, argues that the problem in East Asian regionalism was driven very much by private economic interests and forces in trade, investment, and manufacturing. Accordingly, the reason for the failure in East Asian regionalism is to be found not in institutions, but in the workings of market forces. The market force explanation recognizes the role of material forces in

DOI: 10.4324/9781032613321-8

the shaping of institutions and relations in the production organization. But it fails to see that these market forces of national economies led to the problem of East Asian regionalism through their different positions in the structure of the international economic system. It is the relational economic interests and relative capabilities of the nations that are behind the problem of East Asian regionalism. Both theories miss the role of structural forces and dynamics. I designed the research to investigate these structural forces and to determine how they relate to the problems in East Asian regionalism.

This book first established the concept of international economic structure and the theoretical expectations of the structural force explanation. This book used the GVC analysis and input-output data to construct the three key sets of international economic structures where the positions of the nations can be observed and analyzed. This book also developed substantive empirical material for the institutional preferences and choices of nations in East Asian regionalism. These materials allow us to determine the logical link between the structural forces and the three aspects of the problem in East Asian regionalism.

This book developed three hypotheses to determine the logical relationship between three specific sets of international economic structure and the patterns of weak regionalism. Hypothesis 1 determines whether there was sufficient material basis for East Asia to be a stand-alone regional economic bloc as in the cases of Europe and North America. Hypothesis 2 determines whether the complex levels of global-regional connectivity of the nations were related to the rise of multiple, contending institutional arrangements for transborder production and distribution in the region. Hypothesis 3 requires the investigation of whether the divergence of membership into CP/TPP and RCEP had to do with differences in sectoral focus and priority of the international economic structure of CP/TPP, RCEP, and these East Asian national economies.

Evidence on these three hypotheses found that East Asia lacked the material basis for the region to be a stand-alone economic community. This prevented the region from forming a collective institutional vision for a regional economic community. Furthermore, the region's divergent levels of global/regional connectivity and sectoral focuses and priorities not only weakened its desire for a single region-wide institutional arrangement but also drove the nations involved to prefer various types of institutional arrangements and to agree, in the end, on two overlapping and contending arrangements for the region. My research, thus, successfully identified the structural forces in East Asian regionalism and their logical relationship with the problem in East Asian regionalism.

8.2 Scholarly Significance of the Book

8.2.1 The Study of East Asian Regionalism

This book adds to the scholarship on East Asian regionalism that has until now focused on the power of institutions and market forces. Liberal institutionalism dominates the study of East Asian regionalism with its focus on the enabling role of international institutions and its perception of regionalism as comprising intergovernmental projects of institutional building in managing transnational economic relations and activities. This tradition started with explaining the experience of regional integration in post-War Western Europe. The EU is regarded as an example of successful regional integration. In this framework, regional economic integration is a standardized process of institutional development in five stages, from a free trade area to a customs union, to a common market, to an economic and monetary union, and finally to a political union (Balassa, 1961). Perceived from this framework, the problem of East Asian regionalism was institutional. The domination of the liberal institutional explanations is part of the explanation for the lack of advance in the study of East Asian regionalism.

In more recent years, market force explanations emerged to challenge the liberal institutional theory. Market force theory shifts from a focus on intergovernmental forces in East Asian regionalism as a public sector project to forces in the private sector: trade, investment, and manufacturing. Market forces analysis of East Asian regionalism broadens the field of study to include many different dynamics and forces that influenced the development of regionalism in East Asia. My research here takes the study of East Asian regionalism a step further to call attention to some of the other forces behind the development of East Asian regionalism that are not captured in the two dominant theoretical frameworks.

The structural theory in this book is also a bottom-up approach, as with the market force theory. There are, however, significant differences between these two explanations. Market force theory adopts a realist perspective and focuses on the economic forces of the nations on their own. The structural explanation here is more concerned with the relative interests and capabilities of states and the effects of the structural function of these connected forces. My research thereby brings in a different theory of the causes of the problem in East Asian regionalism and evidence for structural forces influencing the development of East Asian regionalism.

Findings in this book suggest that weak regionalism served the production networks in East Asia well. It was the different positions of the national economies in international economic structures that significantly influenced the interests and capabilities of states in East Asian regionalism. This set of structural forces influenced individual states not to act on the same project for a single set of institutional arrangements for East Asia, but rather to opt for many different and conflicting initiatives for regional institutional arrangement. This circumstance, as presented in my research, led to the ambiguity in the purpose of East Asian regionalism, the proliferation of competing institutional initiatives, and the inability of a single, region-wide organization for the economic community in East Asia to develop. My research brings structural forces into the explanations of East Asian regionalism and offers a deeper understanding of what drives East Asian regionalism, the forms it takes, and its emergent outcomes.

8.2.2 Structural and Institutional Analysis of the International Political Economy

This book develops a concept of the international economic structure and an analytical framework that connects structural forces and dynamics, on the one hand, and states' behavior in regional institutional building, on the other hand. This study uses global value chains analysis and Inter-Country Input-Output data constructing international economic structures and analyzing their effects on states' institutional preferences. This structural analysis fits particularly well for this project that requires effective ways of describing international economic structures and assessing their effects on states' institutional behavior.

This structural analysis and investigation bring new methods of analyzing international economic structures and new indicators and measurements in determining their effects on states' actions and interactions. Kenneth Waltz defines an international structure as a system-wide distribution of capabilities of states in an "anarchic" international system of sovereign states (Waltz, 1979). Immanuel Wallerstein (1980) uses productive, commercial, and financial capabilities to describe the core-peripheral world economic structure. David Lake (1984) uses the relative size and relative productivity of states to describe the international structures in different historical periods of international relations. I use value-added in production networks across different nations to give a more effective account of the national origins of the value-added. More specifically, I use the complex network method to depict the global economic structures and regional concentration rates to determine the position of Europe, North America, and East Asia in the structure. I use the global/regional connectivity method to construct the regional economic structure and levels of the global/regional connectivity to determine the positions of East Asian national economies in the structure. Finally, I use the skyline chart method to construct sectoral economic structures of CP/TPP, RCEP, and individual East Asian national economies and use SSRs and AMSRs to determine positions of the nations in the structures. These three sets of methods and indicators provide a much-improved way of describing and analyzing international economic structures and their effects on states' behavior in and approach to East Asian regionalism.

Moreover, this book also offers a better understanding of the role of institutions in the shaping of international economic order. Dominant liberal institutional analysis such as that of Robert Keohane and Lisa Martin sees international institutions as the primary shaper for the states' international behavior and, more specifically, drivers for international cooperation. Institutions in this book are seen as the consequences of states' actions and interactions driven primarily by structural forces. They are also seen here as instruments for states engaged in intergovernmental negotiations and projects in East Asian regionalism. In determining the effects of the international structures on the institutional preferences of states in East Asian regionalism, I explore the effects of the global economic structure on East Asia as a production unit and the inability of a single and region-wide organization for the economic community in East Asia to develop. I then investigate how the dynamics of the regional economic structure led to multiple contending initiatives for institutional arrangements in the region. Finally, I examine the effects of different types of sectoral economic structures on the divergence of the states' institutional preferences over CP/TPP and RCEP. My institutional analysis here suggests a more nuanced understanding of the relationship between structural dynamics and institutional outcomes. While both have their roles in the shaping of an economic order for industrial production, it is more realistic to see institutions as interstate arrangements arising from the working of the underlying structural forces.

8.2.3 Understandings of World Economic System

Lastly, this book also makes contributions to our understanding of how the world economic system works. The study of the world economic system has been dominated by two leading traditions of scholarship: Wallerstein's core-periphery theory and the world economic system of multilateral institutionalism. Wallerstein was the first to introduce the concept of the world economic structure into the understanding of the international economic system. For Wallerstein, the world economic system is structured into core and peripheral areas, driven by the logic and dynamics of industrial capitalism. It is difficult, if not impossible, for nations to change their position within this hierarchical structure. My research utilizes the structural thinking of the international economic system. I develop a more precise definition of the international economic structures and more contemporary sets of methods and indicators in analyzing an international economic structure and its effects. My research suggests that shifts in power concentration and changes of nations' position in the structure are not only possible but indeed the very fundamental logic of how the international economic structure works.

The dynamics of East Asian growth have provided an ideal case study to explore how the international economic structure and impact on nations' production activities across borders, which Wallerstein's structure theory does not address properly. Industrial growth in East Asia happened in the hierarchical world economic structure built on unequal exchange. These East Asian states started in the "peripheral areas", moved from being peripheral states to semi-peripheral states in waves, and became world core economic states.

Empirical evidence in this book supports a key theoretical assumption underlying my project, this being that international economic structures are dynamic, constantly searching for equilibrium in the power distribution. These dynamics are primarily driven by the different rates of growth of nations in industrial, financial, and trading capabilities. From 1995 to 2015, the international economic structure in East Asia evolved from a Japan-led unipolar pattern to a US-Japan bipolar one, and further to a China-Japan-US tripolar one. Moreover, a country is not always in the same core or peripheral position in the core-periphery structure. The structure of the textile industry, for example, evolved from a multipolar and galaxy type to a China-centered hub-and-spoke pattern. In the case of the electronics industry, the structure transformed from a Japan-led flying goose model to another kind of hierarchy, where China became the hub of final assembly, absorbing key components from the US, Japan, South Korea, and Taiwan. The structure of the automobile industry remained tripolar over time. Although the hierarchic structure and the core-and-periphery relationship have not changed, the distribution patterns vary over time and evolved differently in different sectors.

In addition to Wallerstein's core-periphery conception of the world economic system, this book is also an improvement over the multilateral institutional understanding of the international economic system. Multilateral institutionalism envisages the international economic system to operate under the institutional environment embedded in international institutions set up through multilateral international organizations. East Asian regionalism was advanced as a multilateral undertaking project of international institutional building on the assumption of "the participation, commitment, and consent of multiple nations of equal vetoing power" (Huang, 2019, p. 153) or the principle of national equality and sovereignty. This book empirically demonstrates that East Asian states are not equal in international economic interests and capabilities because they are in different positions in the hierarchic international economic structure. These different positions determine their interests and attitudes toward international institutions and different institutional arrangements for the transborder organization of production and distribution in the region. My research improved the multilateral institutionalist conception of the international economic system through theoretical discussion and empirical investigation. I have established that the working of the international economic system is heavily influenced by the underlying distribution of power among the states, more so than by the rules and norms they manage to agree upon to discipline themselves.

Bibliography

Acharya, A. (1998). Culture, security, multilateralism: The 'ASEAN Way' and regional order. *Contemporary Security Policy, 19*(1), 55–84. https://doi.org/10.1080/13523269808404179

Acharya, A. (2009). *Whose ideas matter? Agency and power in Asian regionalism*. Cornell University Press. https://doi.org/10.7591/j.ctt7zf8x

Acharya, A., & Johnston, A. (2007). *Crafting cooperation: Regional institutions in comparative perspective*. Cambridge University Press. https://doi.org/10.1017/CBO9780511491436

ADB. (2012). *Asian economic integration monitor: July 2012*. Asian Development Bank. Retrieved from: https://www.adb.org/sites/default/files/publication/29923/aem-201207.pdf

ADB. (2013). Beyond factory Asia: Fuelling growth in a changing world. Retrieved from https://www.adb.org/sites/default/files/publication/30223/beyond-factory-asia-fuelling-growth.pdf

ADB. (2017). *The Asian bond markets initiative: Policy maker achievements and challenges*. Asian Development Bank. Retrieved from: https://www.adb.org/sites/default/files/publication/322536/asian-bond-markets-initiative.pdf

ADB. (2020). *ADB-multiregional input-output tables* [Data set]. Asian Development Bank. https://mrio.adbx.online

ADB. (2021). *Multiregional input-output tables* [Data set]. Asian Development Bank. https://kidb.adb.org/mrio

Aggarwal, V., & Urata, S. (2013). *Bilateral trade agreements in the Asia-Pacific: Origins, evolution, and implications*. Routledge. https://doi.org/10.4324/9781315020976

Ahmad, T. (2021). *Indonesian global value chain policy: Learning from China's experiences*. ECIDC Project Paper (No. 9). Retrieved from: https://unctad.org/system/files/official-document/BRI-Project_RP09_en.pdf

Akamatsu, K. (1962). A historical pattern of economic growth in developing countries. *The Developing Economies, 1*(s1), 3–25. https://doi.org/10.1111/j.1746-1049.1962.tb01020.x

Amako, S., Matsuoka, S., & Horiuchi K. (2013). *Regional integration in East Asia: Theoretical and historical perspectives*. UN University. Retrieved from: https://digitallibrary.un.org/record/749079?v=pdf

Ando, M. (2020). Further development of international production networks and job allocation in Japan. *Public Policy Review, 16*(1), 135–162. Retrieved from: https://www.mof.go.jp/english/pri/publication/pp_review/ppr16_01_07.pdf

Ando, M., & Kimura, F. (2003). *The formation of international production and distribution networks in East Asia* (Working Paper No. 10167). Retrieved from: National Bureau of Economic Research website: http://www.nber.org/papers/w10167

Ando, M., & Kimura, F. (2012). International production/distribution networks in East Asia and domestic operations: Evidence from Japanese firms. In Stern (Ed.),

Quantitative analysis of newly evolving patterns of international trade: Fragmentation; offshoring of activities; and vertical intra-industry trade (pp. 239–279). World Scientific.

Ando, M., & Kimura, F. (2013a). Expanding fragmentation of production in East Asia and domestic operations: Further evidence from Japanese manufacturing firms. *Journal of International Commerce, Economics and Policy*, *4*(1). https://doi.org/10.1142/S1793993313500014

Ando, M., & Kimura, F. (2013b). Production linkage of Asia and Europe via Central and Eastern Europe. *Journal of Economic Integration*, *28*(2), 204–240. https://doi.org/10.11130/jei.2013.28.2.204

Ando, M., & Kimura, F. (2014). Evolution of machinery production networks: Linkage of North America with East Asia. *Asian Economic Papers*, *13*(3), 121–160. https://doi.org/10.1162/ASEP_a_00299

APEC. (2017), *Impact of TPP's e-commerce chapter on APEC's e-commerce*. Asia Pacific Economic Cooperation Report (No. APEC#218-CT-01.4). Retrieved from: https://www.apec.org/Publications/2018/05/Impact-of-TPPs-E-commerce-Chapter-on-APECs-E-commerce

Artner, A. (2017). Role of Indonesia in the evolution of ASEAN. *The Journal of East Asian Affairs*, *31*(1), 1–38. http://www.jstor.org/stable/44321271

ASEAN-China Expert Group on Economic Cooperation. (2001). Forging closer ASEAN-China economic relations in the twenty-first century. Retrieved from: https://www.asean.org/wp-content/uploads/images/archive/newdata/asean_chi.pdf

Asia Regional Integration Center. (2019). *Intra-regional trade share* [Data set]. https://aric.adb.org/integrationindicators

Athukorala, P.-C. (2009). Trends and patterns of foreign direct investments in Asia: A comparative perspective. *The Journal of Applied Economic Research*, *3*(4), 365–408. https://doi.org/10.1177%2F097380100900300403

Athukorala, P.-C. (2010). The rise of China and East Asian export performance. In P.-C. Athukorala (Ed.), *The rise of Asia: Trade and investment in global perspective* (pp. 267–291). Routledge.

Athukorala, P.-C. (2011). Production networks and trade patterns in East Asia: Regionalization or globalization? *Asian Economic Papers*, *10*(1), 65–95. https://doi.org/10.1162/ASEP_a_00045

Athukorala, P.-C. (2014). Global production sharing and trade patterns in East Asia. In I. N. Kaur, & N. Singh (Eds.), *The Oxford handbook of the economics of the Pacific Rim* (pp. 333–361). Oxford University Press. https://doi.org/10.1093/oxfordhb/9780199751990.013.014

Athukorala, P.-C., & Yamashita, N. (2006). Production fragmentation and trade integration: East Asia in a global context. *The North American Journal of Economics and Finance*, *17*(3), 233–256. https://doi.org/10.1016/j.najef.2006.07.002

Awanohara, S. (1991). Rich man, poor man. *Far Eastern Economic Review*, *154*(40), 13.

Ayub, A. J., & Jalil, I. N. (2018). Recent trends in trade and trade agreements: Global value chains and mega-regional agreements. In P. Sauvé (Ed.), *Malaysia's trade governance at a crossroads* (pp. 75–110). Khazanah Research Institute. Retrieved from: http://www.krinstitute.org/assets/contentMS/img/template/editor/3%20GVC.pdf

Azhar, K. (2020, December 3). RCEP benefits Malaysia but watch out for competition from Vietnam, Indonesia. *The Edge Markets*. Retrieved from: https://www.theedgemarkets.com/article/rcep-benefits-malaysia-watch-out-competition-vietnam-indonesia

Balassa, B. (1961). *The theory of economic integration*. George Allen & Unwin Ltd.

Baldwin, R. (1993). A domino theory of regionalism (Working Paper No. 4465). Retrieved from National Bureau of Economic Research website: http://www.nber.org/papers/w4465

Baldwin, R. (2008). Managing the noodle bowl: The fragility of East Asian regionalism. *The Singapore Economic Review*, *53*(03), 449–478. https://doi.org/10.1142/S0217590808003063

Baldwin, R. (2011). 21st century regionalism: Filling the gap between 21st century trade and 20th century trade rules (Staff Working Papers No. ERSD-2011-08). Retrieved from WTO website: https://www.wto.org/english/res_e/reser_e/ersd201108_e.pdf

Baldwin, R., & Lopez-Gonzalez, J. (2015). Supply-chain trade: A portrait of global patterns and several testable hypotheses. *World Economy*, *38*(11), 1682–1721. https://doi.org/10.1111/twec.12189

Baldwin, R., & Okubo, T. (2014). Networked FDI: Sales and sourcing patterns of Japanese foreign affiliates. *World Economy*, *37*(8), 1051–1080. https://doi.org/10.1111/twec.12116

Bamber, P., Fernandez-Stark, K., Gereffi, G., & Guinn, A. (2014). Connecting local producers in developing countries to regional and global value chains. OECD Trade Policy Papers (No.160). https://doi.org/10.1787/5jzb95f1885l-en

Bark, T. (2012, March 8). *Strategic value of the KORUS FTA*. Retrieved from the Government of South Korea website: https://www.korea.kr/briefing/speechView.do?newsId=132023871

Beeson, M. (2006). American hegemony and regionalism: The rise of East Asia and the end of the Asia-Pacific. *Geopolitics*, *11*(4), 541–560. https://doi.org/10.1080/14650040600890727

Bernard, M., & Ravenhill, J. (1995). Beyond product cycles and flying geese: Regionalization, hierarchy, and the industrialization of East Asia. *World Politics*, *47*(2), 171–209. https://doi.org/10.1017/S0043887100016075

Borrus, M., Ernst, D., & Haggard, S. (2000). Introduction: Cross-border production networks and the industrial integration of the Asia-Pacific region. In Michael Borrus, D. Ernst, & S. Haggard (Eds.), *International production networks in Asia: Rivalry or riches?* (pp. 1–29). Routledge. https://doi.org/10.4324/9780203361115

Bradford, A. (2007). Regime theory. *Max Planck Encyclopedia of Public International Law*. Retrieved from Columbia Law School Scholarship Archive: https://scholarship.law.columbia.edu/faculty_scholarship/1970

Breslin, S., & Higgott, R. (2000). Studying regions: Learning from the old, constructing the new. *New Political Economy*, *5(3)*, 333–352. https://doi.org/10.1080/713687784

Breslin, S., Higgott, R., & Rosamond, B. (2002). Regions in comparative perspective. In S. Breslin, C. W. Hughes, N. Phillips, & B. Rosamond (Eds.), *New regionalism in the global political economy* (pp. 1–19). Routledge. https://doi.org/10.4324/9780203361672

Cai, K. (2010). *The politics of economic regionalism: Explaining regional economic integration in East Asia*. Palgrave Macmillan.

Cai, P. (2017). Understanding China's Belt and Road Initiative. Retrieved from Lowy Institute website: https://www.lowyinstitute.org/publications/understanding-belt-and-road-initiative

Calder, K., & Ye, M. (2010). *The making of Northeast Asia*. Stanford University Press. https://doi.org/10.1515/9780804775052

Camroux, D. (2012). Regionalism in Asia as disguised multilateralism: A critical analysis of the East Asia Summit and the Trans-Pacific Partnership. *The International Spectator*, *47*(1), 97–115. https://doi.org/10.1080/03932729.2012.655010

Capannelli, G., & Kawai, M. (2014). The political economy of Asian regionalism: Issues and challenges. In G. Capannelli & M. Kawai (Eds.), *The political economy of Asian regionalism* (pp. 1–18). Springer. https://doi.org/10.1007/978-4-431-54568-2

Capannelli, G., & Tan, S. S. (2012). Institutions for Asian integration: Innovation and reform (ADBI Working Paper No. 375). Retrieved from Asian Development Bank website: https://www.adb.org/sites/default/files/publication/156230/adbi-wp375.pdf

Cartwright, M. (2017, May 18). The death of the Trans-Pacific Partnership and the contradictions of neoliberalism. *E-International Relations*. Retrieved from Graduate Institute of International and Development Studies website: https://www.e-ir.info/2017/05/18/the-death-of-the-trans-pacific-partnership-and-the-contradictions-of-neoliberal/

Castle, M., Quesne, S. L., & Leslie, J. (2016). Divergent paths of state-society relations in European and trans-Tasman economic integration. *Journal of European Integration*, *38*(1), 41–59. https://doi.org/10.1080/07036337.2015.1057819

Cha, V. (2018). *Powerplay: The origin of the American alliance system in Asia*. Princeton University Press. https://doi-org.helicon.vuw.ac.nz/10.2307/j.ctvc778dz

Chen, L. (2008). The market driven trade liberalization and East Asian regional integration (HEID Working Paper No. 12/2008). Retrieved from: https://cris.unu.edu/market-driven-trade-liberalisation-and-east-asian-regional-integration

Cheong, I. (2008). Korea's position in the ASEAN+3 process: Review of performance and policy implications. *The Journal of East Asian Affairs*, *22*(2), 63–95. http://www.jstor.org/stable/23257897

Chiang, M.-H. (2016). Sustaining Hong Kong's services amid the changing dynamics of China's economy. *China Perspectives*. Advance online publication. https://doi.org/10.4000/chinaperspectives.6978

Chin, G., & Stubbs, R. (2011). China, regional institution-building and the China ASEAN Free Trade Area. *Regional Studies*, *18*(3), 277–298. http://www.jstor.org/stable/23050605

Chirathivat, S., & Mallikamas, S. (2004). Thailand's FTA Strategy: Current development and future challenges. *ASEAN Economic Bulletin*, *21*(1), 37–53. http://www.jstor.org/stable/25773801

Choi, B.-I., & Oh, J. S. (2017). Reversed asymmetry in Japan's and Korea's FTAs: TPP and beyond. *Pacific Focus*, *32*(2), 232–258. https://doi.org/10.1111/pafo.12091

Chongkittavorn, K. (2020, August 15). Thailand is not ready for the CP/TPP. *Bangkok Post*. https://www.bangkokpost.com/opinion/opinion/1973987/thailand-is-not-ready-for-the-cptpp

Chowdhury, A. (1988). Textiles and electronics industries in ASEAN: A profile. *ASEAN Economic Bulletin*, *4*(3), 241–251. https://www.jstor.org/stable/25770169

Clark, C. (1951). *The conditions of economic progress*. MacMillan.

Coe, N. M., Dicken, P., & Hess, M. (2008). Global production networks: Realizing the potential. *Journal of Economic Geography*, *8*(3), 271–295. https://doi.org/10.1093/jeg/lbn002

Cumings, B. (1984). The origins and development of the Northeast Asian political economy: Industrial sectors, product cycles, and political consequences. *International Organization*, *38*(1), 1–40. https://doi.org/10.1017/S0020818300004264

Daniels, L. V. (2020). Repercussions of the US-China conflict on the multilateral order. In B. Lippert, & V. Perthes (Eds.), *Strategic rivalry between United States and China: Causes, trajectories, and implications for Europe* (pp. 43–47). Stiftung Wissenschaft und Politik, German Institute for International and Security Affairs. https://doi.org/10.18449/2020RP04

Dedrick, J., & Kraemer, K. L. (1998). *Asia's computer challenge: Threat or opportunity for the United States & the world*. Oxford University Press.

Dedrick, J., Kraemer, K. L., & Linden, G. (2010). Who profits from innovation in global value chains? A study of the iPod and notebook PCs. *Industrial and Corporate Change*, *19*(1), 81–116. https://doi.org/10.2139/ssrn.1125024

Dent, C. M. (1997). Economic relations between the EU and East Asia: Past, present and future. *Intereconomics*, *32*(1), 7–13. https://doi.org/10.1007/BF02929815

Dent, C. M. (2016). *East Asian regionalism*. Routledge.

Deprez, Sophie (2018). The strategic vision behind Vietnam's international trade integration. *Journal of Current Southeast Asian Affairs*, *37*(2), 3–38. https://doi.org/10.1177%2F186810341803700201

Dieter, H. (2006). Report on East Asian integration: Opportunities and obstacles for enhanced economic cooperation. *Notre Europe Studies and Research Paper* (No. 47). Retrieved from: https://institutdelors.eu/wp-content/uploads/2020/08/etud47en.pdf

Dieter, H., & Higgott, R. (2003). Exploring alternative theories of economic regionalism: From trade to finance in Asian co-operation? *Review of International Political Economy*, *10*(3), 430–454. https://doi.org/10.1080/09692290308422

Dietzenbacher, E., Los, B., Stehrer, R., Timmer, M., & De Vries, G. (2013). The construction of world input-output Tables in the WIOD Project. *Economic Systems Research*, *25*(1), 71–98. https://doi.org/10.1080/09535314.2012.761180

Djidin, D. A. (1997). The political economy of Indonesia's new economic policy. *Journal of Contemporary Asia*, *27*(1), 14–36. https://doi.org/10.1080/00472339780000031

Doner, R. (1991). *Driving a bargain: Automobile industrialization and Japanese firms in Southeast Asia*. University of California Press.

Doner, R., & Wad, P. (2014). Financial crises and automotive industry development in Southeast Asia. *Journal of Contemporary Asia*, *44*(4), 664–687. https://doi.org/10.1080/00472336.2014.923635

Drysdale, P. (2017). ASEAN: The experiment in open regionalism that succeeded. In R. S. Maria, S. Urata, & S. I. Ponciano (Eds.), The ASEAN Economic Community into 2025 and beyond (pp. 64–86). Economic Research Institute for ASEAN and East Asia.

Drysdale, P., & Garnaut, R. (1993). The Pacific: An application of a general theory of economic integration. In C. F. Bergsten & M. Noland (Eds.), *Pacific dynamism and the international economic system* (Vol. 183, pp. 183–224). Peterson Institute for International Economics.

Drysdale, P., & Vines, D. (1998). *Europe, East Asia, and APEC: A shared global agenda?* Cambridge University Press.

Dunning, J. H. (1980). Toward an eclectic theory of international production: Some empirical tests. *Journal of International Business Studies*, *11*(1), 9–31. https://doi.org/10.1057/palgrave.jibs.8490593

Elms, D. (2020). Using RCEP: Swimsuits and textile trade. *Talking Trade*. Retrieved from Asian Trade Center website: http://asiantradecentre.org/talkingtrade/using-rcep-swimsuits-and-textile-trade

Elms, D. K. (2021). Getting RCEP across the line. *World Trade Review*, *20*(3), 373–380. https://doi.org/10.1017/S1474745620000592

Elms, D. K., & Nguyen, M. H. (2019). The evolution of the regional comprehensive economic partnership. In D. Mukherjee (Ed.), *Economic integration in Asia: Key prospects and challenges with the Regional Comprehensive Economic Partnership* (pp. 7–26). Routledge.

ERIA. (2012). Regional Comprehensive Economic Partnership. *ERIA Research Institute Network Statement* (No. 2). Retrieved from: https://www.eria.org/uploads/media/research-networks/2nd-RIN-Statement_Submission-on_26-Nov-2012.pdf

Ernst & Young Tax Consultants. (2021). *RCEP: Regional trade opportunities for Malaysia*. Retrieved from: https://www.ey.com/en_my/take-5-business-alert/rcep-regional-trade-opportunities-for-malaysia

Ernst, D. (2002). Global Production Networks in East Asia's electronics industry and upgrading perspectives in Malaysia. *East-West Center Working Papers, Economics Series* (No. 44). Retrieved from: https://www.eastwestcenter.org/system/tdf/private/ECONwp044.pdf?file=1&type=node&id=31847

Ernst, D., & Ravenhill, J. (2000). Convergence and diversity: How globalization reshapes Asian production networks. In M. Borrus, D. Ernst, & S. Haggard (Eds.), *International production networks in Asia: Rivalry or riches* (pp. 223–253). Routledge.

Escaith, H., Inomata, S., & Miroudot, S. (2018). Evolution of production networks in the Asia-Pacific region: A vision in value-added and employment dimensions. In S. Armstrong & T. Westland (Eds.), *Asian economic integration in an era of global uncertainty* (pp. 155–183). ANU Press.

EU. (n.d.). The EU in brief. Retrieved from: https://europa.eu/european-union/about-eu/eu-in-brief_en

Evans, P. (2005). Between regionalism and regionalization: Policy networks and the nascent East Asian institutional identity. In P. J. Katzenstein & T. J. Pempel (Eds.), *Remapping East Asia: The construction of a region* (pp. 195–215). Cornell University Press.

Ferrarini, B. (2013). Vertical trade maps. *Asian Economic Journal*, *27*(2), 105–123. https://doi.org/10.1111/asej.12005

Ferrarini, B., & Hummels, D. (Eds.). (2014). *Asia and global production networks: Implications for trade, incomes and economic vulnerability*. Edward Elgar Publishing. Retrieved from: https://www.adb.org/sites/default/files/publication/149221/asia-andglobal-production-networks.pdf

Fildes, N., & Lucas, L. (2019). US charges against Huawei hit global supply chain. *Financial Times*. Retrieved from: https://www.ft.com/content/c5de8c08-23bd-11e9-b329-c7e6ceb5ffdf

Frankel, J. A., & Wei, S.-J. (1997). The new regionalism and Asia: Impact and options. In A. Panagariya, M. G. Quibria, & N. Rao (Eds.), *The global trading system and developing Asia* (pp. 83–130). Oxford University Press.

Fujita, M. (2007). Development of East Asian regional economies: A view from spatial economics. In M. Fujita (Ed.), *Regional integration in East Asia* (pp. 64–88). Springer.

Fukao, K., Ishido, H., & Ito, K. (2003). Vertical intra-industry trade and foreign direct investment in East Asia. *Journal of the Japanese and International Economies*, *17*(4), 468–506. https://doi.org/10.1016/j.jjie.2003.09.004

Fukunaga, Y., & Isono, I. (2013). Taking ASEAN+1 FTAs towards the RCEP: A mapping study. *ERIA Discussion Paper Series* (No. 2). Retrieved from: https://www.eria.org/ERIA-DP-2013-02.pdf

Gereffi, G. (2018). International trade and industrial upgrading in the apparel commodity chain. In G. Gereffi (Ed.), *Global value chains and development: Redefining the contours of 21st century capitalism* (pp. 72–107). Cambridge University Press.

Gereffi, G., & Frederick, S. (2010). *The global apparel value chain, trade and the crisis: Challenges and opportunities for developing countries*. World Bank Policy Research Working Paper (No. 5281). Retrieved from: https://ssrn.com/abstract=1596491

Gereffi, G., Humphrey, J., & Sturgeon, T. (2005). The governance of global value chains. *Review of International Political Economy*, *12*(1), 78–104. https://doi.org/10.1080/09692290500049805

Gereffi, G., & Memedovic, O. (2003). *The global apparel value chain: What prospects for upgrading by developing countries?* United Nations Industrial Development sectoral studies series. Retrieved from: https://ssrn.com/abstract=413820

Gilpin, R. (1981). *War and change in world politics*. Cambridge University Press.

Gilpin, R. (1993). The debate about the new world economic order. In D. Unger & P. Blackburn (Eds.), *Japan's emerging global role*. Lynn Rienner Publishers.

Gilpin, R. (1995). Economic change and the challenge of uncertainty. In R. S. Ross (Ed.), *East Asia in transition: Toward a new regional order* (pp. 3–20). Routledge.

Grimes, W. W. (2006). East Asian financial regionalism in support of the global financial architecture? The political economy of regional nesting. *Journal of East Asian Studies*, *6*(3), 353–380. https://doi.org/10.1017/S1598240800004628

Haas, E. B. (1958). *The uniting of Europe*. Stanford University Press.

Haas, E. B. (1961). International integration: The European and the universal process. *International Organization*, *15*(3), 366–392. https://doi.org/10.1017/S0020818300002198

Haddad, M. (2007). Trade integration in East Asia: The role of China and production networks. Policy Research Working Papers (March 2007). https://doi.org/10.1596/1813-9450-4160

Haggard, S. (2000). *The political economy of the Asian financial crisis*. Columbia University Press.

Hall, P. A., & Taylor, R. C. R. (1996). Political science and the three new institutionalisms. *Political Studies*, *44*(5), 936–957. https://doi.org/10.1111/j.1467-9248.1996.tb00343.x

Hamanaka, S. (2014). Trans-Pacific Partnership versus Regional Comprehensive Economic Partnership: Control of membership and agenda setting. *ADB Working Paper series on Regional Economic Integration*. https://www.adb.org/sites/default/files/publication/152753/reiwp-146.pdf

Hansen, A. (2016). Driving development? The problems and promises of the car in Vietnam. *Journal of Contemporary Asia*, *46*(4), 551–569. https://doi.org/10.1080/00472336.2016.1151916

He, B. (2004). East Asian ideas of regionalism: A normative critique. *Australian Journal of International Affairs*, *58*(1), 105–125. https://doi.org/10.1080/1035771032000184791

He, K., & Feng, H. (2018). Game of institutional balancing: China, the AIIB, and the future of global governance. *The RSIS Working Paper Series* (No. 314). www.jstor.org/stable/resrep19929

Heywood, A. (2014). *Global politics*. Palgrave Macmillan.

Higgott, R. (2016). Regional worlds, regional institutions: Towards the regional economic institutionalisation of East Asia? *CSGR Working Paper* (No. 280). https://warwick.ac.uk/fac/soc/pais/research/researchcentres/csgr/papers/280-16.pdf

Hiratsuka, D., & Kimura, F. (2008). From de facto to de jure economic integration in East Asia: Past, present and future. In D. Hiratsuka & F. Kimura (Eds.), *East Asia's Economic Integration: Progress and Benefit* (pp. 1–25). Springer.

Horn, H., Mavroidis, P. C., & Sapir, A. (2010). Beyond the WTO? An anatomy of EU and US preferential trade agreements. *The World Economy*, *33*(11), 1565–1588. https://doi.org/10.1111/j.1467-9701.2010.01273.x

Hoshiro, H. (2019). Does regionalization promote regionalism? Evidence from East Asia. *Journal of Contemporary East Asia Studies*, *8*(2), 199–219. https://doi.org/10.1080/24761028.2019.1693944

Huang, X. (2019). *International relations of East Asia: Structures, institutions and international order*. Red Globe Press.

Huang, X. (2020). Structuring of transborder flows of national industrial capital: Japan in the 1970s and 1980s, and China in the 2000s and 2010s. *The Japanese Political Economy*, *46*(2–3), 200–226. https://doi.org/10.1080/2329194X.2020.1814159

Hummels, D., Ishii, J., & Yi, K.-M. (2001). The nature and growth of vertical specialization in world trade. *Journal of International Economics*, *54*(1), 75–96. https://doi.org/10.1016/S0022-1996(00)00093-3

Hund, M. (2003). ASEAN plus three: Towards a new age of pan-East Asian regionalism? A skeptic's appraisal. *The Pacific Review*, *16*(3), 383–417. https://doi.org/10.1080/0951274032000085644

IDE-JETRO. (1995). The automotive industry in Asia: The great leap forward? *Institute of Developing Economies Spot Survey* (No. 3). https://www.ide.go.jp/English/Publish/Reports/Spot/03.html

IDE-JETRO, & WTO. (2011). *Trade patterns and global value chains in East Asia: From trade in goods to trade in tasks*. https://www.wto.org/english/res_e/booksp_e/stat_tradepat_globvalchains_e.pdf

Ignatenko, A., Raei, F., & Mircheva B. (2019). Global value chains: What are the benefits and why do countries participate? IMF Working Paper (No. 2019/018). Retrieved from: https://www.imf.org/en/Publications/WP/Issues/2019/01/18/Global-Value-Chains-What-are-the-Benefits-and-Why-Do-Countries-Participate-46505

Ikenberry, G. J. (2001). *After victory: Institutions, strategic restraint, and the rebuilding of order after major wars*. Princeton University Press.

Ikenberry, G. J. (2008). The rise of China and the future of the West: Can the liberal system survive? *Foreign Affairs*, *87*(1), 23–37. https://www.jstor.org/stable/20020265

Ikenberry, G. J. (2014). *Power, order, and change in world politics*. Cambridge University Press.

Intal, P. S., & Chen, L. (2017). The ASEAN member states and ASEAN economic integration. In P. S. Intal & L. Chen (Eds.), *ASEAN and member states: Transformation and integration* (pp. 62–81). Economic Research Institute for ASEAN and East Asia. https://www.eria.org/ASEAN_50_Vol_3_Complete_Book.pdf

Ishida, M. (2012). Attracting FDI: Experiences of East Asian countries. In H. Lim & Y. Yamada (Eds.), *Economic reforms in Myanmar: Pathways and prospects* (pp. 85–130). Retrieved from Bangkok Research Center of IDE-JETRO website: https://www.ide.go.jp/library/English/Publish/Reports/Brc/pdf/10_03.pdf

Ito, T., & Krueger, A. O. (2000). *The role of foreign direct investment in East Asian economic development*. University of Chicago Press.

JETRO. (n.d.) *Japanese trade and investment statistics* [Data set]. https://www.jetro.go.jp/en/reports/statistics.html

Jetschke, A. (2009). Institutionalizing ASEAN: Celebrating Europe through network governance. *Cambridge Review of International Affairs*, *22*(3), 407–426. https://doi.org/10.1080/09557570903107688

Jiang, H., & Yu, M. (2021). Understanding RCEP and CP/TPP: From the perspective China's dual circulation economic strategy. *China Economic Journal*, *14*(2),144–161. https://doi.org/10.1080/17538963.2021.1933055

Jin, K. (2012). Industrial structure and capital flows. *The American Economic Review*, *102*(5), 2111–2146. https://doi.org/10.1257/aer.102.5.2111

Johnson, R. C., & Noguera, G. (2012). Accounting for intermediates: Production sharing and trade in value added. *Journal of International Economics*, *86*(2), 224–236. https://doi.org/10.1016/j.jinteco.2011.10.003

Johnston, A. I. (2012). What (if anything) does East Asia tell us about international relations theory? *Annual Review of Political Science*, *15*(1), 53–78. https://doi.org/10.1146/annurev.polisci.040908.120058

Kasahara, S. (2013). The Asian developmental state and the flying geese paradigm. *UNCTAD Discussion Papers*. Retrieved from: https://unctad.org/system/files/official-document/osgdp20133_en.pdf

Kasahara, S. (2019). *A critical evaluation of the flying geese paradigm: The evolving framework of the model and its application to East Asian regional development and beyond*. [Doctoral thesis, Erasmus University Rotterdam]. http://hdl.handle.net/1765/123636

Katada, S. N., & Solís, M. (2010). Domestic sources of Japanese foreign policy activism: Loss avoidance and demand coherence. *International Relations of the Asia-Pacific*, *10*(1), 129–157. https://doi.org/10.1093/irap/lcp009

Katzenstein, P. J. (1997). Introduction: Asian regionalism in comparative perspective. In P. J. Katzenstein & S. Takashi (Eds.), *Network power: Japan and Asia* (pp. 1–44). Cornell University Press.

Katzenstein, P. J. (2015). *A world of regions: Asia and Europe in the American imperium*. Cornell University Press.

Kawai, M. (2005). East Asian economic regionalism: Progress and challenges. *Journal of Asian Economics*, *16*(1), 29–55. https://doi.org/10.1016/j.asieco.2005.01.001

Kawai, M. (2015). From the Chiang Mai Initiative to an Asian Monetary Fund. *ADB Working Paper Series* (No. 527). Retrieved from: https://www.adb.org/sites/default/files/publication/160056/adbi-wp527.pdf

Kawai, M., & Urata, S. (1998). Are trade and direct investment substitutes or complements? An empirical analysis of Japanese manufacturing industries. In H. Lee & D. W. Roland-Holst (Eds.), *Economic development and cooperation in the Pacific Basin: Trade, investment and environmental issues* (pp. 251–295). Cambridge University Press.

Kawai, M., & Wignaraja, G. (2007). ASEAN+3 or ASEAN+6: Which way forward? *ADB Institute Discussion Paper* (No. 77). https://hdl.handle.net/11540/3665

Kawai, M., & Wignaraja, G. (2008). Regionalism as an engine of multilateralism: A case for a single East Asian FTA. *Asian Development Bank Working Paper Series on Regional Economic Integration* (No. 14). Retrieved from: https://www.adb.org/sites/default/files/publication/28471/wp14-east-asian-fta.pdf

Kawai, M., & Wignaraja, G. (2010). Asian FTAs: Trends, prospects, and challenges. *ADB Working Paper Series* (No. 226). Retrieved from: https://www.adb.org/sites/default/files/publication/28273/economics-wp226.pdf

Kawai, M., & Wignaraja, G. (2014). Trade policy and growth in Asia. *ADBI Working Paper* (No. 495). https://doi.org/10.2139/ssrn.2482100

Keohane, R. O. (1984). *After hegemony: Cooperation and discord in the world political economy*. Princeton University Press.

Keohane, R. O. (1989). *International institutions and state power: Essays in international relations theory*. Westview Press.

Keohane, R. O. (2012). Twenty years of institutional liberalism. *International Relations*, *26*(2), 125–138. https://doi.org/10.1177%2F0047117812438451

Keohane, R. O., & Martin, L. L. (2003). Institutional theory as a research program. In C. Elman & M. F. Elman (Eds.), *Progress in international relations theory: Appraising the field* (pp. 71–108). MIT Press.

Keohane, R. O., & Nye, J. S. (1989). *Power and interdependence* (2nd ed.). Pearson Education.

Khong, Y. F., & Helen, N. (2007). Hanging together, institutional design, and cooperation in Southeast Asia: AFTA and the ARF. In A. Amitav & I. J. Alastair (Eds.), *Crafting cooperation: Regional international institutions in comparative perspective* (pp. 32–82). Cambridge University Press.

Kim, S. Y. (2015). *Deep integration and regional trade agreements*. Oxford University Press.

Kim, Y.-C. (2016). RCEP vs. TPP: The pursuit of Eastern dominance. In Y.-C. Kim (Ed.), *Chinese global production networks in ASEAN* (pp. 19–37). Springer International Publishing. https://doi.org/10.1007/978-3-319-24232-3_2

Kimura, F. (2008). The modality of East Asia's economic integration. In *East Asia's economic integration* (pp. 29–44). Springer.

Klabbers, J. (2014). The emergence of functionalism in international institutional law: Colonial inspirations. *European Journal of International Law*, *25*(3), 645–675. https://doi.org/10.1093/ejil/chu053

Kogut, B. (1985). Designing global strategies: Comparative and competitive value-added chains. *Sloan Management Review*, *26*(4), 15–28. https://doi.org/10.1002/tie.5060280105

Kojima, K. (1973). A macroeconomic approach to foreign direct investment. *Hitotsubashi Journal of Economics*, *14*(1), 1–21. https://doi.org/10.15057/8008

Kono, Y. (2001). Myth and reality: Why Japan strives for multilateralism. Retrieved from the Ministry of Foreign Affairs of Japan website: https://www.mofa.go.jp/announce/fm/kono/speech0101.html

Koopman, R., Wang, Z., & Wei, S.-J. (2014). Tracing value-added and double counting in gross exports. *American Economic Review*, *104*(2), 459–494. https://doi.org/10.1257/aer.104.2.459

Kostoska, O., Mitikj, S., Jovanovski, P., & Kocarev, L. (2020). Core-periphery structure in sectoral international trade networks: A new approach to an old theory. *Plos One*, *15*(4), 1–24. https://doi.org/10.1371/journal.pone.0229547

Krasner, S. D. (1982). Structural causes and regime consequences: Regimes as intervening variables. *International Organization*, *36*(2), 185–205. www.jstor.org/stable/2706520

Krieckhaus, J. (2018). *Geopolitical economy: The South Korean FTA strategy*. University of Michigan Press. https://doi.org/10.3998/mpub.8877143

Ku, S. C. Y. (2010). China and Southeast Asia: The clouds behind the light. In D. Hickey & B. Guo (Eds.), *Dancing with the dragon: China's emergence in the developing world* (pp. 197–222). Lexington Books.

Kwan, C.-H. (2001). *Yen Bloc: Toward economic integration in Asia*. Brookings Institution Press. https://www.jstor.org/stable/10.7864/j.ctt127xx2

Kwan, W. K. (2002, January 10). PM Goh, Koizumi call for Japan-ASEAN pact. *The Straits Times*.
Kwon, T., & Ryou, J. W. (2015). Global value chains of East Asia: Trade in value added and vertical specialization. *Asian Economic Journal*, *29*(2), 121–143. https://doi.org/10.1111/asej.12051
Kwon, Y. (2004). East Asian regionalism focusing on ASEAN plus three. *The Journal of East Asian Affairs*, *18*(1), 98–130. http://www.jstor.org/stable/23257953
Lake, D. A. (1984). Beneath the commerce of nations: A theory of international economic structures. *International Studies Quarterly*, *28*(2), 143–170. https://doi.org/10.2307/2600693
Lardy, N. (1994). *China in the world economy*. Peterson Institute for International Economics. https://doi-org.helicon.vuw.ac.nz/10.1787/9789264062184-zh
Lee, Jessica J. (2015, October 23). The truth about South Korea's TPP shift. *The Diplomat*. Retrieved from: https://thediplomat.com/2015/10/the-truth-about-south-koreas-tpp-shift/
Leong, S. (2000). The East Asian Economic Caucus (EAEC): 'Formalized' regionalism being denied. In B. Hettne, A. Inotai, & O. Sunkel (Eds.), *National perspectives on the new regionalism in the South* (pp. 57–107). Macmillan.
Leontief, W. (1963). The structure of development. *Scientific American*, *209*(3), 148–167. https://doi.org/10.1038/scientificamerican0963-148
Levy, M. A., Young, O. R., & Zurn, M. (1995). The study of international regimes. *European Journal of International Relations*, *1*(3), 267–330. https://doi.org/10.1177/1354066195001003001
Li, W. (2011). Dongya jingji diquzhuyi de zhongjie——zhidu guosheng yu jingji zhenghe de kunjing 东亚经济地区主义的终结?——制度过剩与经济整合的困境 [The end of East Asian economic regionalism? Institutional overreach and the challenges of economic integration]. 当代亚太 [*Journal of Contemporary Asia-Pacific Studies*], *4*, 6–32.
Li, Z. (2013). How foreign direct investment promotes development: The case of the People's Republic of China's inward and outward FDI. *ADB Economics Working Paper Series* (No. 304). Retrieved from: https://hdl.handle.net/11540/2092
Lipsey, R. E. (2006). U.S. firms and East Asian development in the 1990s. In S. Urata, S. Y. Chia, & F. Kimura (Eds.), *Multinationals and economic growth in East Asia: Foreign direct investment, corporate strategies and national economic development* (pp. 105–129). Routledge.
Lipson, C. (1991). Why are some international agreements informal? *International Organization*, *45*(4), 495–538. https://doi.org/10.1017/S0020818300033191
Liu, S. (2003, July 5). Dalu yu xianggang qian CEPA cu liangan jian xin jingji hezuo jizhi 大陆与香港签CEPA促两岸建新经济合作机制 [Mainland-HK CEPA urges the establishment of a new mechanism for cross-strait economic cooperation]. *中国新闻网 [China News Agency]*. Retrieved from: http://business.sohu.com/85/38/article210753885.shtml
Los, B., Timmer, M. P., & de Vries, G. J. (2015). How global are global value chains? A new approach to measure international fragmentation. *Journal of Regional Science*, *55*(1), 66–92. https://doi.org/10.1111/jors.12121
Mansfield, E. D., & Milner, H. V. (1997). *The Political Economy of Regionalism*. Columbia University Press.
Martin, A., & Mercurio, B. (2017). Doha dead and buried in Nairobi: Lessons for the WTO. *Journal of International Trade Law and Policy*, *16* (1), 49–66. https://doi.org/10.1108/JITLP-01-2017-0001
Martin, L. L., & Simmons, B. A. (1998). Theories and empirical studies of international institutions. *International Organization*, *52*(4), 729–757. https://doi.org/10.1162/002081898550734

Marukawa, T. (2002). Japanese FDI and China's industrial development in the automobile, electronics and textile industries. In H. G. Hilpert & R. Haak (Eds.), *Japan and China: Cooperation, competition and conflict* (pp. 174–193). Palgrave Macmillan UK.

Masaki, O., & Kawate, K. (1998). Business development of European companies in Asia. *Japan Research Institute Monthly*, *39*, 37–49. Retrieved from: https://www.jri.co.jp/english/periodical/rim/1998/RIMe199802eucorp/

Mattli, W. (1999a). Explaining regional integration outcomes. *Journal of European Public Policy*, *6*(1), 1–27. https://doi.org/10.1080/135017699343775

Mattli, W. (1999b). *The logic of regional integration: Europe and Beyond*. Cambridge University Press.

McKinsey Global Institute (2012). Manufacturing the future: The next era of global growth and innovation. Retrieved from: https://www.mckinsey.com/capabilities/operations/our-insights/the-future-of-manufacturing

Mearsheimer, J. J. (1994). The false promise of international institutions. *International Security*, *19*(3), 5–49. https://doi.org/10.2307/2539078

Medina, A. F. (2019). The ASEAN automobile industry: Top destinations for manufacturers. *ASEAN Briefing*. Retrieved from: https://www.aseanbriefing.com/news/aseans-automobile-industry/

METI of Japan. (2007, July 12). *White Paper on international economy and trade 2007*. Retrieved from Ministry of Economy, Trade and Industry of Japan website: https://www.meti.go.jp/english/report/downloadfiles/2007WhitePaper/Overview0712.pdf

MFAT of New Zealand. (2021). *RCEP text and resources*. Retrieved from Ministry of Foreign Affairs and Trade of New Zealand website: https://www.mfat.govt.nz/en/trade/free-trade-agreements/free-trade-agreements-concluded-but-not-in-force/regional-comprehensive-economic-partnership-rcep/rcep-text-and-resources/

Mikic, M. (2011). Counter-crisis trade expansion. In S. Rosefielde, M. Kuboniwa, & S. Mizobata (Eds.), *Two Asias: The emerging postcrisis divide* (pp. 295–325). World Scientific Publishing Company.

MOFA. (2015). Japan's foreign policy to promote national and worldwide interests. In *Diplomatic Bluebook 2015* (pp. 174–316). Retrieved from Ministry of Foreign Affairs of Japan website: https://www.mofa.go.jp/files/000106463.pdf

Molle, W. (2017). *The economics of European integration: Theory, practice, policy*. Routledge. https://doi.org/10.4324/9781315196008

Møller, J. Ø. (2008). *European integration: Sharing of experiences*. Institute of Southeast Asian Studies.

Moore, T., & Yang, D. (1999). China, APEC and economic regionalism in the Asia-Pacific. *The Journal of East Asian Affair*, *13*(2), 361–411. http://www.jstor.org/stable/23255534

Moravcsik, A. (1993). Preferences and power in the European Community: A liberal intergovernmentalist approach. *Journal of Common Market Studies*, *31*(4), 473–524. https://doi.org/10.1111/j.1468-5965.1993.tb00477.x

Moravcsik, A. (1997). Taking preferences seriously: A liberal theory of international politics. *International Organization*, *51*(4), 513–553. https://doi.org/10.1162/002081897550447

Moravcsik, A. (1998). *The choice for Europe*. Cornell University Press

MTI of Singapore. (2014, June 18). *Factsheet: What you need to know about Regional Comprehensive Economic Partnership (RCEP)*. Retrieved from Ministry of Trade and Industry of Singapore website: https://www.mti.gov.sg/-/media/MTI/Legislation/Public-Consultations/2014/FACTSHEET-WHAT-YOU-NEED-TO-KNOW-ABOUT/factsheet-on-rcep-june-2014.pdf

Mukherjee, D. (2019). *Economic integration in Asia: Key prospects and challenges with the Regional Comprehensive Economic Partnership*. Routledge

Nair, D. (2009). Regionalism in the Asia Pacific/East Asia: A frustrated regionalism? *Contemporary Southeast Asia*, *31*(1), 110–142. https://www.jstor.org/stable/41288791

Nambiar, S. (2015). The use of free trade agreements by Malaysian firms. In L. Y. Ing, & S. Urata (Eds.), *The use of FTAs in ASEAN: Survey-based analysis* (pp. 123–170). Retrieved from the Economic Research Institute for ASEAN and East Asia website: https://www.eria.org/RPR_FY2013_No.5_Chapter_7.pdf

Nesadurai, H. E. S. (2009). Is depoliticized functional cooperation the key to advancing cooperation in East Asia? Lessons from East Asian financial cooperation. In S. S. Tan (Ed.), *Collaboration under anarchy: Functional regionalism and the security of East Asia* (pp. 11–25). *S. Rajaratnam School of International Studies Monograph (No. 15)*. Retrieved from: https://www.rsis.edu.sg/wp-content/uploads/2014/07/Monograph1513.pdf

Nishitateno, S. (2013). Global production sharing and the FDI-trade nexus: New evidence from the Japanese automobile industry. *Journal of the Japanese and International Economies*, *27*, 64–80. https://doi.org/10.1016/j.jjie.2013.01.001

North, D. C. (1990). *Institutions, institutional change and economic performance*. Cambridge University Press. https://doi.org/10.1017/CBO9780511808678

North, D. C. (1994). Economic performance through time. *The American Economic Review*, *84*(3), 359–368. https://www.jstor.org/stable/2118057

Oba, M. (2019). Further development of Asian regionalism: Institutional hedging in an uncertain era. *Journal of Contemporary East Asia Studies*, *8*(2), 125–140. https://doi.org/10.1080/24761028.2019.1688905

OECD. (2012, December 3). Mapping global value chains. *Policy Dialogue on Aid for Trade*. Retrieved from: https://www.oecd.org/dac/aft/MappingGlobalValueChains_web_usb.pdf

OECD. (2013). Measuring trade in value added. In *Interconnected economies: Benefiting from global value chains* (pp. 53–86). OECD Publishing. Retrieved from: https://www.oecd.org/sti/ind/interconnected-economies-GVCs-synthesis.pdf

OECD. (2018a). *OECD inter-country input-output (ICIO) tables* [Data set]. Organization for Economic Co-operation and Development. http://oe.cd/icio

OECD. (2018b). *Economic outlook for Southeast Asia, China and India 2018: Fostering growth through digitalisation*. OECD Publishing. https://doi.org/9789264286184-en

Okita, S. (1985). *Special presentation: Prospect of Pacific economies*. Paper presented at the 4th Pacific Economic Cooperation Council Conference, Seoul, South Korea. Retrieved from: https://www.grips.ac.jp/forum/module/prsp/FGeese.htm

Ozawa, T. (2001). The "hidden" side of the "flying-geese" model of catch-up growth: Japan's dirigiste institutional setup and a deepening financial morass. *Journal of Asian Economics*, *12*(4), 471–491. http://doi.org/10.1016/S1049-0078(01)00098-7

Ozawa, T. (2003). Pax Americana-led macro-clustering and flying-geese-style catchup in East Asia: Mechanisms of regionalized endogenous growth. *Journal of Asian Economics*, *13*(6), 699–713.

Pacheco Pardo, R., Kim, T., Desmaele, L., Ernst, M., Cantero Dieguez, P., & Villa, R. (2019). Moon Jae-In's Policy Towards Multilateral Institutions: Continuity and Change in South Korea's Global Strategy. KF-VUB Korea Chair Report. Retrieved from: https://www.ies.be/other/moon-jae-ins-policy-towards-multilateral-institutions-continuity-and-change-south-koreas

Pan, H. (2003, June 30). CEPA shi fen shenme yang de dali? CEPA是份什么样的大礼? [What kind of big gift is CEPA?]. *北京青年报 [Beijing Youth Daily]*.

Pang, Z. (2011). Rebalancing relations between East Asian and Trans-Pacific Institutions: Evolving regional architectural features. In L. S. Ho & J. Wong (Eds.), *APEC and the rise of China* (pp. 45–64). World Scientific.

Park, J. (2015,). Korea's linkage strategy between FTA hub policy and middle power leadership in regional economic integration. *Asia Europe Journal*, *13*(4), 379–394. https://doi.org/10.1007/s10308-015-0412-3

Paul, T. V. (2005). Soft balancing in the age of U.S. primacy. *International Security*, *30*(1), 46–71. https://doi.org/10.1162/0162288054894652

Pecht, M. (2006). Development of China's electronics industry. In M. Pecht (Ed.), *China's electronics industry* (pp. 71–92). William Andrew Publishing. https://doi.org/10.1016/B978-081551536-4.50004-6

Pempel, T. J. (2005). Introduction: Emerging webs of regional connectedness. In T. J. Pempel (Ed.), *Remapping East Asia: The construction of a region* (pp. 1–28). Cornell University Press. https://www.jstor.org/stable/10.7591/j.ctv3mtc1f

Petri, P. A. (1993). The East Asian trading bloc: An analytical history. In J. A. Frankel & M. Kahler (Eds.), *Regionalism and rivalry: Japan and the United States in Pacific Asia* (pp. 21–48). The University of Chicago Press.

Petri, P. A., & Plummer, M. G. (2012, June 15). The trans-pacific partnership and Asia-Pacific integration: Policy implications. *Peterson Institute for International Economics Policy Brief.* Retrieved from: https://ssrn.com/abstract=2108399

Petri, P. A., & Plummer, M. G. (2020). East Asia decouples from the United States: Trade war, COVID-19, and East Asia's new trade blocs. *PIIE Working Paper* (No. 20-9). Retrieved from: https://www.piie.com/system/files/documents/wp20-9.pdf

Pitakdumrongkit, K. (2016). Shaping the future of East Asian economic architecture: Views from ASEAN. *Joint U.S.-Korea Academic Studies, 27*, 245–264. https://hdl.handle.net/10356/145353

Plano, J. C., & Olton, R. (1979). *The international relations dictionary*. Western Michigan University.

Ponte, S., & Sturgeon, T. (2014). Explaining governance in global value chains: A modular theory-building effort. *Review of International Political Economy, 21*(1), 195–223. https://doi.org/10.1080/09692290.2013.809596

Puah, C.-H., Kueh, J., & Lau, E. (2007). The implications of emergence of China towards ASEAN-5: FDI-GDP perspective. *Munich Personal RePEc Archive Paper (No. 4550)*, pp. 1–13. Retrieved from: https://mpra.ub.uni-muenchen.de/4550/

Quyet, N. H. (2013). Vietnam's ASEAN strategic objectives since the 1986 doi moi reform. [Doctoral thesis, National Graduate Institute for Policy Studies]. Retrieved from: https://www.grips.ac.jp/cms/wp-content/uploads/2014/04/fulltextdoc10113.pdf

Raj-Reichert, G. (2019). The electronics industry in Indonesia and its integration into global supply chains (Working paper No. 330). Retrieved from International Labor Organization website: https://www.ilo.org/wcmsp5/groups/public/---ed_dialogue/---sector/documents/publication/wcms_732119.pdf

Raj-Reichert, G. (2020). Global value chains, contract manufacturers, and the middle-income trap: The electronics industry in Malaysia. *The Journal of Development Studies, 56*(4), 698–716. https://doi.org/10.1080/00220388.2019.1595599

Rasiah, R., & Ofreneo, R. E. (2009). Introduction: The dynamics of textile and garment manufacturing in Asia. *Journal of Contemporary Asia, 39*(4), 501–511. https://doi.org/10.1080/00472330903076727

Rasiah, R., Xiao-Shan, Y., & Govindaraju, V. G. R. C. (2014). Crisis effects on the electronics industry in Southeast Asia. *Journal of Contemporary Asia, 44*(4), 645–663. https://doi.org/10.1080/00472336.2014.923637

Ravenhill, J. (2001). *APEC and the construction of Pacific Rim regionalism*. Cambridge University Press.

Ravenhill, J. (2016). The political economy of an "Asian" mega-FTA: The Regional Comprehensive Economic Partnership. *Asian Survey, 56*(6), 1077–1100. https://doi.org/10.1525/as.2016.56.6.1077

Rhyu, S.-Y., & Lee, S. (2006). Changing dynamics in Korea-Japan economic relations: Policy ideas and development strategies. *Asian Survey, 46*(2), 195–214. https://doi.org/10.1525/as.2006.46.2.195

Rodrik, D., Subramanian, A., & Trebbi, F. (2004). Institutions rule: The primacy of institutions over geography and integration in economic development. *Journal of Economic Growth, 9*(2), 131–165. https://doi.org/10.1023/b:Joeg.0000031425.72248.85

Rozman, G. (2004). *Northeast Asia's stunted regionalism: Bilateral distrust in the shadow of globalization*. Cambridge University Press. https://doi.org/10.1017/CBO9780511617126

Rüland, J. (2011). Southeast Asian regionalism and global governance: "multilateral Utility" or "hedging utility"? *Contemporary Southeast Asia*, *33*(1), 83–112. https://doi.org/10.1355/cs33-1d

Sahu, P. K. (2016, February 18). Insight: Trans-Pacific Partnership: Should Indonesia join it or not? *The Jakarta Post*. Retrieved from: https://www.thejakartapost.com/news/2016/02/18/insight-trans-pacific-partnership-should-indonesia-join-it-or-not.html

Salidjanova, N. (2015, May 28). China's trade ambitions: Strategy and objectives behind China's pursuit of Free Trade Agreements. *U.S.-China Economic and Security Review Commission Staff Research Report*. Retrieved from: https://www.uscc.gov/sites/default/files/Research/China's%20Trade%20Ambitions%20-%2005.28%2015.pdf

Sasuga, K. (2013). Japan's FDI and the development of the automobile industry in China: Firms, production structure, and government. In X. Huang (Eds.), *Modern economic development in Japan and China* (pp. 118–144). Springer. https://doi.org/10.1057/9781137323088

Shen, M. (2017, March 9). Lifting global free trade from the 'noodle bowl'. *The East Asia Forum Quarterly*. Retrieved from: https://www.eastasiaforum.org/2017/03/09/lifting-global-free-trade-from-the-noodle-bowl/

Shen, M. (2018). Evaluation of regional economic integration in East Asia. In S. Armstrong & T. Westland (Eds.), *Asian economic integration in an era of global uncertainty* (pp. 259–292). Australian National University Press. http://doi.org/10.22459/AEIEGU.01.2018

Shira, Dezan (2021, March 31). Vietnam's free trade agreements – opportunities for your business. *Vietnam Briefing*. Retrieved from: https://www.vietnam-briefing.com/news/vietnam-free-trade-agreements-opportunities-for-your-business.html/

Smith, D. A. (1996). Going south: Global restructuring and garment production in three East Asian cases. *Asian Perspective*, *20*(2), 211–241. https://www.jstor.org/stable/42704106

Song, H. (2012). New challenges to the export oriented growth model. In Y. Zhang, F. Kimura, & S. Oum (Eds.), *Moving toward a new development model for East Asia - the role of domestic policy and regional cooperation* (pp. 27–54). Economic Research Institute for ASEAN and East Asia. Retrieved from: https://www.eria.org/publications/moving-toward-a-new-development-model-for-east-asia--the-role-of-domestic-policy-and-regional-cooperation/

Stein, A. A. (2008). Neoliberal institutionalism. In C. Reus-Smit & D. Snidal (Eds.), *The Oxford handbook on international relations* (pp. 201–221). Oxford University Press. https://doi.org/10.1093/oxfordhb/9780199219322.001.0001

Stollinger, R., Hanzl-Weiss, D., Leitner, S. M., & Stehrer, R. (2018). Global and regional value chains: How important, how different? The Vienna Institute for International Economic Studies Research Report (No. 427). Retrieved from: https://wiiw.ac.at/global-and-regio-nal-value-chainshow-important-how-different--dlp-4522.pdf

Stubbs, R. (2002). ASEAN plus three: Emerging East Asian regionalism? *Asian Survey*, *42*(3), 440–455. https://doi.org/10.1525/as.2002.42.3.440

Sturgeon, T. J. (2003). Exploring the risks of value chain modularity: Electronics outsourcing during the industry cycle of 1992-2002. MIT Working Paper. Retrieved from: https://www.files.ethz.ch/isn/29602/2003-002.pdf

Sturgeon, T. J. (2007). How globalization drives institutional diversity: The Japanese electronics industry's response to value chain modularity. *Journal of East Asian Studies*, *7*(1), 1–34. https://doi.org/10.1017/S1598240800004835

Sturgeon, T. J., & Kawakami, M. (2011). Global value chains in the electronics industry: Characteristics, crisis, and upgrading opportunities for firms from developing countries. *International Journal of Technological Learning, Innovation and Development*, *4*(1–3), 120–147. https://doi.org/10.1504/IJTLID.2011.041902

Sturgeon, T. J., & Van Biesebroeck, J. (2009). Crisis and protection in the automotive industry: A global value chain perspective. World Bank Policy Research Working Paper (No. 5060). Retrieved from: https://ssrn.com/abstract=1476702

Sum, N.-L. (2002). Globalization, regionalization and cross-border modes of growth in East Asia: The (re-) constitution of 'time-space governance'. In M. Perkmann & N.-L. Sum (Eds.), *Globalization, regionalization and cross-border regions* (pp. 50–76). Palgrave Macmillan. https://doi.org/10.1057/9780230596092_1

Takashi, T. (2012). Rise of Northeast Asian economic regionalism. In S. Bhubhindar (Ed.), Is Northeast Asian regionalism the centre of East Asian regionalism? (pp. 4–5). Special Policy Report of Nanyang Technological University. Retrieved from: https://www.files.ethz.ch/isn/153920/RSIS_NEA%20SPECIAL%20POLICY%20REPORT_A4_041012_BW.pdf

Tan, S. S. (2015). Indonesia among the powers: Will ASEAN still matter to Indonesia? In C. B. Roberts, A. D. Habir, & L. C. Sebastian (Eds.), *Indonesia's ascent: Power, leadership, and the regional order* (pp. 287–307). Palgrave Macmillan UK. https://doi.org/10.1057/9781137397416_14

Tang, C. S., Zimmerman, J. D., & Nelson, J. I. (2009). Managing new product development and supply chain risks: The Boeing 787 case. *Supply Chain Forum*, *10*(2), 74–86. https://doi.org/10.1080/16258312.2009.11517219

Tempest, R. (1996). Barbie and the world economy. *Los Angeles Times*. Retrieved from: https://www.latimes.com/archives/la-xpm-1996-09-22-mn-46610-story.html

Terada, T. (2012). ASEAN Plus Three: Becoming more Like a normal regionalism? In M. Beeson & R. Stubbs (Eds.), *Routledge handbook of Asian regionalism*. Routledge. https://doi.org/10.4324/9780203803608

Terada, T. (2018). How and why Japan has saved the TPP: From Trump Tower to Davos. *The ASAN Open Forum*, *9*(2). Retrieved from: http://www.theasanforum.org/how-and-why-japan-has-saved-the-tpp-from-trump-tower-to-davos/#37

Thangavelu, S. M., Rajan, R., & Parinduri, R. A. (2008). *New trends and patterns of US FDI in Asia*. [Paper presentation]. The Ninth Global Development Network Conference, Brisbane, Australia. Retrieved from: https://crawford.anu.edu.au/acde/events/past/tradeandinvestment/papers/Rajan_Thangavelu.pdf

The White House (2015, October 5). *Statement by the President on the Trans-Pacific Partnership*. Retrieved from: https://obamawhitehouse.archives.gov/the-press-office/2015/10/05/statement-president-trans-pacific-partnership

Thompson, E. C. (2006). Singaporean exceptionalism and its implications for ASEAN regionalism. *Contemporary Southeast Asia*, *28*(2), 183–206. http://www.jstor.org/stable/25798781

Thorbecke, W., & Salike, N. (2013). Foreign direct investment in East Asia. *RIETI Policy Discussion Paper Series* (No. 13-P-003). Retrieved from: https://www.rieti.go.jp/jp/publications/pdp/13p003.pdf

Timmer, M. P., Dietzenbacher, E., Los, B., Stehrer, R., & Vries, G. J. (2015). An illustrated user guide to the world input-output database: The case of global automotive production. *Review of International Economics*, *23*(3), 575–605. https://doi.org/10.1111/roie.12178

Titievskaia, J., Kononenko, V., Navarra, C., Stamegna, C., & Zumer, K. (2020). Slowing down or changing track? Understanding the dynamics of 'slowbalisation'. European Parliamentary Research Services (No. PE 659.383). https://doi.org/10.2861/914072

Tonby, O., Ng, J., & Mancini, M. (2014). *Understanding ASEAN: The manufacturing opportunity*. Retrieved from McKinsey Productivity Sciences Center website: https://www.mckinsey.com/~/media/mckinsey/our%20people/matteo%20mancini/understanding_asean_the_manufacturing_opportunity.pdf

Tseng, W., & Zebregs, H. (2002). Foreign direct investment in China: Some lessons for other countries. IMF Policy Discussion Paper (No. 02/3). Retrieved from: https://www.imf.org/external/pubs/ft/pdp/2002/pdp03.pdf

Uda, K. (2003). スカイライン分析と分析用ツール『Ray』の紹介 [Skyline analysis and introduction to skyline map generating tool "Ray"]. *産業連関 [Input-Output Analysis]*, *11*(2), 63–76. https://doi.org/10.11107/papaios.11.63

Uda, K. (2019). スカイラインチャートなどのグラフ描画プログラムを組む方法 [A Method of constructing a program to graph like a skyline chart]. *産業連関 [Input-Output Analysis]*, *27*(1), 39–58. https://doi.org/10.11107/papaios.27.1_39

Ueki, Y. (2011). Intermediate goods trade in East Asia. In M. Kagami (Ed.), *Intermediate goods trade in East Asia: Economic deepening through FTAs/EPAs* (pp. 24–67). Bangkok Research Center of IDE-JETRO Research Report (No. 5). Retrieved from: https://www.ide.go.jp/English/Publish/Reports/Brc/05.html

UIBE. (2019). *UIBE global value chain (GVC) index database* [Data set]. University of International Business and Economics. https://rigvc.uibe.edu.cn/english/D_E/database_database/index.htm

UN. (2017). 'No alternative to multilateralism', in tackling global issues, Singapore tells UN Assembly. UN News (23 September 2017). Retrieved from: https://news.un.org/en/story/2017/09/566842

UNCTAD. (2020). *Investment statistics and trends* [Data set]. United Nations Conference on Trade and Development. https://unctad.org/topic/investment/investment-statistics-and-trends

Urata, S. (2001). Emergence of an FDI-trade nexus and economic growth in East Asia. In J. E. Stiglitz & S. Yusuf (Eds.), *Rethinking the East Asian miracle* (pp. 409–460). The World Bank and Oxford University Press. Retrieved from: https://hdl.handle.net/10986/13969

Urata, S. (2002). Japan's foreign direct investment and trade in Asia. In V. K. Aggarwal & S. Urata (Eds.), *Winning in Asia, Japanese style: Market and nonmarket strategies for success* (pp. 27–57). Palgrave Macmillan US. https://doi.org/10.1007/978-1-137-10926-2

US-ASEAN Business Council. (n.d.). About CP/TPP and RCEP. Retrieved from: https://www.usasean.org/regions/tpp/about

Vanzetti, D., McGuire, G., & Prabowo. (2005). *Trade policy at the crossroads – The Indonesian story*. UNCTAD Policy Issues in International Trade and Commodities Study Series (No. 28). Retrieved from: https://unctad.org/system/files/official-document/itcdtab29_en.pdf

Wallerstein, I. (1980). *The modern world-system II: Mercantilism and the consolidation of the European world-economy, 1600–1750* (1st ed.). University of California Press.

Wallerstein, I. (1984). *The politics of the world-economy: The states, the movements and the civilizations*. Cambridge University Press.

Waltz, K. N. (1979). *Theory of international politics* (1st ed.). Addison-Wesley Pub. Co..

Wang, M. (2009). Manufacturing FDI and economic growth: Evidence from Asian economies. *Applied Economics*, *41*(8), 991–1002. https://doi.org/10.1080/00036840601019059

Wang, Z. (2017). The economic rise of China: Rule-taker, rule-maker, or rule-breaker? *Asian Survey*, *57*(4), 595–617. https://doi.org/10.1525/as.2017.57.4.595

Wang, Z., Powers, W., & Wei, S.-J. (2009). Value chains in East Asian production networks: An international input-output model based analysis. *United States International Trade Commission Working Paper* (2009–10). Retrieved from: https://citeseerx.ist.psu.edu/viewdoc/download?doi=10.1.1.539.9669&rep=rep1&type=pdf

Webber, D. (2001). Two funerals and a wedding? The ups and downs of regionalism in East Asia and Asia-Pacific after the Asian crisis. *The Pacific Review*, *14*(3), 339–372. https://doi.org/10.1080/09512740110064839

Webber, D. (2010). The regional integration that didn't happen: Cooperation without integration in early twenty-first century East Asia. *The Pacific Review*, *23*(3), 313–333. https://doi.org/10.1080/09512748.2010.481051

Weidenbaum, M. (1996). Greater China: The next economic superpower. In R. A. Batterson, K. W. Chilton, & M. L. Weidenbaum (Eds.), *The dynamic American firm* (pp. 79–87). Springer.

Whiting, K. (2021). An expert explains: What is RCEP, the world's biggest trade deal? Retrieved from World Economic Forum website: https://www.weforum.org/agenda/2021/05/rcep-world-biggest-trade-deal/

Whittaker, D. H., Zhu, T., Sturgeon, T., Tsai, M. H., & Okita, T. (2010). Compressed development. *Studies in Comparative International Development*, *45*(4), 439–467. https://doi.org/10.1007/s12116-010-9074-8

Wilson, J. (2020). Looking ahead: RCEP, regional value chains and Indo-Pacific recovery. Retrieved from Asia Society Australia website: https://asiasociety.org/australia/looking-ahead-rcep-regional-value-chains-and-indo-pacific-recovery

Wissenbach, U. (2013). Barriers to East Asian integration: North East Asia—A non-region? *Journal of Global Policy and Governance*, *2*, 205–221. https://doi.org/10.1007/s40320-013-0042-3

Wong, J., & Chan, S. (2003). China-ASEAN free trade agreement: Shaping future economic relations. *Asian Survey*, *43*(3), 507–526. https://doi.org/10.1525/as.2003.43.3.507

Wonnacott, R. J. (1996). Trade and investment in a hub-and-spoke system versus a free trade area. *The World Economy*, *19*(3), 237–252. https://doi.org/10.1111/j.1467-9701.1996.tb00676.x

Woo, J.-E. (1991). *Race to the swift: State and finance in Korean industrialization*. Columbia University Press.

Wood, J. (2017). What is ASEAN? Retrieved from World Economic Forum website: https://www.weforum.org/agenda/2017/05/what-is-asean-explainer/

World Bank. (1993). *The East Asian miracle: Economic growth and public policy*. Oxford University Press.

Wu, C.-H. (2019). ASEAN at the crossroads: Trap and track between CP/TPP and RCEP. *Journal of International Economic Law*, *23*(1), 97–117. https://doi.org/10.1093/jiel/jgz032

Yamamura, K., & Hatch, W. (1997). A looming entry barrier: Japan's production networks in Asia. *NBR Analysis*, 8(1), 1–28. Retrieved from the National Bureau of Asian Research website: https://www.nbr.org/publication/a-looming-entry-barrier-japans-production-networks-in-asia/

Yeo, L. H. (2010). Institutional regionalism versus networked regionalism: Europe and Asia compared. *International Politics*, *47*(3/4), 324–337. https://doi.org/10.1057/ip.2010.18

Yeung, H. W.-C. (2016). *Strategic coupling: East Asian industrial transformation in the new global economy*. Cornell University Press.

Yilmaz, S., & Li, B. (2020, 2020/09/01). The BRI-led globalization and its implications for East Asian regionalization. *Chinese Political Science Review*, *5*(3), 395–416. https://doi.org/10.1007/s41111-020-00145-2

Yoshimatsu, H. (2005). Japan's Keidanren and free trade agreements: Societal interests and trade policy. *Asian Survey*, *45*(2), 258–278. https://doi.org/10.1525/as.2005.45.2.258

Yoshimatsu, H. (2008). *The political economy of regionalism in East Asia: Integrative explanation for dynamics and challenges*. Palgrave Macmillan London.

Young, O. R. (1991). Political leadership and regime formation: On the development of institutions in international society. *International Organization*, *45*(3), 281–308. https://doi.org/10.1017/S0020818300033117

Yu, H.-S. (2003). Explaining the emergence of new East Asian regionalism: Beyond power and interest-based approaches. *Asian Perspective*, *27*(1), 261–288. https://www.jstor.org/stable/42704404

Yue, P., & Evenett, S. J. (2010). Moving up the value chain: Upgrading China's manufacturing sector. Retrieved from International Institute for Sustainable Development website: https://www.iisd.org/system/files/publications/sts_3_moving_up_the_value_chain.pdf

Yukawa, T. (2017). The ASEAN way as a symbol: An analysis of discourses on the ASEAN norms. *The Pacific Review*, *31*(3), 298–314. https://doi.org/10.1080/09512748.2017.1371211

Zhai, K. (2009). Xiaoma La Dache? Dui dongmeng zai dongya hezuo zhong diwei zuoyong de zairenshi 小马拉大车？——对东盟在东亚合作中地位作用的再认识 [Ponies pulling the cart? Re-interpreting the position of ASEAN in East Asian cooperation]. *外交评论(外交学院学报)* [*Foreign Affairs Review*], *26*(02), 9–15.

Zhang, M. (2016). Growing activism as cooperation facilitator: China-Japan-Korea trilateralism and Korea's middle power diplomacy. *The Korean Journal of International Studies*, *14*(2), 309–337. https://doi.org/10.14731/kjis.2016.08.14.2.309

Zhang, M. (2019). The China–Japan–Korea trilateral free trade agreement: Why did trade negotiations stall? *Pacific Focus*, *34*(2), 204–229. https://doi.org/10.1111/pafo.12142

Zhang, Y. L. (2002). Dong ya diqu hezuo de jincheng ji qianzhan 东亚地区合作的进程及前瞻 [The progress and prospect of regional cooperation in East Asia]. *求是* [Qiushi], *24*, 55–57.

Appendix 1

Full Names of Economy Abbreviations

	East Asian Economies (except Laos and Myanmar)		*EU27 (except Lithuania)*		*North America*		*Others*
BRN	Brunei	AUT	Austria	CAN	Canada	AUS	Australia
CHN	China	BEL	Belgium	MEX	Mexico	ARG	Argentina
HKG	Hong Kong	BGR	Bulgaria	USA	United States	AUS	Australia
IDN	Indonesia	HRV	Croatia			BRA	Brazil
JPN	Japan	CYP	Cyprus			CHL	Chile
KOR	Korea	CZE	Czech Republic			COL	Colombia
KHM	Cambodia	DNK	Denmark			CRI	Costa Rica
MYS	Malaysia	EST	Estonia			IND	India
PHL	Philippines	FIN	Finland			ISL	Iceland
SGP	Singapore	FRA	France			ISR	Israel
THA	Thailand	DEU	Germany			ITA	Italy
TWN	Taiwan	GRC	Greece			MLT	Malta
		HUN	Hungary			MAR	Morocco
		IRL	Ireland			NZL	New Zealand
		ITA	Italy			NOR	Norway
		LVA	Latvia			PER	Peru
		LUX	Luxembourg			ROW	Rest of the world
		MLT	Malta			RUS	Russian Federation
		NLD	Netherlands			SAU	Saudi Arabia
		POL	Poland			ZAF	South Africa
		PRT	Portugal			CHE	Switzerland
		ROU	Romania			TUN	Tunisia
		SVK	Slovak Republic			TUR	Turkey
		SVN	Slovenia				
		ESP	Spain				
		SWE	Sweden				
		GBR	United Kingdom				

Appendix 2

FTAs Involving China, Japan, South Korea, Singapore, Malaysia, Indonesia, the Philippines, and Vietnam (as of December 2020)

FTAs Involving China

Scope	*Partner economies*	*Enter into force*
Bilateral (16)	Mauritius	* Signed (Oct. 2019)
	Georgia	Jan. 2018
	South Korea	Dec. 2015
	Iceland	Jul. 2014
	Peru	Mar. 2010
	Singapore	Jan. 2009
	Chile	Oct. 2006
	Pakistan	Jul. 2007
	ASEAN	Jul. 2005
	Maldives	* Signed (Dec. 2017)
	Australia	Dec. 2015
	Switzerland	Jul. 2014
	Costa Rica	Aug. 2011
	New Zealand	Oct. 2008
	Singapore	Jan. 2009
	Chile	Oct. 2006
Regional (1)	RCEP 15	* Signed (Nov. 2020)

Source: Ministry of Commerce of China, http://fta.mofcom.gov.cn/english/fta_qianshu.shtml

FTAs Involving Japan

Scope	*Partner economies*	*Launch negotiations*	*Sign up*	*Enter into force*
Bilateral (17)	Singapore	Jan. 2001	Jan. 2002	Nov. 2002
	Mexico	Nov. 2002	Sep. 2004	Apr. 2005
	Malaysia	Jan. 2004	Dec. 2005	Jul. 2006
	Chile	Feb. 2006	Mar. 2007	Sep. 2007
	Thailand	Feb. 2004	Apr. 2007	Nov. 2007
	Brunei	Jun. 2006	Jun. 2007	Jul. 2008
	Indonesia	Jul. 2005	Aug. 2007	Jul. 2008
	ASEAN	Jan. 2007	Mar. 2008	Dec. 2008
	Philippines	Feb. 2004	Sep. 2006	Dec. 2008
	Switzerland	May 2007	Feb. 2009	Sep. 2009
	Vietnam	Jan. 2007	Dec. 2008	Oct. 2009
	India	Jan. 2007	Aug. 2011	Aug. 2011
	Peru	May 2009	May 2011	Mar. 2012
	Australia	Apr. 2007	Jun. 2014	Jan. 2015
	Mongolia	Jun. 2012	Feb. 2015	Jun. 2016
	EU	Apr. 2013	Jul. 2018	Feb. 2019
	The UK	Jun. 2020	Oct. 2020	* N.A.
Regional (2)	TPP 12	Jul. 2013	Feb. 2016	* N.A.
	TPP 11/CP/TPP	Jul. 2013	Mar. 2018	Dec. 2018
	RCEP	May 2013	Nov. 2020	* N.A.

Source: Ministry of Foreign Affairs of Japan, https://www.mofa.go.jp/policy/economy/fta/index.html, accessed on 25 Nov. 2020.

Notes: Japan's participation in the TPP negotiations started in July 2013. The TPP negotiations started in March 2010.

FTAs Involving South Korea

Scope	*Partner economies*	*Launch negotiations*	*Sign up*	*Enter into force*
Bilateral (17)	Chile	Dec. 1999	Feb. 2003	Apr. 2004
	Singapore	Jan. 2004	Aug. 2005	Mar. 2006
	EFTA	Jan. 2005	Dec. 2005	Sep. 2006
	ASEAN	Feb. 2005	Aug. 2006	Jun. 2007
	India	Mar. 2006	Aug. 2009	Jan. 2010
	EU	May 2007	Oct. 2010	Jul. 2011
	Peru	Mar. 2009	Mar. 2011	Aug. 2011
	USA	Jun. 2006	Jun. 2007	Mar. 2012
	Turkey	Apr. 2010	Aug. 2012	May 2013
	Australia	May 2009	Apr. 2014	Dec. 2014
	Canada	Jul. 2005	Sep. 2014	Jan. 2015
	China	May 2012	Jun. 2015	Dec. 2015
	New Zealand	Jun. 2009	Mar. 2015	Dec. 2015
	Vietnam	Aug. 2012	May 2015	Dec. 2015
	Columbia	Dec. 2009	Feb. 2013	Jul. 2016
	Central America (5 countries)	Jun. 2015	Feb. 2018	Jan. 2020
	The UK	Dec. 2016	Aug. 2019	* N.A.
Regional (1)	RCEP	May 2013	Nov. 2020	* N.A.

Source: For the complete list of Korea's FTAs, please visit the Korean Ministry of Foreign Affairs site https://www.fta.go.kr//main/situation/kfta/ov/

Notes: EFTA (European Free Trade Association, four countries) includes Switzerland, Norway, Iceland, and Liechtenstein. Central America (five countries) includes Panama, Costa Rica, Honduras, El Salvador, and Nicaragua.

FTAs Involving Singapore

Scope	*Partner economies*	*Enter into force*
Bilateral (16)	New Zealand	Jan. 2001
	Japan	Nov. 2002
	EFTA	Jan. 2003
	Australia	Jul. 2003
	USA	Jan. 2004
	India	Aug. 2005
	Jordan	Aug. 2005
	South Korea	Mar. 2006
	Panama	Jul. 2006
	Peru	Aug. 2009
	China	Jan. 2009
	Costa Rica	Jul. 2013
	Gulf Cooperation Council	Sep. 2013
	Turkey	Oct. 2017
	Sri Lanka	May 2018
	European Union	Nov. 2019

(*continued*)

Scope	*Partner economies*	*Enter into force*
Regional (10)	ASEAN	1993
	ASEAN-China	Jul. 2005
	TPSEP(P4)	May 2006
	ASEAN-South Korea	Jun. 2007
	ASEAN-Japan	Apr. 2008
	ASEAN-Australia-New Zealand	Jan. 2010
	ASEAN-India	May 2011
	TPP	* Signed (Feb. 2016)
	CP/TPP	Dec. 2018
	ASEAN-Hong Kong, China	Jun. 2019
	RCEP 15	* Signed (Nov. 2020)

Source: Enterprise Singapore, https://www.enterprisesg.gov.sg/non-financial-assistance/for-singapore-companies/free-trade-agreements/ftas/singapore-ftas/akfta

Notes: Trans-Pacific Strategic Economic Partnership (TPSEP) Parties include Brunei Darussalam, Chile, New Zealand, and Singapore.

FTAs Involving Malaysia

Scope	*Partner economies*	*Enter into force*
Bilateral (7)	Australia	Jan. 2013
	Chile	Feb. 2012
	India	Jul. 2011
	Japan	Jul. 2006
	New Zealand	Aug. 2010
	Pakistan	Jan. 2008
	Turkey	Aug. 2015
Regional (10)	ASEAN	1993
	ASEAN-China	Jul. 2005
	ASEAN-South Korea	Jun. 2007
	ASEAN-Japan	Apr. 2008
	ASEAN-Australia-New Zealand	Jan. 2010
	ASEAN–India	May 2011
	Group of Eight Developing Countries (D8)	Aug. 2011
	TPP	* Signed (Feb. 2016)
	CP/TPP	Dec. 2018
	ASEAN-Hong Kong, China	Jun. 2019
	RCEP 15	* Signed (Nov. 2020)

Source: Ministry of International Trade and Industry of Malaysia, https://fta.miti.gov.my/index.php/pages/view/4?mid=23

FTAs Involving Thailand

Scope	*Partner economies*	*Enter into force*
Bilateral (7)	China	2003
	India	N.A. (under negotiation)
	Australia	Jan. 2005
	New Zealand	Jul. 2005
	Japan	Nov. 2007
	Peru	Dec. 2011
	Chile	Nov. 2015
Regional (9)	ASEAN	1993
	ASEAN-China	Jul. 2005
	ASEAN-South Korea	Jun. 2007
	ASEAN-Japan	Apr. 2008
	ASEAN-Australia-New Zealand	Jan. 2010
	ASEAN-India	May 2011
	BIMSTEC	2013
	ASEAN-Hong Kong, China	Jun. 2019
	RCEP 15	* Signed (Nov. 2020)

Source: ADB-Asia Regional Integration Center, https://aric.adb.org/fta-country

FTAs Involving Indonesia

Scope	*Partner economies*	*Enter into force*
Bilateral (6)	Japan	Jul. 2008
	Pakistan	Sep. 2013
	Chile	Aug. 2019
	Australia	Jul. 2020
	EFTA	* Signed (Dec. 2018)
	Mozambique	* Signed (Aug. 2019)
Regional (9)	ASEAN	1993
	ASEAN-China	Jul. 2005
	ASEAN-South Korea	Jun. 2007
	ASEAN-Japan	Apr. 2008
	ASEAN-Australia-New Zealand	Jan. 2010
	ASEAN–India	May 2011
	Group of Eight Developing Countries (D8)	Aug. 2011
	ASEAN-Hong Kong, China	Jun. 2019
	RCEP 15	* Signed (Nov. 2020)

Source: ADB-Asia Regional Integration Center, https://aric.adb.org/fta-country

FTAs Involving the Philippines

Scope	*Partner economies*	*Enter into force*
Bilateral (2)	Japan	2008
	European Free Trade Association	2018
Regional (8)	ASEAN	1993
	ASEAN-China	Jul. 2005
	ASEAN-South Korea	Jun. 2007
	ASEAN-Japan	Apr. 2008
	ASEAN-Australia-New Zealand	Jan. 2010
	ASEAN-India	May 2011
	ASEAN-Hong Kong, China	Jun. 2019
	RCEP 15	* Signed (Nov. 2020)

Source: ADB-Asia Regional Integration Center, https://aric.adb.org/fta-country

FTAs Involving Vietnam

Scope	*Partner economies*	*Enter into force*
Bilateral (5)	Japan	2009
	Chie	2012
	South Korea	2015
	Eurasian Economic Union	2016
	European Union	2020
Regional (9)	ASEAN	1993
	ASEAN-China	Jul. 2005
	ASEAN-South Korea	Jun. 2007
	ASEAN-Japan	Apr. 2008
	ASEAN-Australia-New Zealand	Jan. 2010
	ASEAN-India	May 2011
	CP/TPP	2018
	ASEAN-Hong Kong, China	Jun. 2019
	RCEP 15	* Signed (Nov. 2020)

Source: ADB-Asia Regional Integration Center, https://aric.adb.org/fta-country

Index

Pages in *italics* refer to figures, pages in **bold** refer to tables, and pages followed by n refer to notes

For Product Safety Concerns and Information please contact our
EU representative GPSR@taylorandfrancis.com Taylor & Francis
Verlag GmbH, Kaufingerstraße 24, 80331 München, Germany